DATA STRUCTURED PROGRAM DESIGN

Kirk Hansen

Prentice-Hall, Englewood Cliffs, New Jersey 07632

Library of Congress Cataloging-in-Publication Data

HANSEN, KIRK (date)
   Data structured program design.

   Bibliography: p.
   Includes index.
      1. Electronic digital computers—Programming.
   2. Structured programming.   3. Data structures.
   (Computer science)   I. Title.
   QA76.6.H3338 1986   005.1'13   85-25729
   ISBN   0-13-196841-6

Editorial/production supervision and
   interior design: Tracey Orbine and Diana Drew
Cover design: 20/20 Services, Inc.
Manufacturing buyer: Gordon Osbourne
Editorial consulting: Karen Howard Brown

Printed in the United States of America

10   9   8   7   6   5   4   3   2   1

ISBN   0-13-196841-6   025

Prentice-Hall International (UK) Limited, *London*
Prentice-Hall of Australia Pty. Limited, *Sydney*
Prentice-Hall Canada Inc., *Toronto*
Prentice-Hall Hispanoamericana, S.A., *Mexico*
Prentice-Hall of India Private Limited, *New Delhi*
Prentice-Hall of Japan, Inc., *Tokyo*
Prentice-Hall of Southeast Asia Pte. Ltd., *Singapore*
Editora Prentice-Hall do Brasil, Ltda., *Rio de Janeiro*
Whitehall Books Limited, *Wellington, New Zealand*

Contents

Part II
OUTPUT

Part III
INPUT

Part IV
OTHER VOICES

Foreword

By the end of the 1970s, the business of designing software was dominated by four competing schools of thought:

- the *Constantine-Myers-Yourdon-Stevens School:* people who believe a system should take its shape from the pattern of interactions among functions performed by the system
- the *Warnier-Orr-Jackson School:* people who believe a system should take its shape from the structure of the data that drives it
- the *Parnas School:* people who believe a system should be structured so that its modular walls serve to isolate and conceal complexities of data and process
- the *Mugwump School:* people who believe design is for sissies and that the structure of the system should be whatever occurs to the coder while seated at the terminal.

As a result of my writing, I have long been classified as a member of the first of these groups, the "function-structured" school of design. And Kirk Hansen is clearly allied with the second group, the "data-structured" school of design. So, how have I come to be writing a foreword to Kirk's book?

My answer stems from a growing conviction that the first three approaches are all valid, and *all necessary*. The notion of using one of these disciplines to suppress the others is onerous; it amounts to saying, "Truth is so valuable we have to use it sparingly." For a given class of programs, any of the techniques might serve well. But if you're building a great diversity of applications, you need a diversity of approaches. If you're building *systems*, particularly large and complex systems, you need all the help you can get—a trick from Myers here, some Jackson "backtracking" there, a Warnier/Orr approach wherever the data gives a strong hint about process structure, some Parnas thinking to abstract and conceal complexity . . . and more.

That famous software engineer Mao Tse Tung said, "Let a thousand blossoms grow, let a thousand schools of thought contend." Of course, Mao didn't really mean it: He not only suppressed competing schools of thought, he even suppressed flowers, judging them to be "bourgeois." But I do mean it. I believe that as a software builder you need an army of ideas to support you. In particular, no matter what school you belong to, you need the ideas set out in Kirk Hansen's crystalline presentation of *Data Structured Program Design*.

Tom DeMarco
Principal
The Atlantic Systems Guild

A Note from Ken Orr

New ideas, even great new ideas, often take a very long time to become popular. One reason is because it is not enough that an idea be a good one, it must also be communicated to those who need it. Time after time, poor ideas that are well communicated have won out over good ideas poorly presented.

Kirk Hansen has given us the best of both worlds in this book. He has taken a great idea (data structured programming) and communicated it superbly. Not only has Kirk done an excellent job of communicating both the letter and spirit of the Ken Orr Data Structured Systems Development (DSSD®) methodology, he has been able to compare and contrast it with Warnier's and Jackson's approaches to data structured programming as well.

This book is a major contribution to the growing body of software engineering literature. It is clear and informative and, best of all, it is fun to read. Kirk Hansen has demonstrated conclusively that important technical ideas don't have to be boring.

One final note. Throughout the book, Kirk refers to the Ken Orr methodology. In this regard, it is important to point out that the Ken Orr methodology is not the work of a single person, or even that of a single firm. Rather, it is the result of the work of hundreds of people over the last two decades, including Mr. Hansen. I am personally delighted that someone as talented as Kirk Hansen should add his own particular brand of creativity to communicate the DSSD® methodology to a wide audience eager to make programming simple, straightforward, and ultimately scientific.

Ken Orr
Topeka, Kansas

Preface

You can derive the structure of a program from the structure of its data.

The insights that let you do this come from three people: Jean-Dominique Warnier, Michael Jackson, and Ken Orr. This book fully describes Orr's program design techniques and outlines the ideas of Warnier and Jackson.

This book is mainly about how to design programs, not how to code them, so it won't make much difference what programming language you know. But you should be familiar with at least one of the major procedural languages: PL/1, COBOL, FORTRAN, ALGOL, BASIC, Pascal. Where code is needed we use COBOL, since it's the most widely used language among business programmers and is fairly clear even to programmers who have never seen it before. The programs in this book have been compiled with the IBM OS/VS COBOL compiler and run on an IBM 3081.

The book will be more valuable if you keep a paper and pencil handy and try things for yourself as they are discussed. "I hear and I forget. I see and I remember. I do and I understand." It's easy to think you understand something when you're just watching it happen; the only way to know for sure is to try it yourself.

Several chapters contain suggestions for "further reading." These references give author and title only; full publication data may be found in the bibliography at the end of the book.

Finally, an explanation of the title may be in order. Data structured program design is a **structured** technique (a detailed procedure) for deriving the **design** of a **structured program** from the **data structure**. Shuffling the emphasized words gives "data structure structured structured program design," which is accurate but unpronounceable; so one of the structures has swallowed the rest.

NOTES ON THE REVISED EDITION

This Revised Edition has three main changes. First, three sections have been added. They are 6.4, "Hidden Hierarchies"; 14.6, "Using Hidden Hierarchies for Efficiency"; and 14.7, "The Logical Data Structure."

The second change is revision of some terms to match the latest release of Orr's DSSD® method. Specifically:

Logical Process Structure (LPS)	is now	Logical Output Mapping (LOM).
Logical Read Routine (LRR)	is now	Physical Input Mapping (PIM).
Physical Put Routine (PPR)	is now	Physical Output Mapping (POM).

The phrase "read routine" has mostly been changed to "input mapping," but the terms are often used interchangeably.

The third change is the separation of the material on inversion from the main flow of the book. Two principles guide the discussion of inversion in this edition:

1. Don't invert unless you have to. If you're lucky enough to work with a system that makes inversion unnecessary, skip the material on inversion completely.
2. Even if your system makes inversion unavoidable, ignore the inversion material on your first reading of the book.

To this end, Chapter 11 and Part III have been prefaced with suitable warnings, and the chapters in Part III have been reorganized so the inversion material is easier to skip.

ACKNOWLEDGMENTS

This book was the idea of Morris Nelson, vice-president of field operations at Ken Orr and Associates, Inc. I am grateful for his strong support and assistance in bringing it to fruition.

The book borrows heavily from KOA instructional materials, especially for examples and exercises. It owes a great deal to all the KOA instructors, past and present, who have contributed to the instructional material and to the development of the methodology itself. I am especially grateful to Ken Orr, Rick Messinger, and Stiles Roberts for their comments on an earlier draft. Thanks also to Dave Higgins, whose new book, *Designing Structured Programs*, impelled me to clarify my thinking on several points; and to the students in my classes for Ken Orr and Associates, whose questions and comments helped shape the material presented here.

M. Jean-Dominique Warnier kindly read Chapters 18 and 19, which survey parts of his work, and made several corrections. And Jim Batterson of Best Products provided a detailed critique of an earlier draft of the book, which led to several improvements.

I am grateful to Manufacturers Life for cooperating in my association with KOA, and for giving concrete assistance with this book.

Specific thanks go to Ken McEvoy and Bob Stark, who worked with me in our initial encounter with data structured program design. Ken also advised me on certain aspects of Jackson's work for this book. John Campbell's comments led to the revised treatment of inversion in this edition.

Karen Brown provided meticulous and cheerful editing; but her insistence that data names mustn't change between sentences, and that referenced sections should actually exist, has made reading this book less of an adventure than it might have been.

My father's comments on an early draft had a healthy effect on the book's style.

Finally, I thank my wife, Mary-Anne Sillamaa, for her love and support while this book was being written.

Part 1

TWICE OVER LIGHTLY

The basic road map of data structured program design is data structure $\longrightarrow$ process structure $\longrightarrow$ code.

This Part follows the road twice: once to show that it's familiar territory; then again to study the critical role of Warnier/Orr diagrams.

1

You Already Do It

Even if you've never heard of data structured program design, you regularly use its principles. Here's proof in the form of three simple coding exercises. Please take a couple of minutes now to write routines to the following specifications. (COBOL programmers: Procedure Division code is all that's needed.)

Exercise 1

Display the message:

```
HAPPY
NEW
YEAR
```

Exercise 2

Display either the message:

```
GOOD MORNING
```

or the message:

```
GOOD DAY
```

depending on whether or not the hour is less than 12.

Exercise 3

Display the warning:

```
FLY AT ONCE -- ALL IS DISCOVERED
```

15 times.

If you tried the exercises, your solutions probably look somewhat like the following. For Exercise 1:

```
EXERCISE-1.
        DISPLAY "HAPPY".
        DISPLAY "NEW".
        DISPLAY "YEAR".
```

For Exercise 2:

```
EXERCISE-2.
        IF HOUR < 12
            DISPLAY "GOOD MORNING"
        ELSE
            DISPLAY "GOOD DAY".
```

For Exercise 3:

```
EXERCISE-3A.
        PERFORM DISPLAY-WARNING 15 TIMES.

DISPLAY-WARNING.
        DISPLAY "FLY AT ONCE -- ALL IS DISCOVERED".
```

Or perhaps:

```
EXERCISE-3B.
        MOVE 0 TO WARNING-COUNT.
        PERFORM DISPLAY-WARNING-AND-BUMP-COUNT
            UNTIL WARNING-COUNT = 15.

DISPLAY-WARNING-AND-BUMP-COUNT.
        DISPLAY "FLY AT ONCE -- ALL IS DISCOVERED".
        ADD 1 TO WARNING-COUNT.
```

(If you treated each exercise as a stand-alone program, you would include STOP RUN in each solution. Also, depending on the compiler you use, you might have apostrophes ['] instead of quotation marks ["] around the literals.)

As these exercises demonstrate, you already know the three basic rules of data structured design:

1. When the data is a **sequence** (HAPPY, then NEW, then YEAR), use a simple sequence of instructions.
2. When the data is a **selection** (either GOOD MORNING or GOOD DAY), use a conditional instruction (IF. . .THEN. . .ELSE).
3. When the data is a **repetition** (15 copies of "FLY AT ONCE—ALL IS DISCOVERED"), use a looping instruction (PERFORM. . .TIMES or PERFORM. . .UNTIL).

If you have ever encountered structured programming, you will remember that sequence, selection, and repetition are enough to build any program. But that's like knowing nails and boards are enough to build a house. What you want to know is: Where should you use which?

Data structured design tells you. It says: identify the sequences, selections, and repetitions in your data. Then work out the structure of your process logic by applying the three rules given above.

With this approach you'll be able to produce reports, balance files, navigate data bases, manipulate strings of text, and do calculations. If such matters make up much of your programming load, you'll find data structured design valuable.

It's not the be-all and end-all, though, so we'll also touch on some other useful techniques and point to further reading about them.

2

Data Structure

Chapter 1 was the first trip along the path: data structure $\longrightarrow$ process structure $\longrightarrow$ code. In the next three chapters we will follow the path again, stressing the role of the Warnier/Orr diagram.

Warnier/Orr diagrams can represent data structure, process structure, or code. This makes them very useful, not only in handling each phase properly, but also in making the transition from one phase to the next.

This chapter examines the use of Warnier/Orr diagrams in representing data or things. Recall our three messages in the previous chapter; they illustrated the three basic constructs of sequence, selection, and repetition. We'll now see how to diagram each of these constructs, and then look at how to combine them.

2.1 SEQUENTIAL DATA

The first message was:

```
HAPPY
NEW
YEAR
```

We would diagram this like so:

$$\text{MESSAGE 1} \begin{cases} \text{''HAPPY''} \\ \text{''NEW''} \\ \text{''YEAR''} \end{cases}$$

You would read this diagram as follows: MESSAGE 1 consists of the literal "HAPPY" followed by the literal "NEW" followed by the literal "YEAR".

That is, the bracket means "consists of." And you show a sequence by listing the elements of the sequence, one below the other, to the right of the bracket. (Strictly speaking it's a brace, but it's almost always called a bracket.)

Here's another example. Since it is a family newspaper, the *Daily Planet* consists of five separate sections so everybody can have something to read. We can diagram it like this:

$$
\text{DAILY PLANET}
\begin{cases}
\text{NEWS SECTION} \\
\text{SPORTS SECTION} \\
\text{ENTERTAINMENT SECTION} \\
\text{LIFESTYLE SECTION} \\
\text{CLASSIFIED SECTION}
\end{cases}
$$

This time there are no quotes around the words on the right (NEWS SECTION, and so on). That's because they are **names** rather than literals; they represent other things (namely, several pages each).

Note that **order is important**. If our message came out:

```
NEW
HAPPY
YEAR
```

it would be wrong. Similarly, if the *Daily Planet* were printed one day with the classified section at the front, it would mean trouble at the plant.

2.2 CHOICES OF DATA: ALTERNATION

Let's move on to the second example; it shows the second major structure, variously known as selection or alternation. If you recall, we wanted to display either "GOOD MORNING" or "GOOD DAY", depending on whether or not the hour is less than 12. This is diagrammed like so:

$$
\text{MESSAGE 2}
\begin{cases}
\text{"GOOD MORNING"} \\
(0,1) \\
\\
\oplus \\
\\
\text{"GOOD DAY"} \\
(0,1)
\end{cases}
$$

That is, MESSAGE 2 is either "GOOD MORNING" or "GOOD DAY" **but not both**. The symbol $\oplus$ is borrowed from symbolic logic; it's called an "exclusive or." The notation $(0,1)$ under "GOOD MORNING" means that it will be present either zero or one times in MESSAGE 2: either it's there or it isn't. Strictly speaking, this doesn't tell you anything that isn't implied by $\oplus$, but the $(0,1)$ is customarily included.

You may have noticed that we haven't included all the information we were given. The diagram doesn't say under what conditions the message is "GOOD MORNING" and under what conditions it's "GOOD DAY". We include this additional very important data in the following way:

$$
\text{MESSAGE 2} \left\{ \begin{array}{l} \text{"GOOD MORNING"} \\ (0,1)/\mathbf{?1} \\ \oplus \\ \text{"GOOD DAY"} \\ (0,1) \end{array} \right.
$$

?1/ IF HOUR < 12

This is called a footnote or conditional. Footnotes are indicated by question marks in Warnier/Orr diagrams; they will be vitally important when we eventually make the move from process structure to code.

The exclusive or structure extends easily to any situation where something is chosen from a list. For example, suppose you've bought a meal that includes choice of beverage: coffee, tea, milk, or soft drink. You could diagram your choices like this:

$$
\text{BEVERAGE} \left\{ \begin{array}{l} \text{COFFEE} \\ (0,1) \\ \oplus \\ \text{TEA} \\ (0,1) \\ \oplus \\ \text{MILK} \\ (0,1) \\ \oplus \\ \text{SOFT DRINK} \\ (0,1) \end{array} \right.
$$

The choices must be **exhaustive** and **mutually exclusive**. Exhaustive means the list exhausts all the possibilities: you can't have a chocolate soda. Exclusive means each choice excludes all the others: you can't have tea *and* a soft drink.

And that's all we need to say for the moment about diagramming alternatives in data. We'll return to the subject with a more extended discussion shortly.

2.3 REPETITION OF DATA

Our last exercise was to display the warning:

```
FLY AT ONCE -- ALL IS DISCOVERED
```

15 times. This output is diagrammed:

MESSAGE 3 { WARNING { "FLY AT ONCE--ALL IS DISCOVERED"
(15)

The notation (15) means that the warning ("FLY AT ONCE—ALL IS DIS-COVERED") occurs 15 times in succession.

Here's another example. Each week contains seven days. We can write:

WEEK { DAY
(7)

Or consider a sequential file. We might write:

FILE { RECORD
(1,R)

to show that the file has 1 or more records. We introduce the "R" so we'll have a way to refer to the number of records in the file. This will come in handy later.

The diagram would be different if we knew that the file might be empty. Then we'd write:

FILE { RECORD
(0,R)

The repetition factor of (0,R) rather than (1,R) shows that R can be zero: there can be no records at all. Zero is the default; that is, a repetition factor (R) means (0,R).

Note, incidentally, that it would be wrong to write:

FILE { RECORD**S**
(0,R)

where RECORD*S* is plural. The notation (0,R) takes care of the pluralizing; pluralizing RECORD as well just confuses things.

2.4 COMBINING THE THREE BASIC STRUCTURES

So now we've seen how to represent the three basic constructs—sequence, alter-nation, repetition—when they're applied to things or data. It only remains to see how they can be combined. This combination is actually a fourth basic construct: hierarchy, or nesting. To illustrate this, consider the following statement:

You may start with either soup or juice. Then have either a roll or any number of slices of bread; in either case, you may have butter. Your main course will be either the salad plate or a hot selection. If you choose a hot item, you may have two vegetables with it (but if the hot item is a casserole you may have two vegetables only if one of them is potato). If you'd like to have dessert, take either ice cream or a sweet. Beverage is tea, coffee, or milk. You're welcome to all the water you can drink.

Some people ate at this cafeteria for decades without getting the rules completely straight. How much clearer is the following diagram:

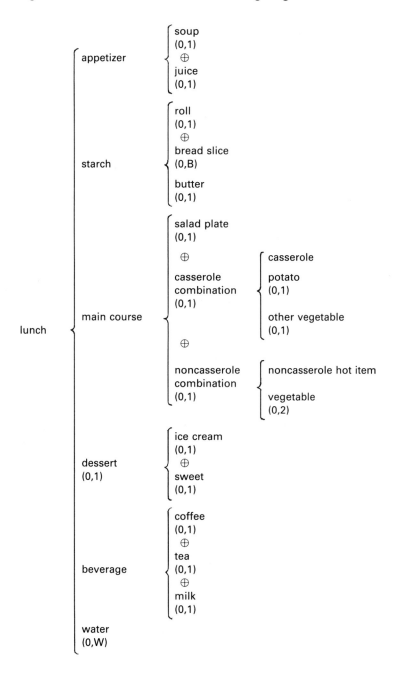

Note the (0,1) below "dessert." It means what you'd think it means: you can have zero or one desserts. If you don't want dessert, you don't have to take it. Similarly with the (0,1) below "potato" and "other vegetable."

You can think of this as a degenerate repetition that can occur, at most, one time. Or you can think of it as shorthand for an alternation:

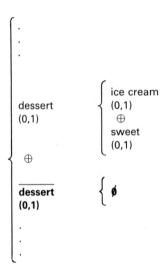

The bar is the normal way of saying "NOT" in Warnier/Orr diagrams; thus:

```
‾‾‾‾‾‾‾
dessert
```

means "not dessert." The symbol Ø, meaning "null," says that "not dessert" is empty: it has nothing in it.

2.5 ALTERNATIVE ALTERNATIVES

Here, as promised, is a more extended discussion of ways to diagram alternatives. Recall the diagram of Message 2:

MESSAGE 2 ⎰ "GOOD MORNING"
              (0,1)/?1
              ⊕
              "GOOD DAY"
              (0,1)

?1/ IF HOUR < 12

With the exception of the footnote, it's all data: "GOOD MORNING" or "GOOD DAY".

If we want to stress the conditions, we can draw it a different way. For example, if we want to stress that the first greeting is used in the morning, while the second is for any time when it isn't morning, we can insert **condition names**:

MESSAGE 2
$\left\{\begin{array}{l}\textbf{MORNING} \quad \left\{ \text{ "GOOD MORNING"} \right. \\ (0,1)/?1 \\ \oplus \\ \overline{\textbf{MORNING}} \quad \left\{ \text{ "GOOD DAY"} \right. \\ (0,1) \end{array}\right.$

?1/ IF HOUR < 12

Recall that:

$\overline{\text{MORNING}}$

means "not morning."

What we've done here is add a level to the diagram and use that level to emphasize the condition. We call this a **condition sandwich**: a condition between two layers of data. We've also added some documentation: the fact that HOUR < 12 means MORNING.

There's still a third way of diagramming Message 2. It also creates a condition sandwich, only it does it by inserting the **condition test** rather than the condition name:

MESSAGE 2
$\left\{\begin{array}{l}\textbf{HOUR} < \textbf{12} \quad \left\{ \text{ "GOOD MORNING"} \right. \\ (0,1) \\ \oplus \\ \overline{\textbf{HOUR} < \textbf{12}} \quad \left\{ \text{ "GOOD DAY"} \right. \\ (0,1) \end{array}\right.$

These two diagrams are equivalent to the original one. The one you use will depend on what you're trying to do.

The condition sandwich formats are most common when you have complex conditions. Here's an example. Suppose courtesy is especially important in the morning, so the greeting should be "Good morning, ma'am" or "Good morning, sir." We *could* stick to our original format and write:

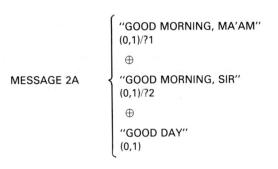

MESSAGE 2A
- "GOOD MORNING, MA'AM"
  (0,1)/?1

  ⊕

  "GOOD MORNING, SIR"
  (0,1)/?2

  ⊕

  "GOOD DAY"
  (0,1)

?1/ IF (HOUR < 12) AND (SEX = "F")
?2/ IF (HOUR < 12) AND (SEX NOT = "F")

But the conditions (footnotes) are getting hard to read. Specifically, it takes a while to figure out that "GOOD DAY" is presented when HOUR NOT < 12. So this is a case where we would probably want to emphasize the conditions. We can build a "Dagwood" condition sandwich: multiple layers of conditions between layers of data. This means either:

MESSAGE 2A
- MORNING
  (0,1)/?1
  - FEMALE
    (0,1)/?2 — { "GOOD MORNING, MA'AM"

    ⊕

    F̶E̶M̶A̶L̶E̶
    (0,1) — { "GOOD MORNING, SIR"

  ⊕

  M̶O̶R̶N̶I̶N̶G̶
  (0,1) — { "GOOD DAY"

?1/ IF HOUR < 12
?2/ IF SEX = "F"

or:

MESSAGE 2A
- HOUR < 12
  (0,1)
  - SEX = "F"
    (0,1) — { "GOOD MORNING, MA'AM"

    ⊕

    S̶E̶X̶ ̶=̶ ̶"̶F̶"̶
    (0,1) — { "GOOD MORNING, SIR"

  ⊕

  H̶O̶U̶R̶ ̶<̶ ̶1̶2̶
  (0,1) — { "GOOD DAY"

No matter how you choose to diagram it, you haven't fully understood a condition until you have specified both its name and its test.

2.6 TERMINOLOGY

And there you are. When dealing with data or other things (as opposed to processes), you now know how to diagram the three basic constructs—sequence, alternation, repetition—and how to combine them into a hierarchy. You can, in short, diagram anything.

Before we leave the subject, it will be useful to establish some terminology. Suppose we have the following Warnier/Orr diagram:

We say that A, B, C, D, E, F, G, and H are the **elements** of this diagram. Elements A, C, D, E, and F (emboldened in the diagram) are called **universals** or **sets**: they are broken down further. Elements B, G, and H are called **atomic items**: they are *not* broken down further in this diagram.

Thus, a universal is any element that has a bracket on its right; an atomic item is an element that does *not* have a bracket on its right. So tight is the correlation that the terms "universal" and "bracket" are sometimes used almost as synonyms.

You will also run across the term **structure**: it means anything that can be represented by a Warnier/Orr diagram.

The universal-atom distinction lets us state a rule of Warnier/Orr diagrams: atoms never alternate; atoms never repeat. This will sometimes mean you have to create a universal where you didn't think one was needed. As the catch phrase has it: "Alternations and repetitions always spawn brackets." Notice, for example, the empty brackets that appear in the summary table in the next section.

This rule is required to make Orr's coding rules (and data base design techniques) work; and once we get to Part II, we will follow it conscientiously. To keep the exposition straightforward in Part I, we are allowing ourselves an occasional lapse.

2.7 SUMMARY

As we follow the path from data structure through process structure to code, we will use Warnier/Orr diagrams at each step. This chapter described the use of Warnier/Orr diagrams for data or things:

HIERARCHY	SEQUENCE	ALTERNATION	REPETITION
{	A { B C D	E { F (0,1) ⊕ G (0,1)	J { K (6)
consists of	A consists of B followed by C followed by D	E consists of either F or G but not both	J consists of K repeated 6 times

A condition name (MORNING) or condition test (HOUR < 12) can be interpolated between two layers of data to make a condition sandwich:

MESSAGE 2 {
MORNING (0,1)/?1 { "GOOD MORNING"
⊕
MORNING (0,1) { "GOOD DAY"

?1/ IF HOUR < 12

A footnote (?1/) can be used to state the condition test.

2.8 EXERCISES

Unless there are other instructions, draw a Warnier/Orr diagram of the structure described in each exercise.

1. Mr. Burfel's class is lined up for fire drill: first all the girls, then all the boys. The girls are divided into three groups: the eight-year-olds, then the nine-year-olds, then the ten-year-olds. The dark-haired boys are in front of the fair-haired boys.

2. A COBOL program consists of an Identification Division, an Environment Division, a Data Division, and a Procedure Division, in that order. The Data Division can contain

a File Section, Working-Storage Section, and Linkage Section. Only the Working-Storage Section is compulsory; but if more than one section is present, their order must be the one mentioned. The Procedure Division consists of one or more sections; each of these sections consists one or more paragraphs.

3. The description of a COBOL program in Exercise 2 is, of course, incomplete: for example, it doesn't describe the contents of the Identification Division. It is also wrong: when describing the contents of the Procedure Division, it fails to mention the PROCEDURE DIVISION header. Draw a Warnier/Orr diagram that accurately shows the combinations of Procedure Division sections and paragraphs with and without headers, as accepted by your compiler. How much work do you think it would be to draw a complete and accurate Warnier/Orr diagram covering all permissible COBOL programs? Would you ever want to do such a thing? When?

4. On the twelfth day of Christmas my true love gave to me twelve drummers drumming, eleven lords a-leaping, ten ladies dancing, nine pipers piping, eight maids a-milking, seven swans a-swimming, six geese a-laying, five golden rings, four calling birds, three French hens, two turtle doves, and a partridge in a pear tree.

5. The parade will be led by the Marching and Chowder Society. Next will be four segments, each consisting of a band (either a brass band or a pipe band) followed by three floats. Then will come the giant duck. Bringing up the rear will be the parade marshal, if we can find him.

6. The company file consists of one or more records. Each record is either a sales record or an inventory record. A sales record contains part number, date, customer name, and agent number. An inventory record consists of part number, stock on hand, and reorder point.

FURTHER READING

A reference guide to all aspects of Warnier/Orr diagrams appears in the appendix of *Structured Requirements Definition* by Ken Orr. (As mentioned in the Preface, complete publication information on all "further reading" suggestions can be found in the bibliography.)

3

Process Structure

We continue the second trip down the road: data structure $\longrightarrow$ process structure $\longrightarrow$ code. We've seen how Warnier/Orr diagrams describe the structure of data. This chapter will describe how to use them on processes—that is, on logic flow.

In fact, there's not much to learn; processes use the same diagrams with the same four basic constructs. For example, the processes to produce the three sample messages of Chapter 1 are diagrammed like this:

```
                    ┌ DISPLAY "HAPPY"
PRODUCE            ┤  DISPLAY "NEW"
MESSAGE 1          └ DISPLAY "YEAR"
```

```
                    ┌ DISPLAY "GOOD MORNING"
                    │  (0,1)/?1
                    │
PRODUCE            ┤  ⊕
MESSAGE 2          │
                    │  DISPLAY "GOOD DAY"
                    └  (0,1)
```

?1/ IF HOUR < 12

```
PRODUCE            ┌ PRODUCE WARNING    ┌ DISPLAY "FLY AT ONCE"
MESSAGE 3          ┤  (15)              ┤
```

So the basics present no surprises at all.   Nevertheless, there is more to say.

3.1 SEQUENCE OF PROCESSES

Here is the Warnier/Orr diagram for PRODUCE MESSAGE 1, along with an equivalent flowchart:

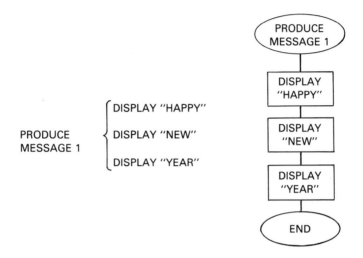

Why are we drawing flowcharts, which have been out of fashion for years? Mainly because they provide a sort of common language: they let you test your understanding of the order of flow in Warnier/Orr process diagrams.   This will come in especially handy when we discuss repetitions.   If you don't know much about flowcharts, count yourself lucky and just skim the references to them.

A second reason for discussing flowcharts is historical.   When Jacopini proved that sequence, alternation, repetition, and hierarchy are enough to accomplish anything, he proved it in terms of flowcharts.   It is interesting to see how Warnier/Orr diagrams express the control structures Jacopini required.   It would doubtless be still more satisfying to understand Jacopini's proof itself; if you would like to try, see the paper by Bohm and Jacopini cited under "Further Reading" at the end of the chapter.

3.2 ALTERNATIVES IN PROCESSES

We again lead off with Warnier/Orr diagram and flowchart side by side:

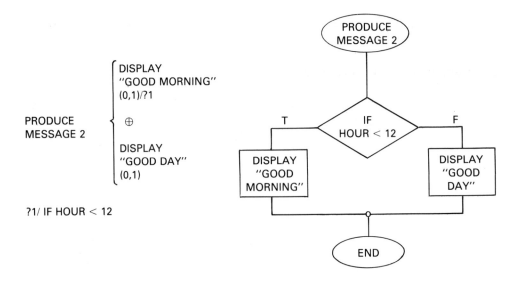

PRODUCE
MESSAGE 2 $\left\{\begin{array}{l}\text{DISPLAY}\\\text{"GOOD MORNING"}\\(0,1)/?1\\[8pt]\oplus\\[8pt]\text{DISPLAY}\\\text{"GOOD DAY"}\\(0,1)\end{array}\right.$

?1/ IF HOUR < 12

In Chapter 2 we came up with three different ways of diagramming alternatives in data. As you'd expect, we can carry any of them over into diagramming alternative processes. We've already carried over the first form—data only—to get the "process only" version above. The condition sandwich forms come over just as easily. The condition-name format gives:

PRODUCE
MESSAGE 2 $\left\{\begin{array}{ll}\text{MORNING}\\(0,1)/?1 & \left\{\text{DISPLAY "GOOD MORNING"}\right.\\[8pt]\oplus\\[8pt]\overline{\text{MORNING}}\\(0,1) & \left\{\text{DISPLAY "GOOD DAY"}\right.\end{array}\right.$

?1/ IF HOUR < 12

and the condition-statement format gives:

PRODUCE
MESSAGE 2 $\left\{\begin{array}{ll}\text{HOUR} < 12\\(0,1) & \left\{\text{DISPLAY "GOOD MORNING"}\right.\\[8pt]\oplus\\[8pt]\overline{\text{HOUR} < 12}\\(0,1) & \left\{\text{DISPLAY "GOOD DAY"}\right.\end{array}\right.$

As with data, these three formats are equivalent; which one you use will depend on what you're trying to do.

As long as we're discussing diagrams of alternative processes, we should mention a classic in the field. Shakespeare, lacking a good diagramming technique, expressed a choice this way:

> To be, or not to be: that is the question:
> Whether 'tis nobler in the mind to suffer
> The slings and arrows of outrageous fortune,
> Or to take arms against a sea of troubles,
> And by opposing end them?

We can replace this rather awkward formulation with a clear and crisp graphical representation:

HAMLET'S FUTURE
{
  TO BE (0,1)/?1 { to suffer the slings and arrows of outrageous fortune
  ⊕
  ‾‾‾‾ TO BE (0,1) { to take arms against a sea of troubles and by opposing end them
}

?1/IF 'TIS NOBLER IN THE MIND

As with data, we can extend process alternatives both down the page and across. First, let's look at down. Suppose you never know how to act with animals. You might carry a diagram to consult as the need arose:

PROCESS ANIMAL
{
  DOG (0,1) { scratch behind its ears
  ⊕
  CAT (0,1) { stroke the fur on its back
  ⊕
  HORSE (0,1) { pat its shoulder
}

On meeting a porcupine you could refine the guide:

PROCESS ANIMAL
{
  DOG (0,1) { scratch behind its ears
  ⊕
  CAT (0,1) { stroke the fur on its back
  ⊕
  HORSE (0,1) { pat its shoulder
  ⊕
  ELSE (0,1) { skip
}

The word "skip" often appears in Warnier/Orr diagrams to indicate that no action is required. It is very like the null (∅) we met in the discussion of data structures.

The rule for alternatives in processing is the same as for alternatives in data: the listed choices must be exhaustive and mutually exclusive. The first version of PROCESS ANIMAL had exclusive alternatives: an animal can't be both a dog and a cat. But it wasn't exhaustive: it didn't cover all possible cases.

Now for the other form of extension: across the page. Dagwood condition sandwiches are as easy for processes as they are for data. Remember that we decided to address people as "Sir" or "Ma'am" in the morning? Here's what the process diagram looks like in the condition-name format:

$$
\text{PRODUCE MESSAGE 2A} \begin{cases} \text{MORNING} \\ (0,1)/?1 \\ \\ \oplus \\ \\ \overline{\text{MORNING}} \\ (0,1) \end{cases} \begin{cases} \text{FEMALE} \\ (0,1)/?2 \quad \left\{ \text{DISPLAY "GOOD MORNING, MA'AM"} \right. \\ \oplus \\ \overline{\text{FEMALE}} \\ (0,1) \quad \left\{ \text{DISPLAY "GOOD MORNING, SIR"} \right. \end{cases} \\ \left\{ \text{DISPLAY "GOOD DAY"} \right.
$$

?1/ IF HOUR < 12
?2/ IF SEX = "F"

It is equally easy to bring the condition-statement format across from data to process.

3.3 REPETITIONS IN PROCESSES

There are also some interesting extensions to what we've already said about diagramming **repetitions** of processes. Here is our Warnier/Orr diagram for PRODUCE MESSAGE 3, along with an equivalent flowchart:

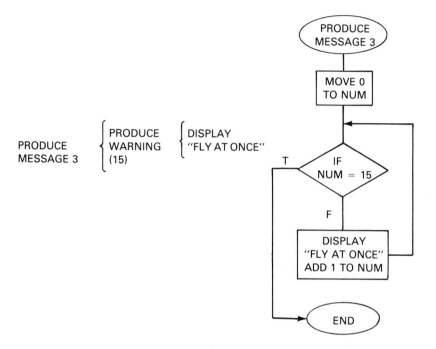

PRODUCE
MESSAGE 3 { PRODUCE
WARNING
(15) { DISPLAY
"FLY AT ONCE"

The first thing you probably noticed is how much more concise the Warnier/Orr form is. It is only fair to point out that this is the worst possible case from a flowcharting point of view; the two techniques sometimes give results much closer in size.

The second thing you may notice is the location of the test for IF NUM = 15. Why is it before the instruction DISPLAY "FLY AT ONCE" instead of after it? That is, why is it at the top of the loop rather than at the bottom?

The main reason for testing at the top of a loop is to allow *zero* repetitions. The very first thing that happens when control enters a **top-tested loop** is the checking of the exit condition:

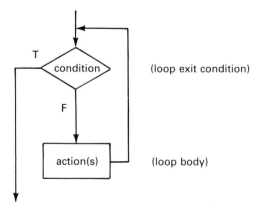

If the condition holds at the very start, the body of the loop is never executed.

But with a **bottom-tested loop**, the loop body is executed once before the condition is tested at all:

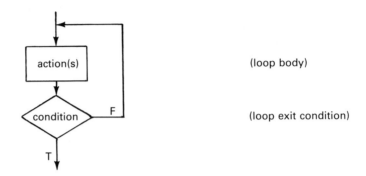

(loop body)

(loop exit condition)

so it's impossible to have zero repetitions.

Allowing for zero repetitions is only of academic interest in the current example: we always want exactly 15 repetitions. But suppose your program had to read a number, then display "FLY AT ONCE" that number of times. If the number could be zero, you'd definitely need a top-tested loop.

This difference between a process that can happen zero times and a process that must happen at least once is very important. You won't be surprised, then, to learn that there's a way of showing it on Warnier/Orr process diagrams. In fact, you won't be surprised to learn what that way is, since we've already used it when diagramming data. A repetition shown as (N) or (0,N) can happen zero times: it is top tested. A repetition shown as (1,N) must happen at least once: it is bottom tested. So we have:

TEST AT	TOP	BOTTOM
MINIMUM TIMES	0	1
WARNIER/ORR	ABLE { BAKE (**0**,B)/?5 { ?5/ UNTIL CHARLIE > DOG	ABLE { BAKE (**1**,B)/?5 { ?5/ UNTIL CHARLIE > DOG
FLOWCHART		

Notice that the exit condition "UNTIL CHARLIE > DOG" appears as a footnote in Warnier/Orr diagrams of repetitions, in the same way that a selection condition is footnoted when diagramming alternatives.

Finally, we note that the question of whether loops should in general be executed zero-to-n times vs. one-to-n times arouses passionate feelings. If you aspire to coercing general agreement on the subject, you might warm up on a less controversial topic. Perhaps religion or politics.

3.4 COMBINING STRUCTURES: HIERARCHY

It would be a dull world if everything were a sequence or an alternation or a repetition, period. To solve real-world problems we must nest repetitions within sequences, alternations within repetitions, sequences within repetitions within repetitions, and so on, and so on, and so on. You can easily imagine what the resulting diagrams might look like. At any rate, you will see a lot of them in the rest of this book.

3.5 SUMMARY

Warnier/Orr diagrams are used to describe processes. The syntax is essentially the same as for data diagrams.

A top-tested loop is executed **zero**-to-n times; a bottom-tested loop, **one**-to-n times.

3.6 EXERCISES

1. The parade described in Chapter 2, Exercise 5, has an official starter whose job is to make sure the parade leaves the starting point in the right order. Draw a Warnier/Orr diagram that tells the starter what to do. (The diagram should be essentially the same as your answer to Exercise 5 in Chapter 2, with some changes in wording.)

2. While Mr. Burfel's class is lined up for a fire drill, Santa Claus passes along the line. He gives the eight-year-old girls and the fair-haired boys electric trains; he gives the nine-year-old girls and dark-haired boys advice that will last a lifetime. He pats the ten-year-old girls on the head. Draw a Warnier/Orr diagram of this process. (It should have the same structure as your answer to Exercise 1 in Chapter 2.)

3. If you are familiar with flowcharts, use them to diagram the following series of problems:
    (a) A process called PROGRAM consists of task 1 followed by task 2 followed by task 3.
    (b) The same as (a) but task 1 consists of statement A, statement B, and statement C in order.
    (c) The same as (b) but task 2 is defined as statement X if color is green or statement Y if color is not green.
    (d) The same as (c) but task 3 consists of statement L followed by statement M, and task 3 occurs some R times (possibly zero).
    (e) The same as (d) but R must be at least 1.

4. Do Exercise 3 with one or more Warnier/Orr diagrams.

FURTHER READING

In 1965 Jacopini published an intricate mathematical proof in "Flow diagrams, Turing machines, and languages with only two formation rules," (Bohm and Jacopini). He showed that any well formed flowchart can be converted to an equivalent flowchart that uses just sequence, alternation, repetition, and hierarchy. This result provided the theoretical basis for "structured programming."

4

Code

This chapter completes the second trip from data structure through process structure to code, by showing how a Warnier/Orr process structure diagram can be turned into COBOL. One of the coding examples will also provide a chance to discuss handling of a sequential input file.

4.1 THE FIVE RULES

There are five basic rules for turning a program structure diagram into COBOL code:

1. Every universal becomes a paragraph. (Recall that a universal is something to the left of a bracket.)
2. Each universal PERFORMs its constituent universals.
3. **Sequence** is represented by a sequential list of statements.
4. **Alternation** is implemented with IF. . .THEN. . .[ELSE. . .].
5. **Repetition** is implemented with PERFORM. . .UNTIL. . . .

We will work two examples. The first will apply the rules one by one to clarify the meaning of each. The second example will be a more realistic application of the rules.

4.2 RULE BY RULE

Suppose you have derived the following process structure:

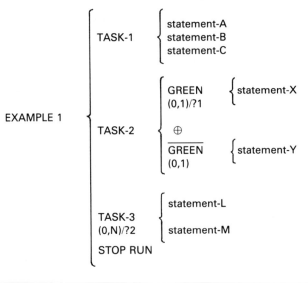

?1/ IF COLOR = "G"
?2/ UNTIL WEIGHT > 50

The statements (-A, -B, -C, etc.) are any COBOL statements you like: ADD, MOVE, UNSTRING, whatever.

We will apply the five rules one by one to create corresponding COBOL code. The first rule says universals become paragraphs, so the code will have the following outline:

```
EXAMPLE 1.
    . . .
    . . .
TASK-1.
    . . .
    . . .
TASK-2.
    . . .
    . . .
TASK-3.
    . . .
    . . .
GREEN.
    . . .
    . . .
NOT-GREEN.
    . . .
    . . .
```

Rule 2 says universals PERFORM their constituent universals. This gives:

```
EXAMPLE-1.
    PERFORM TASK-1
    PERFORM TASK-2
    PERFORM TASK-3
    STOP RUN.
TASK-1.
    . . .
    . . .
TASK-2.
    . . .
    PERFORM GREEN
    . . .
    PERFORM NOT-GREEN
TASK-3.
    . . .
    . . .
GREEN.
    . . .
    . . .
NOT-GREEN.
    . . .
    . . .
```

These PERFORMs obviously need help; we'll repair the damage shortly.

Notice we also applied rule 3: a sequence is represented by a sequential list of statements. That's how we knew enough to write the first three PERFORMs one after the other. Of course this rule applies also to the contents of tasks 1 and 3, and trivially to GREEN and NOT-GREEN. The result is:

```
EXAMPLE-1.
    PERFORM TASK-1
    PERFORM TASK-2
    PERFORM TASK-3
    STOP RUN.

TASK-1.
    statement-A.
    statement-B.
    statement-C.

TASK-2.
    . . .
    PERFORM GREEN
    . . .
    PERFORM NOT-GREEN

TASK-3.
    statement-L.
    statement-M.

GREEN.
    statement-X.

NOT-GREEN.
    statement-Y.
```

Rule 4 says an alternation is implemented with IF. . .THEN . . .[ELSE]. So TASK-2 becomes:

```
TASK-2.
    IF COLOR = "G"
        PERFORM GREEN
    ELSE
        PERFORM NOT-GREEN.
```

Finally we apply rule 5, the one about using PERFORM UNTIL for repetitions. This makes the promised correction to PERFORM TASK-3; and now that we know the PERFORMs are complete, we can terminate them with periods:

```
EXAMPLE-1.
    PERFORM TASK-1.
    PERFORM TASK-2.
    PERFORM TASK-3 UNTIL WEIGHT > 50.
    STOP RUN.

TASK-1.
    statement-A.
    statement-B.
    statement-C.

TASK-2.
    IF COLOR = "G"
        PERFORM GREEN
    ELSE
        PERFORM NOT-GREEN.

TASK-3.
    statement-L.
    statement-M.

GREEN.
    statement-X.

NOT-GREEN.
    statement-Y.
```

This completes the coding.

4.3 TOP-TESTED AND BOTTOM-TESTED LOOPS

We have said that repetition is controlled by PERFORM. . .UNTIL. But recall from Chapter 3 that we often must distinguish top-tested loops from bottom-tested ones.

A top-tested loop will give rise to zero or more repetitions of its body:

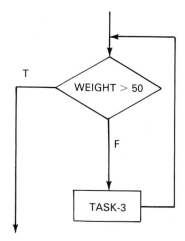

That is the situation we faced in the previous example. And luckily the COBOL PERFORM. . .UNTIL suited our needs: PERFORM. . .UNTIL generates a top-tested loop.

But suppose we instead need a bottom-tested loop. That is, suppose we want to be sure TASK-3 will execute at least once, even if the WEIGHT is greater than 50 at the start:

EXAMPLE 1

```
            ⎧  .
            ⎪  .
            ⎪  .
            ⎨                  ⎧ statement-L
            ⎪  TASK-3          ⎨
            ⎪  (1,N)/?2        ⎩ statement-M
            ⎩
```

?2/ UNTIL WEIGHT > 50

In flowcharting terms, we require:

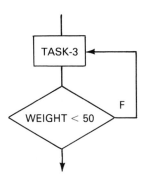

How can we ensure that TASK-3 will be executed at least once?

We ensure it by having a separate PERFORM before the PERFORM . . .UNTIL.   Like this:

```
EXAMPLE-1.
    .
    .
    PERFORM TASK-3.
    PERFORM TASK-3 UNTIL WEIGHT > 50.
```

Then TASK-3 will always be executed once before the exit condition (WEIGHT > 50) is tested for the first time.   This is the general technique for handling bottom-tested loops.

As a postscript, note that you will often see a top-tested loop called a DO WHILE and a bottom-tested loop called a DO UNTIL.   These terms help programmers in PL/1, Pascal, and some other languages remember the proper syntax. But they are confusing for COBOL programmers: remembering that a PER-FORM. . .UNTIL is a DO WHILE, with the condition negated, is more trouble than it's worth.   I suggest you stick to the terms "top tested" and "bottom tested" until you're thoroughly at home with the concepts.

4.4 PARAGRAPH BY PARAGRAPH

Now we'll work a more realistic example, and work it in a more realistic way. Instead of trying to apply one *rule* at a time, we'll code one *bracket* (paragraph) at a time.

As an employee benefit, a company occasionally makes short-term loans to its employees.   Management wants a program to list any current loans, showing employee name and the loan amount.   A typical run might produce this output:

```
LIST OF EMPLOYEE LOANS

ABEL              350.00
CUMMINGS         2625.73
MIKHANOV          985.08
    .                 .
    .                 .
    .                 .

    END OF LOAN LIST
```

The input is a file with one record for each current loan.   Since these loans are rare, the file may well be empty.

Suppose we are given the following process structure diagram.   In a few chapters we will learn how it was derived, but right now the focus is on coding it:

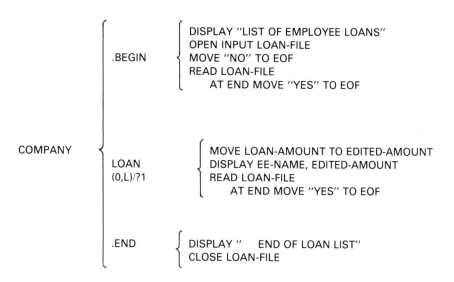

COMPANY
- .BEGIN
  - DISPLAY "LIST OF EMPLOYEE LOANS"
  - OPEN INPUT LOAN-FILE
  - MOVE "NO" TO EOF
  - READ LOAN-FILE
    - AT END MOVE "YES" TO EOF
- LOAN (O,L)/?1
  - MOVE LOAN-AMOUNT TO EDITED-AMOUNT
  - DISPLAY EE-NAME, EDITED-AMOUNT
  - READ LOAN-FILE
    - AT END MOVE "YES" TO EOF
- .END
  - DISPLAY "   END OF LOAN LIST"
  - CLOSE LOAN-FILE

?1/ UNTIL EOF = "YES"

The .BEGIN and .END labels use a common shorthand convention: the dot says to prefix the name of the universal on the left. So .BEGIN becomes COMPANY-BEGIN, and .END becomes COMPANY-END.

Now to write the COBOL code. The only interesting paragraph is the first one, and even it is pretty easy. Applying the rules gives:

```
COMPANY.
    PERFORM COMPANY-BEGIN.
    PERFORM LOAN
        UNTIL EOF = "YES".
    PERFORM COMPANY-END.
    STOP RUN.
```

COBOL demands the insertion of STOP RUN into this main line paragraph.

The other three paragraphs are straight copies from the process structure diagram:

```
COMPANY-BEGIN.
    DISPLAY "LIST OF EMPLOYEE LOANS".
    OPEN INPUT LOAN-FILE.
    MOVE "NO" TO EOF.
    READ LOAN-FILE
        AT END MOVE "YES" TO EOF.

LOAN.
    MOVE LOAN-AMOUNT TO EDITED-AMOUNT.
    DISPLAY EE-NAME, EDITED-AMOUNT.
    READ LOAN-FILE
        AT END MOVE "YES" TO EOF.

COMPANY-END.
    DISPLAY "   END OF LOAN LIST".
    CLOSE LOAN-FILE.
```

This completes the program. Before going further you may want to work out what this program will do if the input file is empty: that is, if there are no loans outstanding.

4.5 HANDLING REPETITIVE INPUT

The loan list problem introduced code for processing a sequential input file. We will now examine this logic in more detail since it's a pattern that will recur frequently. It will be important to recall that we control loops with PER-FORM. . .UNTIL, which tests at the top:

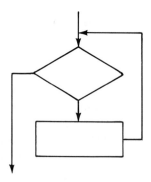

First, how does the logic work if there are no loans current and the input file is empty? At COMPANY-BEGIN we do the following:

```
OPEN INPUT LOAN-FILE.
MOVE "NO" TO EOF.
READ LOAN-FILE
    AT END MOVE "YES" TO EOF.
```

Note that EOF is a field defined in Working-Storage with PICTURE XXX.

The second instruction moves "NO" to EOF. But then the READ, because the file is empty, moves "YES" to EOF.

Then we enter the loop. It's top-tested; it has to be so LOAN can occur **0** to C times. So the exit test in footnote 1 is made: UNTIL EOF = "YES". And of course the condition is true, so we immediately exit from the loop without ever executing its body:

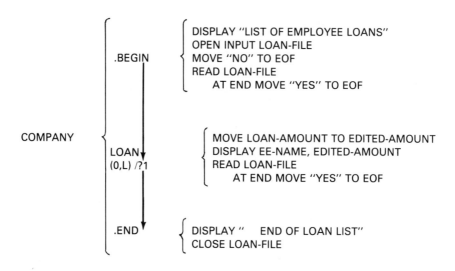

Control falls into COMPANY-END, which cleans up and stops the run. So the structure works just as it should if the input file is empty.

Now, what if there *are* some loans? Once again, COMPANY-BEGIN sets EOF to "NO". This time there *is* a record on the file, so EOF is still "NO" after the first read.

Thus, the test UNTIL EOF = "YES" is false and we enter the body of the LOAN loop. Here we display the name and amount from the first record, then READ again:

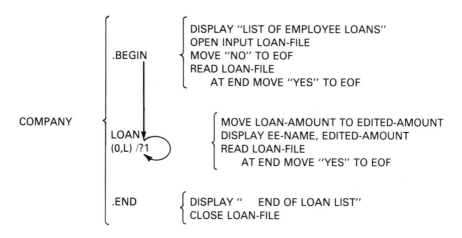

If there is another record on the input file, EOF stays at "NO". The exit condition UNTIL EOF = "YES" is still false, so we re-enter the LOAN loop body to report on this new record. And so on.

Eventually, the READ finds nothing left on the file, so AT END sets EOF to "YES". Then, of course, the exit test UNTIL EOF-READ = "YES" is true; so control passes to COMPANY-END to close the files and stop the run:

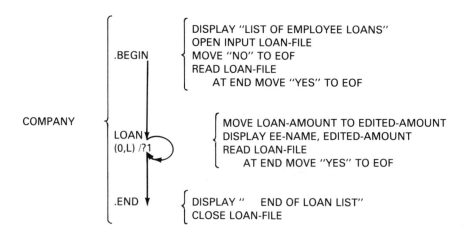

COMPANY

.BEGIN
```
DISPLAY "LIST OF EMPLOYEE LOANS"
OPEN INPUT LOAN-FILE
MOVE "NO" TO EOF
READ LOAN-FILE
    AT END MOVE "YES" TO EOF
```

LOAN
(0,L) /?1
```
MOVE LOAN-AMOUNT TO EDITED-AMOUNT
DISPLAY EE-NAME, EDITED-AMOUNT
READ LOAN-FILE
    AT END MOVE "YES" TO EOF
```

.END
```
DISPLAY "    END OF LOAN LIST"
CLOSE LOAN-FILE
```

?1/ UNTIL EOF = "YES"

Thus, the process structure also works if the input file is not empty.

4.6 NOTES ON REPETITIVE INPUT

A handy catch phrase for the technique we've used is "read once to begin, and again when a record is consumed"; I think the wording is Michael Jackson's. We read once in COMPANY-BEGIN to start things off, and again at the end of LOAN, after the current record has been "consumed" by being used for a display line.

We have seen that the technique works, even for empty files. The loop exit test is made right after COMPANY-BEGIN, before we try to process a nonexistent record. We manage to keep one step ahead of ourselves.

But it's still a bit surprising. The LOAN processing consists of process-then-read; our natural first guess would probably be read-then-process.

The Pascal programmer, for example, may object: "The process structure is modeled on mind-warping COBOL. With a sensible language like Pascal, which sets EOF *simultaneously* with finding the last record (instead of one READ later), you could have:

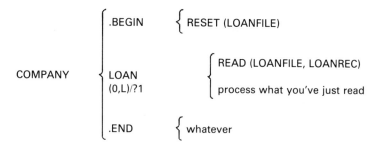

?1/ WHILE NOT EOF(LOANFILE)

Isn't that better?"

You could certainly program this structure easily in Pascal. But problems would arise when you got to multilevel control breaks, which will be discussed in Chapter 9.

Before we leave the subject, it's diverting to note some of the many essentially similar ways of handling the test for end of file:

- Define two more fields: TRUE with value "YES", FALSE with value "NO". Then you can say, for example, AT END MOVE TRUE TO EOF (as long as TRUE and FALSE aren't reserved words in your compiler.)
- Save two bytes by defining EOF as PIC X and using values "Y" and "N" (and change TRUE and FALSE accordingly).
- Use level–88 items to test the value of EOF.
- Instead of EOF, call the switch END-OF-COMPANY or ALL-LOANS-PROCESSED or something of the sort.

If you don't like defining switches, you can dispense with EOF and instead write "AT END MOVE HIGH-VALUES TO EE-NAME". Then you would test for end of file by checking EE-NAME against HIGH-VALUES, possibly using a level-88 item.

Note that this HIGH-VALUES trick is not guaranteed to work. (For example, on IBM mainframes if you move data into a file section record after end of file, you get an SOC4 program check.) To avoid the problem, you might use READ. . .INTO and process the record in Working-Storage.

So there is a wide range of options for handling the end-of-file test. In this book we will continue to use EOF with PIC XXX for consistency, but feel free to adapt it as you see fit.

4.7 SUMMARY

To turn a Warnier/Orr process diagram into COBOL code, follow the five basic rules:

1. Every universal becomes a paragraph.
2. Each universal PERFORMs its constituent universals.
3. A **sequence** becomes a sequential list of statements.
4. An **alternation** becomes an IF. . .THEN. . .[ELSE. . .].
5. A **repetition** that occurs zero or more times is handled by PERFORM . . .UNTIL. To force a repetition of **one**-to-*n* times, use PERFORM . . .PERFORM. . .UNTIL.

The rules for repetitive input are:

1. Read once to begin, and again when a record is consumed.
2. Use AT END on the READ to set the end-of-file signal.

4.8 EXERCISES

1. In the loan-listing example, your user asks you to print some asterisks to the right of any loan amount exceeding $400. All other loans are to be printed just as before. Modify the process structure diagram to handle this change; then produce the updated code.

2. Write COBOL code from this Warnier/Orr diagram:

```
                        ┌ .BEGIN          { MOVE SPACES TO OUT-NAME
                        │                   MOVE 1 TO IN-SUB, OUT-SUB
                        │
                        │  SKIP-BLANK      { ADD 1 TO IN-SUB
                        │  (0,B)/?1
BUILD OUT-NAME         ┤
                        │                   ┌ MOVE IN-CHAR (IN-SUB)
                        │  MOVE-CHAR        │    TO OUT-CHAR (OUT-SUB)
                        │  (0,N)/?2         └ ADD 1 TO IN-SUB, OUT-SUB
                        │
                        └ .END             { COMPUTE OUT-LENGTH = OUT-SUB - 1
```

?1/ UNTIL (IN-SUB > 25) OR (IN-CHAR (IN-SUB) > " ")
?2/ UNTIL (IN-SUB > 25) OR (IN-CHAR (IN-SUB) = " ")

3. What do you suppose the code in Exercise 2 is supposed to do?

4. If you code in a language other than COBOL, formulate rules corresponding to those in Section 4.1 for use in this language.

5. The rule "read once to begin, and again when a record is consumed" is fundamental to our handling of repetitive input structures. It requires that the read logic set an EOF flag to TRUE on the read *after* the one that finds the last record. If you code in a language other than COBOL, devise a READ subroutine or procedure that will do this for you.

Part II

OUTPUT

"What I tell you three times is true."

Lewis Carroll, *The Hunting of the Snark*

This will be the third time along the path from data structure, through process structure, to code. The first, in Chapter 1, was to get the lay of the land; the second, in Chapters 2 to 4, was to master the necessary tools. Now, at last, we will write real programs to produce real-life outputs.

This third trip will take up the bulk of the book. In Part II we see how to derive process structures from output data structures; then in Part III we will turn our attention to the input.

This output-first approach is fundamental to Orr's method. The output is what the user is paying for; processing and input are just unavoidable overheads. The only way to be sure we are doing the right processing, and using the right input, is to get the output right first.

5

Introduction to Logical Output Structure (LOS)

This chapter is about the structure of the output data. Of course we're talking about data structure because it will give us the process structure.

We get away with considering just the *output* data structure by assuming the input structure is the same. Real-life inputs are rarely so cooperative, but we postpone their discussion until Part III.

5.1 DESCRIBING OUTPUTS: USER REQUIREMENTS DEFINITION

We want to produce an output: a report, say. What are we given when it's time to design the report program? We're given whatever was produced during the previous phase of the system life cycle, the user requirements definition. This previous phase goes under many aliases, including functional specification, structured specification, detailed analysis, and external architecture.

This isn't a book on requirements definition. But to discuss design realistically, we have to put it in context: we're designing a program whose behavior is specified by the requirements definition.

So let's return to our question: What are we given when it's time to design a report program? It depends on the habits of our shop, or possibly of the analyst who did the requirements definition. We could be given one or more of the following things:

1. **An "X-9":** A mock-up with variables shown as Xs and 9s. Name might show as XXXXXXXXX; salary as 999,999.

2. **A sample:** A mock-up of the report with realistic data. Name might appear as FRANK MUIR; salary as 36,700.
3. **A bucket chart:** A mock-up with fields named. For example, name could show as | NAME |; salary as | SALARY |.
4. **A data structure diagram:** A Warnier/Orr diagram of the output.

5.2 THE DREADFUL X-9

Suppose the report is a list of projects. An X-9 might look like this:

PROJECT STATUS REPORT		
DEPARTMENT	PROJECT	COST
999	XXX99	99,999.99
999	XXX99	99,999.99
. .	. . .	. . .
. .	. . .	999,999.99
999	XXX99	99,999.99
999	XXX99	99,999.99
. .	. . .	. . .
. .	. . .	999,999.99
. .	. . .	. . .
. .	. . .	. . .
. .	. . .	. . .
GRAND TOTAL		9,999,999.99

Look familiar? If you've spent any time in the systems business, you've seen something like it.

It certainly gives a clear idea of the layout. Mind you, it doesn't identify which particular data elements go where, so in a minute we'll look at a different type of layout that does that.

But there are far deeper problems. If we want to design the *right* program, the one the user needs, then the X-9 is gravely flawed. If the user has only seen an X-9, it's nearly guaranteed that the X-9 is wrong.

Here is a true story. Once upon a time there were some user requirements. They called for about 300 different reports. Each report had been painstakingly X-9ed by the team doing the requirements definition, and duly signed off by the user. But when the design team prepared samples of each report, they found that *all 300 were wrong*.

How could this be? How could such a widely used tool fail so utterly? There seem to be two major X-9 defects that cause problems in user communications.

First, X-9s suppress information. The user might expect departments to be listed in decreasing order of total cost; meanwhile, the designer creates a system showing them in ascending order of department number. Or user and designer could easily have different ideas about whether all the projects for one department are to be grouped together.

The second defect in X-9s is that they don't help users define what they want. Maybe including the name of the project would make the report clearer, for example. But this likely won't occur to someone looking at the X-9. The X-9 isn't realistic; how can we expect a realistic appraisal?

When we look at a **sample**, however, things start to pop. Watch.

5.3 SAMPLES

Here is a sample of this same report:

PROJECT STATUS REPORT		
DEPARTMENT	PROJECT	COST
53	GTO52	3,640.00
53	HEW88	516.12
53	NDP60	67,388.89
		71,545.01
163	HEW88	26,503.15
		26,503.15
307	ABC39	25,924.16
307	FLQ69	38,227.00
307	PDQ05	5,833.75
307	STP77	79,805.95
		149,790.86
. .	. . .	. . .
. .	. . .	. . .
. .	. . .	. . .
GRAND TOTAL		1,317,587.32

The department numbers and project IDs are at least realistic; ideally, they include some real values the user is familiar with. The costs are sensible. A department's projects add up to the department total shown. The grand total is in the right ball park.

The point is, users don't have to make allowances. They can pretend the report has just landed on their desk. If something looks wrong, we want to hear about it.

A user can notice things like project HEW88 appearing under two departments with different amounts—is that valid? Is the project ID adequate information, or would the project name be a useful addition? Is ascending order of department number what the user wants? And so on.

What does this have to do with program design? If you're lucky, nothing. The analyst will already have produced a realistic sample of your report and will have it signed off by the user. But if this hasn't happened, you'd be well advised to make a sample yourself and clear it with the user before proceeding further with program design.

5.4 LOGICAL DATA LAYOUTS (BUCKET CHARTS)

So we'll assume that, one way or another, you have in your possession a realistic sample. Now remember our purely technical criticism of the X-9: it didn't identify the individual data elements by name. This statement, sad to say, applies also to samples, however realistic; and it's to remedy this deficiency that a designer needs the logical data layout or "bucket chart."

For our project report, the bucket chart looks like this:

As you can see, the bucket chart shows which fields appear where. Each bucket defines an atomic data element. If the element is a literal, its value appears in the bucket in quotes; if the element is a variable, its name appears there.

Bucket charts were devised by Jean-Dominique Warnier. As far as the designer is concerned they provide a useful bridge between the sample and the data structure diagram.

5.5 LOS: THE LOGICAL OUTPUT STRUCTURE

We have one final way of describing an output: a data structure diagram. If you want to maximize the return on the time you're investing in this book, take a couple of minutes now to draw a Warnier/Orr diagram of the above report. Then compare it with the following:

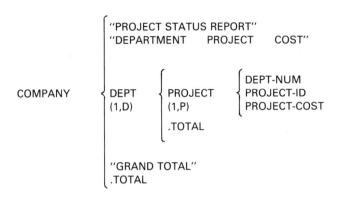

We have again used the dot convention of Chapter 4: the .TOTAL in the COMPANY bracket is COMPANY-TOTAL; the one in the DEPT bracket is DEPT-TOTAL. And recall that the quoted strings are literals: "PROJECT STATUS REPORT" appears exactly as it does on the report.

We call the whole structure COMPANY (rather than, say, REPORT) because the other universals in the diagram refer to organizational entities (like department). Naturally, if you work for a state government, you call the structure STATE instead of COMPANY; if the report covers only projects from one division, you call it DIVISION; and so on.

But those are the easy points. If you tried this exercise before looking at the answer, you had to wrestle with the question: "What about page breaks? How do I show that the report is divided into pages with the headers repeated at the top of each page?" Similarly, you may wonder how to show that "GRAND TOTAL" and COMPANY-TOTAL appear on the same output line; or how to show that the top two literals ("PROJECT. . ." and "DEPARTMENT. . .") are on separate lines. These are tough questions.

Charlie Brown is quoted as saying that no problem is too big to run away from. We are going to run away from these. We will rigorously separate logical questions (*what* appears on the output) from physical ones (*how* the output is arranged); and then we'll put the physical ones on the back burner.

When it comes to reports, for example, we adopt the **one-page rule**: we assume all reports are exactly one page long, so we don't have to worry about page breaks. And we pay no attention to which data elements are on the same line and which are on different lines; we care only about their order of appearance. We don't care whether the output will be printed on paper, displayed on a screen, or transmitted down a telephone line. For a data base output, we ignore the particular data base management system (DBMS) we are using. If the output is an on/off control signal to an electronic device, we don't worry about which voltage level means "on" and which means "off." All such questions are postponed until Chapter 9 or later.

Once we have done this, we are left essentially with a stream of data elements to be produced. The Warnier/Orr diagram of this stream is called the logical output structure or LOS—"logical" because all physical considerations are removed. (LOS is pronounced "ell owe ess," not "loss".)

This logical-before-physical approach is another of Orr's fundamental tenets: the longer we postpone our consideration of the physical, the more immune the design will be to merely physical changes in requirements.

5.6 DIGRESSION: LOSs FOR USER COMMUNICATION

Data structure diagrams are remarkably useful tools, as we said before. And of course we need them for program design, since the data structure will yield the program structure.

But after the discussion of user communication you may be wondering: How good are Warnier/Orr diagrams for communicating with users? They look like the sort of thing a programmer would like; but how could a businessperson possibly understand them?

Very easily, as it turns out. Average users take about a minute to get used to Warnier/Orr diagrams; that's the time it takes you to draw one while they watch. Don't tell them about the wonderful new tool you've found. Don't send them to courses in structured systems design. Don't even set up an informal session to teach them about the diagrams. Just start to draw one, explaining what it means, as you discuss a report with your user.

For example, in discussing the project report you could say the following while taking the actions described in brackets:

> I want to be sure about what's going to be in this report. As I understand it, this report will cover the entire company. [You write COMPANY and draw the major bracket.] There will be a report label saying "PROJECT STATUS REPORT" [write it in] and column headings of "DEPARTMENT", "PROJECT", and "COST" [write them]. Then will come a list of all the departments in the company [write DEPT and draw its bracket]; we don't know how many there are, so let's just say there are D of them [write in (l,D)]. . . .

And so on. Users won't know or care that you're following a set of rules; they'll just see an understandable picture of the report emerging. As one analyst reported, "I've been drawing lots of curly braces . . . and find that my 'user'—an intelligent commercial loan officer with no technical background—is able to grasp them with no explanation given."

Yes, data structure diagrams are excellent communications tools. In fact, Tom DeMarco suggests they're **all** you need for negotiating and communicating data requirements with the user.* He suggests you stick to (essentially) LOSs during the analysis phase, and through design if you can manage it.

That's taking a risk. You can learn something about ducks by looking at a picture. But you learn a lot more by seeing a sample duck. A picture (LOS) may be worth a thousand words, but a sample is worth many pictures. You still need your sample.

* See *Structured Analysis and System Specification*, p. 164. DeMarco represents data structures in his own language, called "Data Dictionary Definition Conventions." The diagrams don't look anything like Warnier/Orr diagrams, but it's possible to translate one into the other.

5.7 MORE LOS PRACTICE

We have seen four ways of communicating with the user to define report outputs, and have discovered that three of them are useful. Naturally, there is more to user requirements than report outputs, but this isn't a book about requirements definition.

It *is* a book about design, and the question we started with is: How are we going to design a report program? You probably have a good idea already. Draw an LOS: a logical output structure diagram. And then—of course—derive the process structure from this data structure. We will have much more to say about deriving the process structure in a couple of chapters. But because LOSs are so critical to the technique, we'll first study them in more depth.

We've just seen that it is sometimes possible to draw the LOS from inspection: look at the bucket chart; draw the Warnier/Orr diagram. In the next chapter we'll see a more formal way of drawing LOSs, but for the moment, let's continue to work by inspection. We'll look at a user change request for this report. Suppose the user gets tired of seeing the department number repeated on every line. Instead, it should just be listed once: for the first project of that department. The bucket chart becomes:

This small change to the report requires a small change to the data structure diagram. Once again, you will get a bigger payoff from your reading time if you try this problem before you look at the answer.

Here is the LOS with the change made:

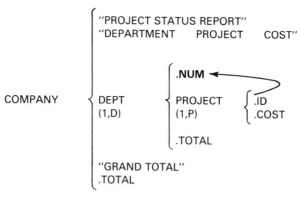

The department number has been moved from appearing once per PROJECT, as it did on the original report. It now appears once per DEPT.

Remember, this is a *logical* output structure. Physically, DEPT-NUM is printed on the same line as PROJECT-ID and PROJECT-COST. That's one reason we have to keep the bucket chart around for the programmer to look at.

5.8 SUMMARY

This chapter introduced two of Orr's key ideas: start with the output, and look at logical structure before physical.

We begin our analysis of a programming problem with the output because the output is the independent variable. Only by being clear about the output can we know what processing to do and what inputs we need.

We must have a common understanding with the user of what the output will be. An LOS (logical output structure) is always useful here. For a report output, we also need samples and bucket charts (logical data layouts). Naturally we hope this has all been taken care of during the requirements definition stage. If it hasn't, we rectify the deficiency before proceeding.

An LOS is a Warnier/Orr diagram of an output. It ignores all physical considerations: page breaks, line groupings, output data base system, and so on.

5.9 EXERCISES

1. Change the bucket chart and the LOS of the project report so the current month and year are shown just below the top header line.
2. Find a report or other output that you have defined or programmed. Draw an LOS for it.
3. Did you ever write a program only to discover it didn't do what the user expected? If so, what might you do differently to reduce the chance of that happening?

FURTHER READING

For a complete description of Orr's method of ascertaining user requirements, including output definition, see his *Structured Requirements Definition*.

6

Logical Output Structure Formalized

In the previous chapter we met the logical output structure: a Warnier/Orr diagram of an output, ignoring physical considerations. We created some LOSs by inspection. In this chapter we discuss Orr's formal method for creating an LOS.

6.1 INTRODUCTION TO LFUD

First we introduce an unofficial name for the technique: LFUD (pronounced "el fudd"). LFUD goes like this:

LFUD $\begin{cases} \textbf{LIST} \text{ all the atoms} \\ \text{give the } \textbf{FREQUENCY} \text{ of each atom} \\ \text{do the } \textbf{UNIVERSAL} \text{ analysis} \\ \text{draw the } \textbf{DIAGRAM} \end{cases}$

To find out what this means we will work through some examples. We start with the project report from Chapter 5, using the last version we saw, the one in which department number is printed only on the first line of a department.

The basic idea behind LFUD is this: every element in a Warnier/Orr diagram is either an atom (not divided further) or a universal (which is divided). If you work out all the atoms and universals and how they relate to each other, you have your diagram.

Step 1. List. LFUD begins with the atoms; the first step is to list all of them. An atom, remember, is something that can't be decomposed further: it's a basic unit of information. In the case of a report, the atoms will be the data elements. All the data elements of a report will be identified on its logical data layout (bucket chart). Here they are for the project report:

DATA ELEMENT	DETAILS
REPORT-TITLE	"PROJECT STATUS REPORT"
COLUMN-HEADINGS	"DEPARTMENT PROJECT..."
DEPT-NUM	
PROJECT-ID	
PROJECT-COST	
DEPT-TOTAL	
COMPANY-TOTAL-LABEL	"GRAND TOTAL"
COMPANY-TOTAL	

Notice that we included the values of any literals. You don't have to give the complete value of each—the first few words will do, since the complete literal will be clear from the sample or bucket chart.

Some people just place the literal values in quotes in the data element column and don't bother to name them at all:

DATA ELEMENT
"PROJECT STATUS REPORT"
"DEPARTMENT   PROJECT. . ."
DEPT-NUM
PROJECT-ID
PROJECT-COST
DEPT-TOTAL
"GRAND TOTAL"
COMPANY-TOTAL

Our goal is to turn a bucket chart into a Warnier/Orr diagram. We have listed the atomic elements for the diagram. Now we have to identify the universals—the brackets—and figure out how these universals fit together.

Step 2: Frequency. What will the universals be? If something appears, say, once per company, there had better be a bracket called COMPANY in the final diagram. If something else appears once per department, we'll need a DEPT bracket. So as our second step of LFUD we identify the frequency with which each atom *appears*, where frequency means "once per what?":

DATA ELEMENT	APPEARS	DETAILS
REPORT-TITLE	1/COMPANY(B)	"PROJECT STATUS REPORT"
COLUMN-HEADINGS	1/COMPANY(B)	"DEPARTMENT PROJECT. ."
DEPT-NUM	1/DEPT(B)	
PROJECT-ID	1/PROJECT	
PROJECT-COST	1/PROJECT	
DEPT-TOTAL	1/DEPT(E)	
COMPANY-TOTAL-LABEL	1/COMPANY(E)	"GRAND TOTAL"
COMPANY-TOTAL	1/COMPANY(E)	

The "APPEARS" column is interpreted like this:

```
1/PROJECT     = "appears once per project"
1/DEPT (B)    = "appears once per department at DEPT-BEGIN"
1/COMPANY (E) = "appears once per company at COMPANY-END"
```

If you find it troubling that REPORT-TITLE appears once per COMPANY rather than once per PAGE, you're in good—er—company. It certainly seems artificial. But remember the one-page rule: draw the LOS as if the report is one page long. The restriction will be removed in plenty of time to write an accurate program.

Step 3: Universal Analysis. We are now ready for the third step of LFUD: universal analysis. Recall our reason for listing the frequency—the "once-per-what?"—of each data element: the "whats" will become the universals.

Thus, in the case of the project report the universals will be:

```
COMPANY
DEPT
PROJECT
```

Now we have to figure out which brackets will fit inside which: that is, how these universals relate to each other in the report. We start by finding the leftmost bracket, the one that will contain all the others. We need a universal that occurs exactly once; and of course COMPANY fills the bill:

UNIVERSAL	OCCURS
COMPANY	1
DEPT	
PROJECT	

As for the other two universals: DEPT appears one-to-D times per COMPANY and PROJECT appears one-to-P times per DEPT:

UNIVERSAL	OCCURS
COMPANY	1
DEPT	1,D/COMPANY
PROJECT	1,P/DEPT

And there we are—the universal analysis is completed.

Perhaps you were troubled by the glib assumption that PROJECT appears one-to-P times per DEPT. In real life you would have to ask your user. Maybe the user wants every department listed, even if it has *no* active projects. In that case of course PROJECT would occur **zero**-to-P times per department; so we would write:

```
PROJECT        0,P/DEPT
```

The same goes for DEPT within COMPANY.

Step 4: Diagram. If the user approves the above statements, we're ready to move on to the fourth step of LFUD: Draw the diagram.

This divides into two parts: (1) create a place for everything and (2) put everything in its place. We create a place for everything by drawing the brackets the universal analysis demands. For the project report, the universal analysis shows there will be three brackets fitting together like this:

```
COMPANY   ┤ DEPT    ┤ PROJECT  ┤
          | (1,D)   | (1,P)    |
```

And now we put everything in its place. "Everything" means all the atoms in our list from Step 1. Inserting them is a mechanical operation:

```
              ┤ REPORT-TITLE
              | COLUMN-HEADINGS
              |
              |           ┤ .NUM
              |           |              ┤ .ID
COMPANY       ┤ DEPT      ┤ PROJECT      ┤ .COST
              | (1,D)     | (1,P)        |
              |           |
              |           | .TOTAL
              |
              | .TOTAL-LABEL
              | .TOTAL
```

Note the underlining that has appeared in the LOS. This shows **sort sequence**. The LOS purports to be a complete description of the logical output, so it has to show the order in which the output appears. The underlining indicates that departments are sequenced in DEPT-NUM order, and that a given department's projects are ordered by PROJECT-ID.

And there we have it: a logical output structure formally derived by the LFUD process. Of course in this case there was little need for a formal process. We proved that earlier, when we drew the diagram directly from the logical data layout. But for complicated outputs the method comes in very handy; and even in simpler cases it helps avoid careless errors.

We must note a few of points before proceeding. First, LFUD isn't hocus-pocus. It's a straightforward technique to keep us from slipping up. You should always be able to come pretty close to the LOS by inspection—the way we did with the project report in the previous chapter. If you draw every diagram by inspection, as well as by LFUD, the duplication will provide a useful check on the accuracy of your work.

Second, nothing about outputs makes them uniquely suited to LFUD. LFUD can be an aid in drawing *any* kind of Warnier/Orr diagram. We will use it in two or three different ways before the book is finished.

Finally, we noted in Section 2.6 that the terms "universal" and "set" are used interchangeably. You can now see why we have opted for "universal": LFSD would be much harder to pronounce.

6.2 ACCOUNTING REPORT

The user wants the accounting entries for a day listed in account-number order. The sample looks like this:

```
┌─────────────────────────────────────────────────────┐
│        ACCOUNTING ENTRIES FOR JULY 17, 1985          │
│                                                       │
│   ACCOUNT              DEBIT          CREDIT          │
│                                                       │
│   1234-42-3384         200.00                         │
│   1234-42-3384                        1430.00         │
│   2436-38-1942         550.95                         │
│   3719-81-1759                         567.55         │
│   5711-74-3986                         347.62         │
│   6570-12-2415         697.47                         │
│   8800-90-1000        1318.18                         │
│   8800-90-1000                        1256.85         │
│   8800-90-1000         835.92                         │
└─────────────────────────────────────────────────────┘
```

The bucket chart is:

```
┌─────────────────────────────────────────────────────────┐
│     |"ACCOUNTING ENTRIES FOR"|  |REPORT-DATE|            │
│                                                           │
│  | "ACCOUNT              DEBIT              CREDIT" |     │
│                                                           │
│  | ACCOUNT-NUMBER |  | DEBIT-AMOUNT |                     │
│  |_____|  |_____|  |CREDIT-AMOUNT|   │
│  |_____|  |_____|                    │
│  |_____|  |_____|                    │
└─────────────────────────────────────────────────────────┘
```

As we run through LFUD, notice the treatment of alternation. Here is the list of elements:

DATA ELEMENT		DETAILS
REPORT-TITLE REPORT-DATE COLUMN-HEADINGS ACCOUNT-NUMBER DEBIT-AMOUNT CREDIT-AMOUNT		"ACCOUNTING ENTRIES FOR" "ACCOUNT DEBIT. . ."

Now add the frequencies:

DATA ELEMENT	APPEARS	DETAILS
REPORT-TITLE	1/COMPANY(B)	"ACCOUNTING ENTRIES FOR"
REPORT-DATE	1/COMPANY(B)	
COLUMN-HEADINGS	1/COMPANY(B)	"ACCOUNT DEBIT..."
ACCOUNT-NUMBER	1/ENTRY	
DEBIT-AMOUNT	**1/DEBIT**	
CREDIT-AMOUNT	**1/CREDIT**	

Notice that DEBIT-AMOUNT appears once per debit; CREDIT-AMOUNT appears once per credit.

Next, the universals:

UNIVERSAL	OCCURS
COMPANY	1
ENTRY	1,E/COMPANY
DEBIT	**0,1**/ENTRY
CREDIT	**0,1**/ENTRY

Notice that DEBIT and CREDIT are both **0,1**/ENTRY. We haven't seen that before.

Finally, the diagram. First, we create a place for everything:

COMPANY { ENTRY (1,E) { DEBIT (0,1) { ⊕ CREDIT (0,1) {

We've used some information that wasn't in the universal analysis: DEBIT and CREDIT are related by an **exclusive or** (⊕). We know from basic accounting (or from the user) that every entry is a debit or a credit, but not both.

Now everything goes in its place:

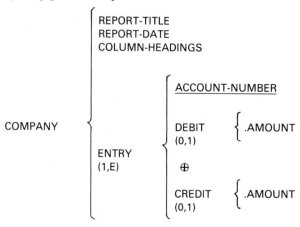

COMPANY { REPORT-TITLE REPORT-DATE COLUMN-HEADINGS ENTRY (1,E) { ACCOUNT-NUMBER DEBIT (0,1) { .AMOUNT ⊕ CREDIT (0,1) { .AMOUNT

(Once again we have used underlining to show the sequence of the output: the entries are in order by ACCOUNT-NUMBER.) Debit amount and credit amount are mutually exclusive fields on the outputs, so they generate mutually exclusive brackets on the LOS.

Of course, it *might* happen that the input file has only one field—AMOUNT, say—that represents a debit if it's negative but a credit if it's positive. This fact about the *physical input* structure would have absolutely no effect on the *logical output* structure. (It would, however, affect the logical read routine, which will be described in Part III.)

6.3 EXPENSE REPORT

The user wants a monthly listing of expenses. Here is the sample:

```
                    MONTHLY EXPENSE REPORT              PAGE    1
                         MAY   1987


EXPENSE CATEGORY
DATE            SUPPLIER        ITEM                        COST

OFFICE SUPPLIES

05-10-87        PRINTERS INC.   BUSINESS CARDS             50.00
05-10-87        PRINTERS INC.   LETTERHEAD                 75.00
05-25-87        COMPUSTORE      DISKETTES                  90.00

                                TOTAL FOR OFFICE SUPPLIES  215.00
   •                •               •                         •
   •                •               •                         •
   •                •               •                         •

TRAVEL EXPENSES

05-03-87        JENKINS         CARSON CITY, NV            525.00
05-03-87        STEVENSON       LANSING,MI                 375.26
05-21-87        MILLBROOK       PRINCE ALBERT, SASK        400.18

                                TOTAL FOR TRAVEL EXPENSES  1,300.44
                                    •                         •
                                    •                         •
                                    •                         •
                                GRAND TOTAL                45,907.95
```

Notice that the expense items are grouped into categories; each category begins with its name and ends with the total expense amount for that category. The report order is category, then date, then supplier, then item.

Here is the bucket chart:

```
                    |"MONTHLY EXPENSE REPORT"|        |"PAGE"| |PAGE-NO|

                          |REPORT MONTH|
|"EXPENSE CATEGORY"|

|"DATE        SUPPLIER            ITEM                    COST"        |



|  CATEGORY-NAME  |
|ITEM-DATE| |SUPPLIER-NAME|  |    ITEM-DESCRIPTION    |  |ITEM-AMOUNT|
|_____|  |_____|    |_____|  |_____|
|_____|  |_____|    |_____|  |_____|

     .          .                    .                      .
     .          .                    .                      .
                |"TOTAL FOR"|   |CATEGORY-NAME|      |CATEGORY-TOTAL|
                                      .
                                      .
                                |"GRAND TOTAL"|      |COMPANY-TOTAL|
```

And now we can begin LFUD. Here is the list of data elements, along with the frequency of each:

DATA ELEMENT	APPEARS	DETAILS
REPORT-TITLE	1/COMPANY	"MONTHLY EXPENSE REPORT"
PAGE-LABEL	**1/COMPANY**	"PAGE"
PAGE-NO	**1/COMPANY**	
REPORT-MONTH	"	
COLUMN-HEADINGS	"	"EXPENSE CATEGORY"
		"DATE SUPPLIER . . ."
CATEGORY-NAME	**1/CATEGORY**	
ITEM-DATE	1/ITEM	
SUPPLIER-NAME	"	
ITEM-DESCRIPTION	"	
ITEM-AMOUNT	"	
CATEGORY-TOTAL-LABEL	1/CATEGORY	"TOTAL FOR"
CATEGORY-NAME	"	
CATEGORY-TOTAL	"	
COMPANY-TOTAL-LABEL	1/COMPANY	"GRAND TOTAL"
COMPANY-TOTAL	"	

Note the frequencies of page number and page label. It's tempting to say they appear once per page. But remember the one-page rule: for the purposes of the LOS, we assume the report is one page long. Therefore once per page = once per company (since this report covers the whole company); so 1/COMPANY is the frequency we use.

The report sample showed that the CATEGORY-NAME appears twice for each category: once at the beginning, once at the end. But we must always show frequency of appearance as *once* per something. That's why in the above table CATEGORY-NAME appears twice: once for the beginning appearance, once for the ending one.

The universal analysis is straightforward. There are only three different things in the "appears" column and they relate like this:

UNIVERSAL	OCCURS
COMPANY	1
CATEGORY	1,C/COMPANY
ITEM	1,I/CATEGORY

So now we can draw the diagram. First, we must find a place for everything:

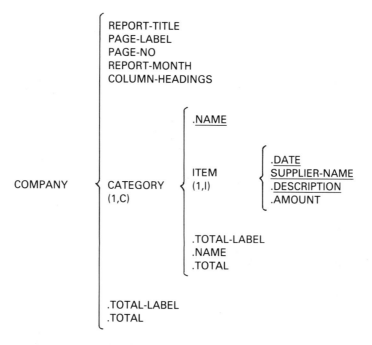

and then put everything in its place:

As usual, the underlining indicates sequencing, but here it looks a bit different from the previous examples. There are three underlined fields within ITEM. They indicate that the ITEMs in a given category are sequenced by DATE; within DATE, by SUPPLIER-NAME; and within SUPPLIER-NAME, by DESCRIPTION.

This is probably a good place to mention a few other extensions to the underlining notation. For instance, suppose the items are in *descending* order by date. We can write:

$$
\left\{
\begin{array}{l}
\cdots \\[6pt]
\begin{array}{l} \text{ITEM} \\ (1,\mathrm{I}) \end{array}
\left\{
\begin{array}{l}
\underline{.\text{DATE}}_{\text{D}} \\
\underline{\text{SUPPLIER-NAME}} \\
\underline{.\text{DESCRIPTION}} \\
.\text{AMOUNT}
\end{array}
\right. \\[24pt]
\cdots
\end{array}
\right.
$$

Or suppose the sequence is changed to DATE within DESCRIPTION within SUPPLIER-NAME:

$$
\left\{
\begin{array}{l}
\cdots \\[6pt]
\begin{array}{l} \text{ITEM} \\ (1,\mathrm{I}) \end{array}
\left\{
\begin{array}{l}
\underline{.\text{DATE}}_{3} \\
\underline{\text{SUPPLIER-NAME}}_{1} \\
\underline{.\text{DESCRIPTION}}_{2} \\
.\text{AMOUNT}
\end{array}
\right. \\[24pt]
\cdots
\end{array}
\right.
$$

Finally, you can mix the D and the integers in the obvious way:

$$
\left\{
\begin{array}{l}
\cdots \\[6pt]
\begin{array}{l} \text{ITEM} \\ (1,\mathrm{I}) \end{array}
\left\{
\begin{array}{l}
\underline{.\text{DATE}}_{\text{D}3} \\
\underline{\text{SUPPLIER-NAME}}_{1} \\
\underline{.\text{DESCRIPTION}}_{2} \\
.\text{AMOUNT}
\end{array}
\right. \\[24pt]
\cdots
\end{array}
\right.
$$

6.4 HIDDEN HIERARCHIES

It may be useful to introduce the idea of hidden hierarchy at this point. We will make no serious use of it until Part III ("Input"), but it will be good to have the groundwork in place.

Recall the accounting report of Section 6.2. We came up with this LOS:

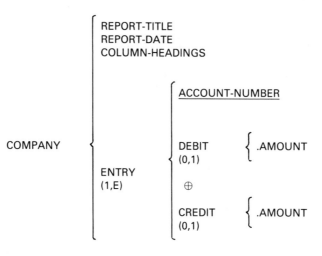

The underlining indicates that the entries are sequenced by ACCOUNT-NUMBER. Of course, one result of this sequencing is that all entries for the same account number are grouped together:

ACCOUNTING ENTRIES FOR JULY 17, 1985		
ACCOUNT	DEBIT	CREDIT
1234-42-3384	200.00	
1234-42-3384		1430.00
2436-38-1942	550.95	
3719-81-1759		567.55
5711-74-3986		347.62
6570-12-2415	697.47	
8800-90-1000	1318.18	
8800-90-1000		1256.85
8800-90-1000	835.92	

If we wish, we can redraw the LOS to point out the "hidden hierarchy" created by this grouping:

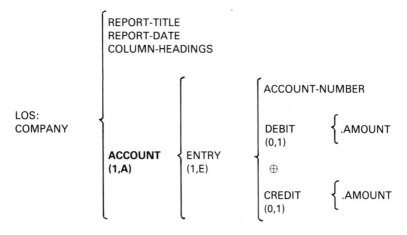

Notice that the ACCOUNT bracket contains no atomic elements. No *field* appears at this level; that's why the LFUD process didn't identify it.

Now let's look at the expense report from Section 6.3. Its LOS was:

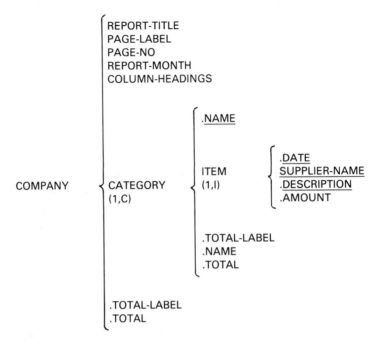

Here the sequencing by DATE and by SUPPLIER-NAME has introduced two hidden hierarchies, which we can add to the diagram if we wish:

There are no hidden hierarchies in the Project List that we discussed in Section 6.1. The hierarchies that would be created by the sequencing fields—namely, DEPT and PROJECT—already exist.

If an LOS has hidden hierarchies, a diagram that makes them explicit by giving each of them its own bracket is certainly an accurate picture of the output. But these extra levels are not normally drawn as part of the LOS: the LFUD method results in an LOS that only has a bracket for each level at which an item *appears*. We use the underlining convention to indicate sequence, and leave the resultant grouping implicit.

So why are we discussing hidden hierarchies at all? The first reason is that when you draw an LOS by inspection (rather than by the LFUD method), there is a tendency to include the hidden hierarchies. Knowing about the concept lets you ignore purely cosmetic differences between the inspection and LFUD versions of the same diagram.

A second and more important reason for discussing hidden hierarchies is that they will appear again when we discuss the input mapping in Part III.

6.5 SUMMARY

The logical output structure is a picture of an output: a Warnier/Orr diagram ignoring all physical characteristics. You can derive it by applying LFUD, and adding a couple of important bits of documentation. The process is illustrated below.

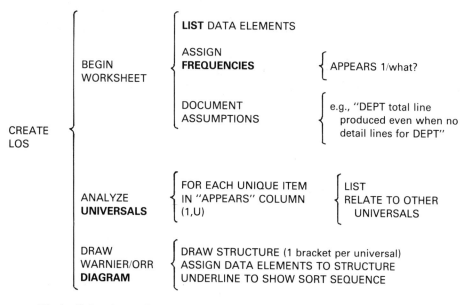

Underlining is used on the LOS to show sequencing. Sequencing can result in "hidden hierarchies": levels of grouping that were not exposed by the LFUD process.

The "worksheet" referred to in the diagram above is a preprinted "Output Definition Form," available from Ken Orr and Associates, that you can use in deriving the logical output structure.

The worksheet is also useful in deriving the logical output mapping (LOM), which is the next topic we will discuss. Because you always proceed to the LOM from the LOS, there is no point in rigorously separating the fields on the worksheet needed for the LOS from those needed for the LOM. Thus, the Ken Orr and Associates guidelines on creating an LOS call for more information than is shown above; the extra information is needed for the LOM.

6.6 EXERCISES

Use LFUD to draw the LOS for one or more of the outputs that you have had to program on the job.

7

Logical Output Mapping (LOM)

The goal, of course, is to derive **process** structure from the output structures we have been constructing. In this chapter we will see how to work out a **logical** process structure: one that is independent of language, computer, and operating system. Subsequent chapters will discuss how to turn this logical structure into a physical one that can be coded from.

Orr's company now refers to processes as "mappings." The term is borrowed from mathematics, where a mapping (also called a function or an operation) can be viewed as transforming an independent variable into a dependent variable. Similarly, a computing process transforms input to output.

So "mapping" is used to refer to processes, programs, and routines. Specifically, what was formerly known as the logical process structure is now called the logical output mapping (LOM). It is the subject of this chapter.

We will again start by doing a problem intuitively, and then get more formal.

7.1 THE PROJECT REPORT

As before, the problem for intuition is the project report from Chapter 5. The logical data layout is:

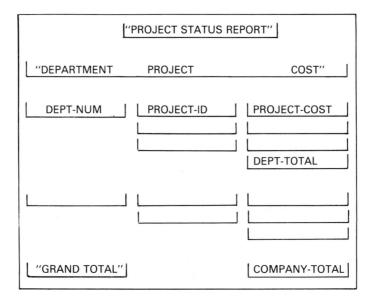

The LOS, as developed in Chapters 5 and 6, is:

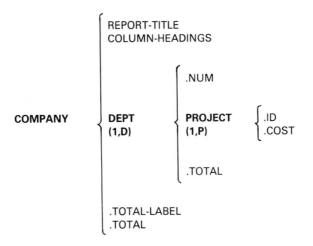

If data structure yields process structure, the process structure must be:

COMPANY { DEPT { PROJECT {
         { (1,D) { (1,P)   {

This is correct but Spartan. When there's a repetition, there is almost always housekeeping required—for example, initializing beforehand and producing totals afterward. We create .BEGIN and .END brackets to give such items comfortable homes:

```
          ┌ .BEGIN {
          │
          │                    ┌ .BEGIN {
          │                    │
COMPANY  ⟨  DEPT              ⟨ PROJECT
          │   (1,D)            │  (1,P)              {
          │                    │
          │                    │  .END   {
          │                    └
          │
          └ .END   {
```

This gives a place for everything; now to put everything in its place. We'll start with the **calculations**. There are department totals and a company total; these have to be initialized and accumulated. Here is one way to do it:

```
          ┌ .BEGIN { SET COMPANY-TOTAL TO 0
          │
          │              ┌ .BEGIN { SET DEPT-TOTAL TO 0
          │              │
COMPANY  ⟨  DEPT         ⟨ PROJECT       { ADD PROJECT-COST TO DEPT-TOTAL
          │   (1,D)      │  (1,P)
          │              │
          │              │  .END   { ADD DEPT-TOTAL TO COMPANY-TOTAL
          │              └
          │
          └ .END   {
```

The totals will then be cleared at the appropriate places: COMPANY-TOTAL at COMPANY-BEGIN, and DEPT-TOTAL at DEPT-BEGIN. Then as each project comes through, its cost is added to DEPT-TOTAL. And at the end of each DEPT, the department's total is added to COMPANY-TOTAL.

(Alternatively, we could have inserted "ADD PROJECT-COST TO COM-PANY-TOTAL" in the PROJECT bracket and dropped "ADD DEPT-TOTAL TO COMPANY-TOTAL" from DEPT-END. It would be less efficient, but logically equivalent.)

That takes care of the calculations; now for some output. It is handled by the emphasized statements in the following diagram:

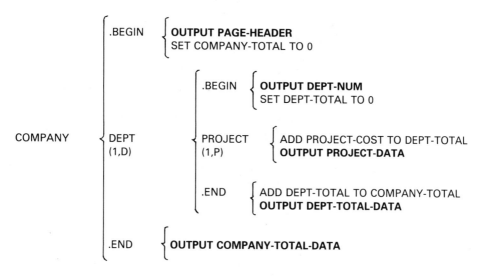

Synonyms for OUTPUT would be PRINT, PRODUCE, or FORMAT AND PRINT. This is a **logical** output operation: we are still not paying attention to page breaks, line formats, channel skips, and so on. (Speaking of page breaks, notice that "OUTPUT PAGE-HEADER" is shown once—at COMPANY-BE-GIN—in keeping with the one-page rule.)

There is one **output** command for each group of items that appears together on the LOS. So, for example, DEPT-NUM has its own output statement, separate from PROJECT-DATA, because the two entities appear in different universals.

Of course when we move to physical implementation, it is possible that an entire print line, containing DEPT-NUM (or blanks) and the PROJECT-DATA, will be printed at once. Possible, but not necessary. We leave that to the skill of the programmer.

Finally, the process needs some **input**. To keep things simple, we will insert the minimum number of instructions that will work correctly.

We assume the simplest possible input. This is a single file of records, all with the same format. If you're old enough to remember key punches, you can think of it as a file of punched cards. The simplest input file will look like this:

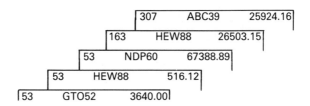

Each of these cards is called a **logical record**. The ordered collection of logical records is called the **logical input file**, or sometimes the **ideal file**. The term "ideal" refers to the fact that such a file would make life very simple for whoever has to code from the LOM.

Notice that DEPARTMENT-NUMBER is repeated on every logical record, even though the output shows it only once per department. Such redundancy is typical of the "ideal" file. As an extreme example, if the CURRENT-DATE is needed only once—say at the top of the report—it will appear on every logical record. A file with this much redundancy falls short of many people's notion of ideal; so in this book we will normally stick with the phrase "logical input file," or LIF.

The logical input file has the same hierarchical structure as the LOS. Thus, for the project list, the LIF is:

LIF: COMPANY { DEPT (1,D) { PROJECT (1,P) { DEPT-NUM / PROJECT-ID / PROJECT-COST

The LIF always has the same structure as the LOS. But it contains only the *required* data elements; and these are pushed all the way to the right.

With such an input file, we can immediately apply the read-once-to-begin-again-when-consumed rule developed in Chapter 4:

COMPANY {
.BEGIN { **GET LOGICAL RECORD** / OUTPUT PAGE-HEADER / SET COMPANY-TOTAL TO 0

DEPT (1,D) {
.BEGIN { OUTPUT DEPT-NUM / SET DEPT-TOTAL TO 0
PROJECT (1,P) { ADD PROJECT-COST TO DEPT-TOTAL / OUTPUT PROJECT-DATA / **GET LOGICAL RECORD**
.END { ADD DEPT-TOTAL TO COMPANY-TOTAL / OUTPUT DEPT-TOTAL-DATA
}

.END { OUTPUT COMPANY-TOTAL-DATA
}

The interesting point was figuring out when the previous record has been consumed. Pretty clearly, it's consumed when its detail line has been written; hence the placement of the second GET LOGICAL RECORD immediately after OUTPUT PROJECT-DATA.

7.2 DATA ELEMENT TYPES

Here is the forest that may have got lost in the trees:

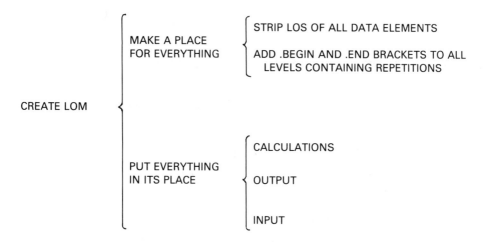

There was a lot of arm waving during the discussion of calculations, output, and input. Let's begin to make the method more rigorous by identifying which data elements can be output as they are, which need calculating, and which need to be input. We add a column to the table developed in Chapter 6 and use it to identify each data element as a literal ("L"), calculated ("C"), or required on input ("*"):

DATA ELEMENT	APPEARS	TYPE	DETAILS
REPORT-TITLE	1/COMPANY	L	"PROJECT STATUS REPORT"
COLUMN-HEADINGS	1/COMPANY	L	"DEPARTMENT PROJECT..."
DEPT-NUM	1/DEPT	*	
PROJECT-ID	1/PROJECT	*	
PROJECT-COST	1/PROJECT	*	
DEPT-TOTAL	1/DEPT	C	
COMPANY-TOTAL-LABEL	1/COMPANY	L	"GRAND TOTAL"
COMPANY-TOTAL	1/COMPANY	C	

Rules for setting an element's **type** are straightforward:

1. If it appears in quotes on a bucket chart, the element is Literal.
2. If it can be derived from other data elements **on the output**, it's Calculated.
3. Otherwise, it's Required (symbol "*").

There is actually a fourth type: if a required field duplicates another required field on the report, the second—and any subsequent—occurrence is called Redundant, symbol **R**. Redundant fields are rare, but we will meet one in the Expense Report.

7.3 WHAT TO DO WITH THE DATA ELEMENTS

Now we will look at how the analysis of element types will help fill the brackets of the logical output mapping.

Type L: Literal. You already know everything there is to know about literals. Along with all the other elements on the worksheet, they will be handled by **output** statements. They need no special attention.

Type C: Calculated. There is more to say, or at least to ask, about calculated data elements—namely: What is the calculation? Simple calculations can be documented right on the worksheet (table) we're developing. Just show what statements are needed and when they must be executed. For example, calculating DEPT-TOTAL needs two instructions:

```
SET DEPT-TOTAL TO 0              executed 1/DEPT (B)
ADD PROJECT-COST TO DEPT-TOTAL   executed 1/PROJECT
```

where 1/DEPT (B) means once per DEPT at DEPT-BEGIN, as usual. (Note that we don't purport to be writing COBOL in the logical output mapping; specifically the above "set" is not a COBOL SET statement.)

We insert these instructions, along with their frequencies of execution, in the columns of the worksheet to the right of DEPT-TOTAL:

DATA ELEMENT	APPEARS	†	DETAILS	EXECUTED
REPORT-TITLE	1/COMPANY	L	"PROJECT STATUS REPORT"	
COLUMN-HEADINGS	1/COMPANY	L	"DEPARTMENT PROJECT..."	
DEPT-NUM	1/DEPT	*		
PROJECT-ID	1/PROJECT	*		
PROJECT-COST	1/PROJECT	*		
DEPT-TOTAL	1/DEPT	C	1.SET DEPT-TOTAL TO 0	1/DEPT (B)
			2.ADD PROJECT-COST TO	1/PROJECT
			DEPT-TOTAL	
COMPANY-TOTAL-LABEL	1/COMPANY	L	"GRAND TOTAL"	
COMPANY-TOTAL	1/COMPANY	C	1.SET COMPANY-TOTAL TO 0	1/COMPANY (B)
			2.ADD DEPT-TOTAL TO	1/DEPT (E)
			COMPANY-TOTAL	

(The dagger [†] has been used as the column heading for Type, to save space.)

The initialization and computation of each calculated field should be documented. These calculation instructions will then make their way into the LOM at the locations indicated: 1/DEPT (B) and so on.

More complex calculations can't be squeezed onto the worksheet, so they are documented elsewhere and the documentation is referred to in the details column of the worksheet. Chapter 12 gives techniques for documenting complex calculations.

Type *: Required. So much for calculated data elements. What about required ones? The hardest thing here is accepting the simplicity: if an element isn't a literal and can't be derived from other fields on the output, then it's required. This rule is easy to accept for the project report. But what about the report shown here in its entirety?

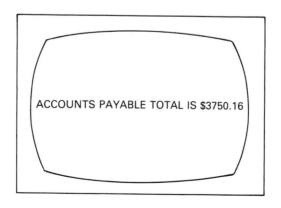

ACCOUNTS PAYABLE TOTAL IS $3750.16

That's all: just one line stating the sum of the amounts payable by our company. It does not, however, list these amounts individually. The logical data layout is:

```
┌─────────────────────────────────────────┐
│ │"ACCOUNTS PAYABLE TOTAL IS"│  │AP-TOTAL│ │
└─────────────────────────────────────────┘
```

and the worksheet is:

DATA ELEMENT	APPEARS	†	DETAILS
TOTAL-LABEL AP-TOTAL	1/COMPANY 1/COMPANY	L *	"ACCOUNTS PAYABLE TOTAL IS"

AP-TOTAL is a **required** field. Of course somebody or some process must have calculated it; but they didn't calculate it from other fields on this report.

We can call this the "brick-wall rule": build a brick wall around your output; then you worry only about calculations inside the wall. You neither know nor care about what goes on outside. All communication with the outside world will eventually be done by the physical input mapping (PIM), which we will meet in Part III. Anything the LOM can't calculate from other data elements on the output, it will **require** the LRR to deliver; i.e., such data elements will have type *.

As we said in Section 7.1, required fields are assumed to be arranged in the LIF (logical input file). The LIF has the same hierarchical structure as the LOS; its atoms are the required elements, pushed all the way to the right.

The LOM gets the records from the LIF with GET LOGICAL RECORD instructions. These are placed according to the standard rule for repetitive inputs: read once to begin, and again when a record is consumed.

7.4 ACCOUNTING REPORT

We now turn to the LOM for the accounting report that we met in Section 6.2. Its LOS was:

$$
\text{COMPANY}
\left\{
\begin{array}{l}
\text{REPORT-TITLE} \\
\text{REPORT-DATE} \\
\text{COLUMN-HEADINGS} \\[2em]
\text{ENTRY} \\
\text{(1,E)}
\left\{
\begin{array}{l}
\text{ACCOUNT-NUMBER} \\[1em]
\text{DEBIT} \quad \left\{ \text{.AMOUNT} \right. \\
\text{(0,1)} \\[1em]
\oplus \\[1em]
\text{CREDIT} \quad \left\{ \text{.AMOUNT} \right. \\
\text{(0,1)}
\end{array}
\right.
\end{array}
\right.
$$

The outline of the LOM comes from stripping the data elements and adding .BEGIN and .END brackets:

$$
\text{COMPANY}
\left\{
\begin{array}{l}
\text{.BEGIN} \quad \Big\{ \\[2em]
\text{ENTRY} \\
\text{(1,E)}
\left\{
\begin{array}{l}
\text{DEBIT} \quad \Big\{ \\
\text{(0,1)} \\[1em]
\oplus \\[1em]
\text{CREDIT} \quad \Big\{ \\
\text{(0,1)}
\end{array}
\right. \\[2em]
\text{.END} \quad \Big\{
\end{array}
\right.
$$

The next step is to complete the worksheet:

DATA ELEMENT	APPEARS	†	DETAILS
REPORT-TITLE	1/COMPANY	L	"ACCOUNTING ENTRIES FOR"
REPORT-DATE	"	*	
COLUMN-HEADINGS	"	L	"ACCOUNT DEBIT..."
ACCOUNT-NUMBER	1/ENTRY	*	
DEBIT-AMOUNT	1/DEBIT	*	
CREDIT-AMOUNT	1/CREDIT	*	

We can now deal with calculations, output, and input. The calculations are especially easy; there aren't any. Output is straightforward:

Here, as elsewhere, the output instruction encompasses any required formatting (to suppress leading zeros, insert decimals, or the like). Notice that OUTPUT PAGE-HEADER is responsible for the report title, report date, and column headers. They constitute a cluster: a group of items that appear together on the LOS and that are always produced together.

Finally, the input. Read once to begin, and again when a record is consumed:

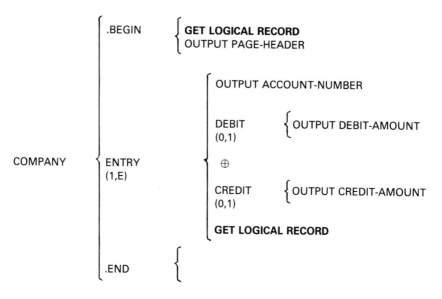

And this completes the LOM for the accounting report.

7.5 EXPENSE REPORT

Finally, we will derive the LOM for the expense report of Section 6.3. The LOS had this basic structure:

COMPANY { CATEGORY (1,C) { ITEM (1,I) {

So the basic LOM shape is:

COMPANY { .BEGIN {

CATEGORY (1,C) { .BEGIN {

ITEM (1,I) {

.END {

.END {

The complete worksheet for the expense report is:

DATA ELEMENT	APPEARS	†	DETAILS	EXECUTED
REPORT-TITLE	1/COMPANY	L	"MONTHLY EXPENSE REPORT"	
PAGE-LABEL	"	L	"PAGE"	
PAGE-NO	"	C	1.SET PAGE-NO TO 1	1/COMPANY (B)
			2.ADD 1 TO PAGE-NO	1/PAGE
REPORT-MONTH	"	*		
COLUMN-HEADINGS	"	L	"CATEGORY "	
			"DATE SUPPLIER"	
CATEGORY-NAME	1/CATEGORY	*		
ITEM-DATE	1/ITEM	*		
SUPPLIER-NAME	"	*		
ITEM-DESCRIPTION	"	*		
ITEM-AMOUNT	"	*		
CATEGORY-TOTAL-LABEL	1/CATEGORY	L	"TOTAL FOR"	
CATEGORY-NAME	"	R		
CATEGORY-TOTAL	"	C	1.SET CATEGORY-TOTAL TO 0	1/CATEGORY (B)
			2.ADD ITEM-AMOUNT TO	1/ITEM
			CATEGORY-TOTAL	
COMPANY-TOTAL-LABEL	1/COMPANY	L	"GRAND TOTAL"	
COMPANY-TOTAL	"	C	1.SET COMPANY-TOTAL TO 0	1/COMPANY (B)
			2.ADD CATEGORY-TOTAL TO	1/CATEGORY (E)
			COMPANY-TOTAL	

Note the frequency of the instruction "ADD 1 TO PAGE-NO": it is shown as 1/PAGE, which is stretching the one-page rule some. It turns out there is no comfortable home for the page-number handling in the structure we will derive; we'll see what to do about that in Chapters 10 and 11.

Here is the expense report LOM with the calculation, output, and input instructions:

```
                 ┌          ┌ GET LOGICAL RECORD
                 │ .BEGIN  ─┤ OUTPUT PAGE-HEADER
                 │          └ SET COMPANY-TOTAL TO 0
                 │
                 │              ┌          ┌ SET CATEGORY-TOTAL TO 0
                 │              │ .BEGIN  ─┤ OUTPUT CATEGORY-NAME-DATA
                 │              │          └
                 │              │
                 │              │                ┌ ADD ITEM-AMOUNT TO
COMPANY         ─┤ CATEGORY    ─┤ ITEM          ─┤   CATEGORY-TOTAL
                 │ (1,C)        │ (1,I)          │ OUTPUT ITEM-DATA
                 │              │                └ GET LOGICAL RECORD
                 │              │
                 │              │          ┌ OUTPUT CATEGORY-TOTAL-DATA
                 │              │ .END    ─┤ ADD CATEGORY-AMOUNT TO
                 │              └          └   COMPANY-TOTAL
                 │
                 │ .END     ─{ OUTPUT COMPANY-TOTAL-DATA
                 └
```

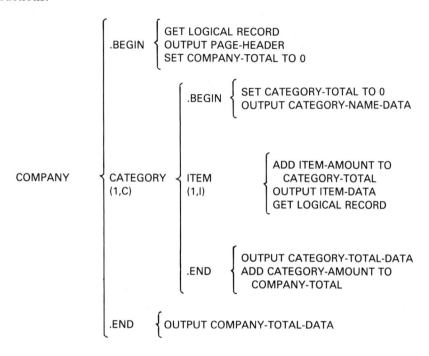

7.6 WHAT NOW?

This completes the development of the LOM. But what's it good for? We certainly can't code from it directly: it's a **logical** output mapping. It's time to get physical.

We add physical detail to the LOM to get what has been called the **augmented LOM** (or ALOM). How much detail we have to add will depend on who is doing the coding. The more background they share with us, the fewer extra levels of brackets we must add to the LOM to specify details of such things as output production.

But at an irreducible minimum, there must be answers to the following questions before the program can be created:

1. How do you create logic to correctly control alternations and repetitions—particularly nested repetitions such as PROJECT within DEPARTMENT?
2. How do you deal with the physical structure of the output? For report outputs, how do you discard the one-page rule?

3. How do you document and program calculations more complex than working out totals?

4. How do you design a read routine ("input mapping") to access whatever physical files you may have to work with, and pass you the logical input file consisting of the required fields?

The rest of Part II deals with the first three of these problems; Part III deals with the last, the creation of the read routine.

Because we will want to include coding samples in the discussion of the other issues, our first step will be to go into coding in more detail.

7.7 SUMMARY

The following diagram summarizes the steps in creating the LOM:

```
              ⎧ COMPLETE        ⎧ ALLOCATE TYPE (L, C, *, R) TO EACH ELEMENT
              ⎪ WORKSHEET       ⎨ DOCUMENT CALCULATION RULES FOR C-TYPE
              ⎪
              ⎪                  ⎧ STRIP LOS OF ALL DATA ELEMENTS
              ⎪ MAKE A          ⎪ ADD .BEGIN AND .END BRACKETS
              ⎪ PLACE FOR       ⎨    TO ALL LEVELS CONTAINING REPETITIONS
              ⎪ EVERYTHING      ⎩
CREATE LOM  ⎨
              ⎪                  ⎧ CALCULATIONS  { AS DOCUMENTED ON WORKSHEET
              ⎪                  ⎪
              ⎪                  ⎪                ⎧ "OUTPUT" STATEMENT FOR
              ⎪ PUT             ⎪ OUTPUT        ⎨    EACH GROUP OF ADJACENT
              ⎪ EVERYTHING      ⎨                ⎩    ITEMS ON THE LOS
              ⎪ IN ITS          ⎪
              ⎪ PLACE           ⎪                ⎧ "GET LOGICAL RECORD":
              ⎪                  ⎪ INPUT         ⎨    ONCE TO BEGIN,
              ⎩                  ⎩                ⎩    AGAIN WHEN CONSUMED
```

The LIF (logical input file) is just the LOS with the required (*) data elements shifted all the way to the right, and all other elements (L,C,R) omitted.

7.8 EXERCISES

1. Create the LOMs for the outputs you identified in the Chapter 6 exercises.
2. Diagram the LIF for the Expense Report.

8

More on Coding

On this, our final and most detailed trip from data structure through process structure to code, we should pay attention to some additional ways of translating process diagrams into COBOL. You may not choose to use them all, but each can be helpful in its place. And help is definitely needed. It is possible to adhere religiously to the rules in Chapter 4 and still produce "write-only" code that no mere human can follow.

In Chapter 4 the first rule of COBOL creation was: every universal becomes a paragraph. We now replace this with a more elaborate understanding: a universal can be less than a paragraph or exactly a paragraph. And paragraphs can be grouped into larger units.

8.1 ABSORPTION

How can a universal be less than a paragraph? By the miracle of "lexical inclusion in the superordinate." This fine phrase of Yourdon and Constantine means: you can replace a PERFORM by the contents of the performed paragraph. We will call this replacement "absorption."

Recall Example 1 from Chapter 4, our original look at coding:

```
EXAMPLE-1.
    PERFORM TASK-1.
    PERFORM TASK-2.
    PERFORM TASK-3 UNTIL WEIGHT > 50.
    STOP RUN.

TASK-1.
    statement-A.
    statement-B.
    statement-C.

TASK-2.
    IF COLOR = "G"
        PERFORM GREEN
    ELSE
        PERFORM NOT-GREEN.

TASK-3.
    statement-L.
    statement-M.

GREEN.
    statement-X.

NOT-GREEN.
    statement-Y.
```

This has six paragraphs for seven COBOL statements; many people would think this is spreading things a bit thin. A trivial example like this, of course, presents no real difficulties. But in a large program you can easily get PERFORMs nested many levels deep, and that causes a lot of minds to boggle.

Here is a way to reduce the number of levels. We can simplify the above structure by absorbing the contents of paragraphs GREEN and NOT-GREEN into TASK-2:

```
EXAMPLE-1.
    PERFORM TASK-1.
    PERFORM TASK-2.
    PERFORM TASK-3 UNTIL WEIGHT > 50.
    STOP RUN.

TASK-1.
    statement-A.
    statement-B.
    statement-C.

TASK-2.
    IF COLOR = "G"
*       (--GREEN--)
        statement-X
    ELSE
        statement-Y.

TASK-3.
    statement-L.
    statement-M.
```

Note the comment (--GREEN--) inserted into TASK-2. It's all very well to absorb paragraphs, but we can't throw away valuable information. It won't be obvious to the next person that "G" means GREEN; it could as easily be GRAY or GOLD.

Some people might take absorption even further. For example, they might come up with:

```
EXAMPLE-1.

*    (TASK-1)
         statement-A.
         statement-B.
         statement-C.

*    (TASK-2)
         IF COLOR = "G"
*            (--GREEN--)
             statement-X
         ELSE
             statement-Y.

     PERFORM TASK-3 UNTIL WEIGHT > 50.

     STOP RUN.

TASK-3.
     statement-L.
     statement-M.
```

And others might be totally opposed to absorption. For example, if your shop saves its Warnier/Orr diagrams and has a one-paragraph-per-bracket standard, then absorption will play hob with cross referencing between diagrams and programs.

So how much absorbing you do is a matter of taste. But if you do decide to absorb, use comments so the reader knows what you've done.

Incidentally, intermixing comments and code is difficult to do in COBOL; they tend to get in each other's way. PL/1, Pascal, and ALGOL are more satisfactory; they let you put comments on the right-hand side of a line containing code.

One shop solves the problem by putting all compile listings through a special print program. This program translates comments to lower case, leaving the code in UPPER CASE.

The eye then distinguishes comments from code with no conscious effort. If your printer has lower-case characters, you might want to create such a print program. Or you might find that your editor and compiler let you enter your comments in lower case.

8.2 CLUSTERING AND SECTIONS

We have just seen that brackets don't have to become paragraphs; instead, bracket contents can be absorbed into the higher-level paragraph, along with an explanatory comment.

There's another issue we have to deal with. It's fine to produce a program consisting of a dozen or so paragraphs; but what if your process diagram has dozens of brackets, or hundreds, or thousands? It often will for a large system. You will have dozens (hundreds, thousands) of paragraphs PERFORMing each other. How will you arrange them?

The rules in Chapter 4 place no constraints on you. As long as the highest level paragraph (i.e., the leftmost universal) comes first in the Procedure Division, you can arrange the other paragraphs in any order you like: the PERFORM chains will all still work properly.

So how will you use your freedom? You can write paragraph names on 3 × 5 cards and shuffle them, or consult a table of random digits, or perhaps arrange the paragraphs alphabetically. But none of these techniques lets the reader develop a real feel for the structure of the program.

If you are concerned that people be able to read your code easily, I recommend that you group your paragraphs into logical clusters.

A cluster is smaller than the forest but bigger than a tree. It helps you write comprehensible code because it lets you divide the code into an intellectually manageable number of units. Instead of, say, 60 fiercely independent paragraphs, you and the reader only have to cope with perhaps 10 clusters.

Once you have formed a cluster, set it off so the reader can identify it. Start it on a new page, put asterisks around its title—do something to let the reader's eye find the breaks between groups without a conscious effort.

Normally, only the first paragraph in a cluster should be PERFORMed from outside. If any other paragraph must be PERFORMed from outside the cluster, then move that paragraph and its subordinates out into a cluster all their own. The reader should be able to tell from the lead paragraph whether there is any need to pay attention to the cluster at all.

Where do clusters come from? Often, they come from grouping a paragraph with some of the paragraphs that appear just to the right of it on the Warnier/Orr process diagram. For example, suppose you are programming the following diagram:

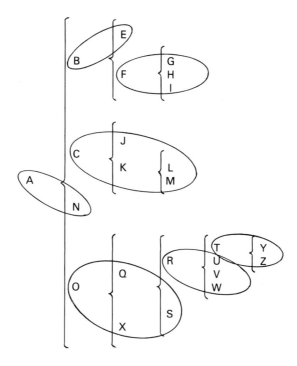

You might conceivably group this logic into seven clusters according to the circles in the above diagram. Or you might use some altogether different grouping, depending on your knowledge of the application.

Suppose for the moment that you will use the circled clusters. Then your program will have the following "organization chart." Each box represents a cluster that consists of the paragraphs shown in it: The "lead" paragraph is shown above the line. For example, one cluster consists of A (the lead paragraph) and N; another consists of R (lead), along with U, V, and W. The lines joining the boxes indicate PERFORMs: at least one statement in the O cluster performs paragraph R:

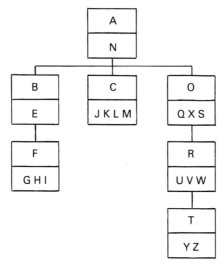

Incidentally, many people think that code should be divided into units that take no more than one page of source listing. The cluster can be used to provide this level of structure; it is then limited to, say, 50 lines of COBOL code to be sure it will fit on one page. My former colleague Ken McEvoy goes further and offers the "twenty is plenty" rule: No more than 20 lines of COBOL statements on one page. The other 30 lines are made up of section or paragraph headers, comments, and white space. (White space means blank lines inserted to improve readability by separating groups of statements.)

Some people find it helpful to implement their clusters as COBOL sections. A COBOL section begins with a section header and runs to the next section header. Suppose you decide to make a section out of paragraph ABLE and its subordinates BAKER, CHARLIE, and DOG. The section would look like this:

```
ABLE SECTION.
       ...        (code from the
       ...         original ABLE
       ...         paragraph)
       ...
GO TO EXIT-SECTION.

BAKER.
       ...
       ...

CHARLIE.
       ...
       ...

DOG.
       ...
       ...


EXIT-SECTION. EXIT.


SOME-OTHER SECTION.
       ...
       ...
       ...
```

Note that EXIT-SECTION is *not* a COBOL reserved word. It's just a handy name for the last paragraph in a section. You can get more information on sections from your COBOL manual.

8.3 "MODULES"

So we've dealt with paragraphs and clusters/sections. But there is one more unit of COBOL structure to distinguish, and here the terminology gets confusing. A lengthy and sophisticated decision-making process (which came up tails) has given us the following two terms:

1. **Module.** A module is the basic unit of COBOL code. It consists of four divisions: Identification, Environment, Data, and Procedure.

   The COBOL standard calls such a unit a "program"; various other people call it a "subprogram," a "separately compilable [sub]program," and heaven knows what else. But we'll call it a module. This seems to have been common terminology during the 60s. (During the 70s "module" was often used to mean any piece of code that could be invoked as a unit.)

2. **Program.** We will use "program" to mean a group of modules linked together. Modules pass control to each other with CALL and GOBACK statements, and receive data from their callers by using linkage sections.

   If module MOD1 calls MOD2 and MOD3; and MOD3, in turn, calls MOD4 and MOD5; then we can diagram the relationship like this:
   (Don't confuse this diagram with the previous one, which showed clusters or sections PERFORMing each other. This diagram shows modules CALLing each other. A module is bigger than a section.)

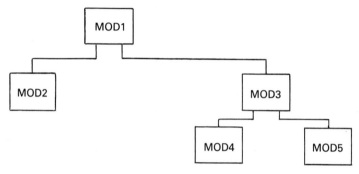

The combination of MOD1 through MOD5 is what we call a program. The COBOL standard calls the combination a "run-unit." Other people call it a "module" or "executable load program"; IBM Job Control Language calls it a PGM; and there must be lots of other names for it.

Note that it's quite possible for a program to consist of exactly one module.

The point of this discussion is: the module provides another unit of structure, bigger than a section and smaller than a program. Once your program gets past a few hundred lines, you should think seriously about dividing it into modules.

In the light of this discussion of sections and modules, we refine our Rule 1 ("each universal becomes a paragraph") as follows:

Rule 1 extended. Each universal either (a) becomes a paragraph, or (b) is absorbed into a performing paragraph.

Paragraphs are clustered; sections and modules can be used to implement clustering.

If you decide to use sections and modules, you may appreciate some guidelines to get you started. Note first that there are lots of reasons other than clarity for using sections and modules: segmentation, overlay, sort input and output procedures, and so on.

And when none of these apply, there are still many logical criteria to use in arranging your program into clusters and modules. But when all else fails, it may be helpful to observe this guideline:

$$\text{PROGRAM} \begin{cases} & \end{cases} \begin{array}{l} \text{MODULE} \\ (1,20) \end{array} \begin{cases} & \end{cases} \begin{array}{l} \text{CLUSTER} \\ (1,12) \end{array} \begin{cases} & \end{cases} \begin{array}{l} \text{PARAGRAPH} \\ (1,10) \end{array}$$

These aren't absolute limits; they're more like 90-percent rules. That is, 90 percent of programs have no more than 20 modules; 90 percent of modules have no more than 12 clusters; 90 percent of clusters have no more than 10 paragraphs.

This has been a rapid skim over the surface of COBOL "packaging" considerations. It's an extensive subject and beyond the scope of this book; the suggestions for further reading at the end of the chapter point to more detailed discussions. But the guidelines outlined here can be helpful in getting started.

POSTSCRIPT

The proposed COBOL-8X standard gives you something bigger than a module and smaller than a program: it will let you have multiple modules in one compilable source member. It sounds good, but any guidelines on how to use it would be purely speculative. The standard also introduces many other new features into COBOL with the goal of supporting structured programming. Specifically, such features as END-IF and END-PERFORM remove current constraints on absorption.

8.4 SUMMARY

A paragraph can be absorbed into the paragraph that PERFORMs it (unless the PERFORM specifies UNTIL. . ., or complications arise from nested ifs).

Lengthy source programs can be made more readable by grouping the paragraphs into logical units. You can do your own grouping armed only with page breaks and comment cards. Or you can use features provided by COBOL: sections and modules.

8.5 EXERCISES

1. Would it be useful to have yet another unit of grouping—the page, say—between paragraph and section? Why or why not?

2. What standards for naming conventions and layout would you set for paragraphs, sections, and modules? Specifically, how would you mark the beginning of a new section or cluster visually?

3. What nonnumeric criteria can you think of for deciding how to group paragraphs? How could you use the position of the universal in the diagram hierarchy in making such decisions?

4. Suppose you decide your code doesn't have to be readable: you want maintainers to read the Warnier/Orr diagrams, not the program. What can you do to help the maintenance programmer move easily from the diagrams to the appropriate spot in the code?

5. If you code in a language other than COBOL, what levels of grouping does your language provide? Are they adequate? What guidelines can you suggest about their use?

FURTHER READING

Structured Design by Yourdon and Constantine introduces the concept of "cohesion" as a criterion to govern grouping of routines. Note that their use of the term "module" differs from ours.

"On the Criteria to Be Used in Decomposing Systems into Modules" by Parnas offers a different approach to identifying logical groups. "To achieve an efficient implementation we must abandon the assumption that a module is one or more subroutines, and instead allow subroutines and programs to be assembled collections of code from various modules."

9

Looping and Control Breaks

In Chapter 8 we met some additional coding techniques. We can now get on with the job of "augmenting" the logical output mapping to get something we can code from. A key part of this transformation is providing **footnotes** or **conditionals**.

Each alternation and repetition on an LOM needs a footnote before it can be programmed. The footnote on an alternation provides a condition test that decides which alternative to take (?1/ IF COLOR = "G"); the footnote on a repetition gives the loop exit condition (?2/ UNTIL WEIGHT > 50).

Footnoting alternations is usually straightforward. If you have trouble with one, you might want to look at Warnier's ideas on processing phases (Section 19.4) and Jackson's ideas on backtracking (Chapter 21).

Footnoting repetitions, especially nested ones, takes some getting used to. It is the subject of this chapter.

9.1 NESTED LOOPS IN THE PROJECT REPORT

The read-once-to-begin-again-when-consumed rule was used in Chapter 7 to place the GET LOGICAL RECORD statements. But this rule was derived in Chapter 4 only for a simple one-level structure (the loans file). How do we know it can be made to work for a two-level structure like project within department?

In this chapter we will settle the question by pushing the output process structure all the way to code.

Stripped of most details, the LOM for the project report looks like this:

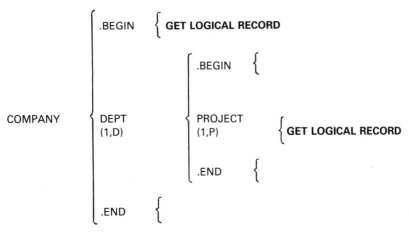

To simplify the discussion we assume there is a physical file sorted in the correct order, so we can use COBOL READ instead of creating a physical input mapping. Then, just as with the loan report in Chapter 4, we expand the GETs:

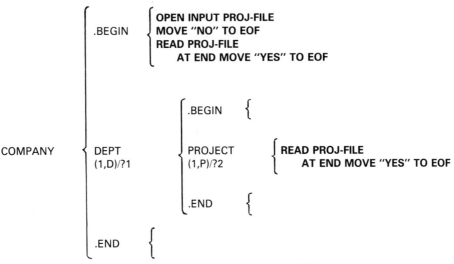

Now we have to work out the footnotes ?1 and ?2.

The first is easy because it's the same as for the loan report. We want to process departments until we reach end-of-file:

```
?1/ UNTIL EOF = "YES"
```

The fact that DEPT has a PROJECT loop within it doesn't change anything; the test still works.

(Granted, the instruction:

```
AT END MOVE "YES" TO EOF
```

in the PROJECT bracket isn't done immediately before the exit test is made. But the only logic between it and the test is DEPT-END, which has nothing to do with the input file; it merely prints a footer line and increments a total. The test for EOF = "YES" will still do the job.)

What about footnote 2? How will we know when we've processed the last project for a department so control can pass to DEPT-END? Basically, we want to write:

```
?2/ UNTIL DEPT CHANGES
```

Thus, whenever we finish processing a project, we check to see if the next input record is for a different department; if it is, then control falls through to DEPT-END.

Unfortunately, UNTIL DEPT CHANGES is not a valid COBOL instruction; we need to elaborate. We set up a field in Working-Storage called CURR-DEPT#. (You can't use the # symbol in COBOL names, but it makes the diagrams easier to read.) Then, if the department in the input buffer (COBOL File Section) is called IN-DEPT#, we do the following:

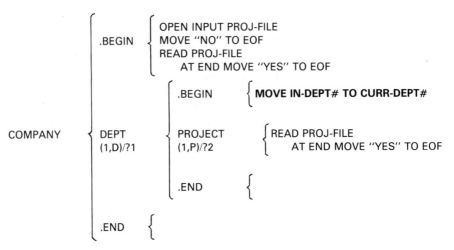

Then we're tempted to write:

```
?2/ UNTIL IN-DEPT# > CURR-DEPT#
```

(This assumes the departments are in DEPT# order, so we can test for IN-DEPT# *greater than* CURR-DEPT#. If the departments are in some other order, the test will have to be IN-DEPT# *not equal to* CURR-DEPT#.)

But the footnote shown above still isn't quite right. Think of what happens after the last read, the one that finds end-of-file. There won't be any new record in the input buffer. What will happen when test ?2 is made?

If you're lucky, the system will hang. On IBM mainframes, for example, accessing a field in the File Section after end-of-file results in system completion code 0C4.

If you're less lucky, the system will use the value of the last record in the buffer. Of course this will give you an endless loop, since CURR-DEPT# equals the value of IN-DEPT# on that record.

So the choice is between an infinite loop and a hang. To evade the problem, we write:

At least on IBM mainframes, this works fine. The tests are made in the order specified; once the machine finds EOF = "YES" is satisfied, it realizes the entire condition is true and stops testing. Of course, the EOF = "YES" test prevents any endless loop.

If this doesn't work with your system, the simplest solution is to transfer the definition of IN-REC from the File Section to Working-Storage. Then change the READ to:

```
READ PROJ-FILE INTO IN-REC
     AT END MOVE "YES" TO EOF.
```

All tests now involve working storage, so there's no danger of hanging.

9.2 MODEL LOGIC

We have now discussed just about all the principles of control-break logic. The best way to sum it up is with a sample you can use for reference. It is for a three-level problem: DIVISION, SECTION, PERSON:

```
COMPANY
    .BEGIN
        MOVE "NO" TO EOF
        OPEN INPUT PERSON-FILE
        READ PERSON-FILE
            AT END MOVE "YES" TO EOF
        OUTPUT COMPANY-HEADER

    DIVISION (D)/?1
        .BEGIN
            MOVE IN-DIV# TO CURR-DIV#
            OUTPUT DIVISION-HEADER

        SECTION (S)/?2
            .BEGIN
                MOVE IN-SEC# TO CURR-SEC#
                OUTPUT SECTION-HEADER

            PERSON (P)/?3
                PROCESS PERSON
                OUTPUT PERSON-DATA
                READ PERSON-FILE
                    AT END MOVE "YES" TO EOF

            .END
                OUTPUT SECTION-FOOTER

        .END
            OUTPUT DIVISION-FOOTER

    .END
        OUTPUT COMPANY-FOOTER
        CLOSE PERSON-FILE
```

?1/ UNTIL EOF = "YES"
?2/ UNTIL (EOF = "YES") OR (IN-DIV# > CURR-DIV#)
?3/ UNTIL (EOF = "YES") OR (IN-DIV# > CURR-DIV#) OR (IN-SEC# > CURR-SEC#)

Notice footnote 3:

```
?3/ UNTIL (EOF="YES") OR (IN-DIV# > CURR-DIV#) OR (IN-SEC# > CURR-SEC#)
```

Of course, the test for EOF = "YES" is necessary for the reasons we have discussed. But why the test for IN-DIV# > CURR-DIV#? It is needed because the input file might be:

DIV#	SEC#
36	1
36	3
36	7
108	7
108	15

If we tested only for IN-SEC# > CURR-SEC#, we wouldn't catch the change in DIV# between lines 3 and 4, since divisions 36 and 108 both have sections numbered 7. Thus the rule: *any loop condition must also test for control breaks at all higher levels*.

This model logic could be coded in the following way:

```
    COMPANY.

*       (COMPANY-BEGIN)
            MOVE "NO" TO EOF.
            OPEN INPUT PERSON-FILE.
            READ PERSON-FILE
                AT END MOVE "YES" TO EOF.
            output company-header

        PERFORM DO-DIVISION UNTIL EOF = "YES".

*       (COMPANY-END)
            output company-footer
            CLOSE PERSON-FILE.

        STOP RUN.


    DO-DIVISION.

*       (DIVISION-BEGIN)
            MOVE IN-DIV-NUM TO CURR-DIV-NUM.
            output division-header

        PERFORM DO-SECTION UNTIL EOF = "YES"
                            OR IN-DIV-NUM NOT = CURR-DIV-NUM.

*       (DIVISION-END)
            output division-footer


    DO-SECTION.

*       (SECTION-BEGIN)
            MOVE IN-SEC-NUM TO CURR-SEC-NUM.
            output section-header

        PERFORM DO-PERSON UNTIL EOF = "YES"
                          OR IN-DIV-NUM NOT = CURR-DIV-NUM
                          OR IN-SEC-NUM NOT = CURR-SEC-NUM.

*       (SECTION-END)
            output section-footer

    DO-PERSON.
            process person
            output person-data
            READ PERSON-FILE
                AT END MOVE "YES" TO EOF.
```

COBOL instructions are written in UPPER CASE; statements needing expansion into COBOL are shown in lower case. To avoid using reserved words (DIVISION, SECTION) as paragraph names, we have prefixed them with DO-.

The above code makes use of the absorption technique we introduced in Chapter 8. For example, DIVISION-BEGIN does not have a paragraph to itself; instead it has been absorbed into DO-DIVISION. Exercise 3 at the end of the chapter deals with this matter.

9.3 COMPOUND KEYS

If you find the testing of all higher levels of control field unsatisfying, you may like the following approach. In any case it's instructive.

Remember where those complicated footnotes came from? We wanted to write:

```
?1/  UNTIL END OF FILE
?2/  UNTIL DIVISION CHANGES
?3/  UNTIL SECTION CHANGES
```

It turns out that a "change" has to include checking for a change at any higher level. What this really means is: the true division key is the EOF switch joined to DIV#; the true section key is the division key joined to SEC#.

So the key structure looks like:

SECTION KEY		
DIVISION KEY		
EOF	DIV#	SEC#
NO	9	11
NO	36	2
NO	36	7
NO	108	7
NO	145	26
•	•	•
•	•	•
•	•	•
NO	876	13
YES	876	13

where EOF is just the highest level of key. To write a program using this insight, we need to declare the following items in working storage:

```
01  CURR-SEC-KEY.
    02  CURR-DIV-KEY.
        03  CURR-EOF        PIC XXX.
        03  CURR-DIV-NUM    PIC ....
    02  CURR-SEC-NUM        PIC ....

01  NEW-SEC-KEY.
    02  NEW-DIV-KEY.
        03  NEW-EOF         PIC XXX.
        03  NEW-DIV-NUM     PIC ....
    02  NEW-SEC-NUM         PIC ....
```

The Warnier/Orr diagram is now:

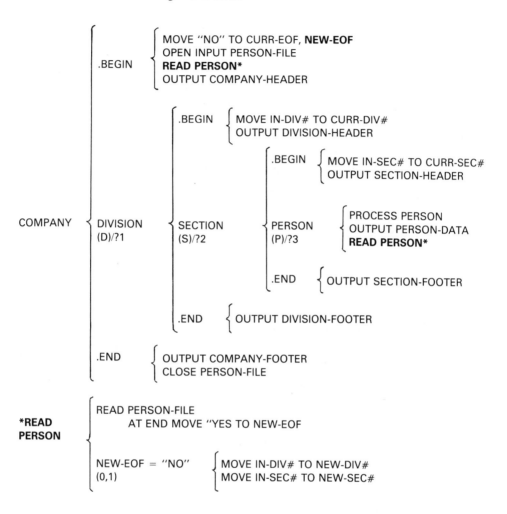

And now the payoff, such as it is. The footnotes become:

```
?1/ UNTIL NEW-EOF = "YES"
?2/ UNTIL NEW-DIV-KEY > CURR-DIV-KEY
?3/ UNTIL NEW-SEC-KEY > CURR-SEC-KEY
```

That was a lot of work to save a few characters in the loop exit footnotes. But the idea of compound keys is important; we'll be seeing it again.

By the way, the IF NEW-EOF = "NO" test in *READ PERSON is needed only if your system hangs when you access a buffer after AT END. Even then you can avoid the problem by using READ. . .INTO.

9.4 SUMMARY

This chapter established that nested loops can be made to work and that they don't affect the validity of the read-once-to-begin-again-when-consumed rule.

We created a control field for each level—for example, CURR-DIV-NUM for DIVISION. Because it is set in DIVISION-BEGIN, CURR-DIV-NUM always contains the number of the division currently being processed. Thus, it can be used when we need to test the incoming record for a control break.

In fact, this control field is more generally useful: we can use it anytime we need to know what division we're working on. For example it would be the source for division number in the DIVISION footer line.

We found that any loop condition must also test for control breaks at all higher levels.

9.5 EXERCISES

1. Expand one or both of the control-break models in this chapter to include computation of totals at all levels.

2. Code and test one of the models. How easily could you create a COBOL skeleton that could be quickly modified for any new multilevel request? How useful would such a model be?

3. The sample "code" for the control-break logic used the absorption technique from Chapter 8. Redo it without absorption. Which version do you prefer? Why?

10

Concurrency

We have used the **logical** output structure to derive the logical output mapping. That is, we postponed consideration of the physical structure of the output: page breaks on reports, physical hierarchy on output data bases, and the like.

We now move on to consider the physical structure. Orr's basic insight here is that the output has physical and logical natures *simultaneously*. In this chapter we will see how these two aspects of the output can be treated if we have the right support software. In the next chapter we will see how to deal with them in the world that most of us, in fact, inhabit.

To make the discussion of physical structures concrete, we focus on the question: How shall we get rid of the one-page rule? Of course this question is not the key point: if it were, we could just look at a PRINT-A-LINE subroutine that handles page breaks and move on to something else. We want to develop concepts and techniques that can be used in more general cases.

10.1 CONCURRENT DATA STRUCTURES

So far we have dealt with the three basic structures—sequence, alternation, repetition—and their combination into hierarchies. We now introduce a new structure: **concurrency**. As usual, we will first look at the data structure and then investigate process structures for handling it.

The students of Elmdale Public School are preparing for their excursion to the waxworks. They are lined up in the school yard by grade level:

GRADE	1	2	3	4	5	6
LINE-UP	. . . .					

Each dot represents one student. We can represent this as a Warnier/Orr diagram:

$$\text{LINE-UP} \left\{ \begin{array}{l} \text{GRADE} \\ \text{(6)} \end{array} \right. \left\{ \begin{array}{l} \text{STUDENT} \\ \text{(S)} \end{array} \right.$$

The students will travel to the waxworks in small buses, each of which holds 8 students. To allocate students to buses, the line is left in exactly the same order but divided into groups of 8:

GRADE	1	2	3	4	5	6
LINE-UP	. . . .	. . . .	. . . .	. . . .	. . . .	
BUS LOAD						

So we can diagram the line-up this way:

$$\text{LINE-UP} \left\{ \begin{array}{l} \text{BUSLOAD} \\ \text{(B)} \end{array} \right. \left\{ \begin{array}{l} \text{PASSENGER} \\ \text{(8)} \end{array} \right.$$

We have now drawn two different diagrams of the same line-up. Which one is correct?

Obviously, the answer is *both*. The line-up has two separate structures: an academic structure based on who's in which grade, and a transportation structure based on who will ride in which bus. And it has both of these structures at the same time; the line wasn't reordered when it was divided into busloads.

Warnier/Orr diagrams represent such **concurrent** structures by a plus sign: +. There's no circle around it; it's just a plus sign. (Warnier/Orr diagrams show several different things by plus signs in various forms. You must be careful to distinguish them.) So we can draw:

$$.\text{INE-UP} \left\{ \begin{array}{l} \text{ACADEMIC} \left\{ \begin{array}{l} \text{GRADE} \\ \text{(6)} \end{array} \right. \left\{ \begin{array}{l} \text{STUDENT} \\ \text{(S)} \end{array} \right. \\[2em] + \\[2em] \text{TRANSPORT} \left\{ \begin{array}{l} \text{BUSLOAD} \\ \text{(B)} \end{array} \right. \left\{ \begin{array}{l} \text{PASSENGER} \\ \text{(8)} \end{array} \right. \end{array} \right.$$

Note that STUDENTs and PASSENGERs are the same thing. This will be important when we move on to concurrent process structures.

The plus sign, then, is our new symbol to show that the upper and lower brackets apply at the same time: they're just different ways of looking at the same thing.

In fact, that's too strict. They don't have to show exactly the same thing; it's enough that both structures are present simultaneously. For example, suppose each bus driver were to come and stand at the head of his busload of students in the line. Then we would normally permit ourselves to write:

```
                ┌ ACADEMIC   ┌ GRADE     ┌ STUDENT   ┌
                │            │ (6)       │ (S)       │
                │            └           └           └
LINE-UP  ┤      │  +
                │                                    ┌ DRIVER
                │ TRANSPORT  ┌ BUSLOAD   ┌           │
                └            │ (B)       │ PASSENGER │
                             └           └ (8)       └
```

The DRIVER isn't a member of the ACADEMIC structure at all.

Here is another example of concurrency. When they're not on field trips, the students have classes. There are six class periods in the morning and six in the afternoon; each period lasts 35 minutes (one of them is used for lunch). So, the school day has two concurrent structures:

```
             ┌ SCHEDULE  ┌ HALFDAY  ┌ PERIOD  ┌ MINUTE  ┌
             │           │ (2)      │ (6)     │ (35)    │
             │           └          └         └         └
SCHOOLDAY ┤  │  +
             │ CLOCK     ┌ HOUR     ┌ MINUTE  ┌
             └           │ (7)      │ (60)    │
                         └          └         └
```

Once again the rightmost universals (MINUTE) correspond; and once again this would have an impact on process structures, as we'll see shortly.

Here is our final example of data concurrency, and the one that set us off on this path in the first place. It's the project report again, with some reality injected. We abandon the one-page rule and admit that the report will be divided into pages. In fact, it will have two concurrent structures: a logical structure of DEPTs and PROJECTs and whatnot, and a physical structure of PAGEs—like this:

```
                    ┌ LOGICAL   ┌ COMPANY  ┌ DEPT    ┌ PROJECT  ┌
                    │           │          │ (1,D)   │ (1,PR)   │
                    │           └          └         └          └
PROJECT   ┤         │  +
REPORT              │ PHYSICAL  ┌ REPORT   ┌ PAGE    ┌
                    └           │          │ (1,PA)  │
                                └          └         └
```

This completes our look at concurrent data structures. Of course, the reason for looking at them is that we want to derive process structures ("mappings") to deal with them. We certainly know how to derive the process structure for a data structure composed only of the three basic operations of sequence, alternation, and repetition. In fact, we've carried such structures all the way to COBOL code. But how do we handle the process structure for concurrency?

10.2 CONCURRENT STRUCTURES: MELDING

Well, it depends. What it depends on is whether the two concurrent structures match; if they do, the problem is trivial. If, for example, you are writing a program to send a one-page, personalized letter to each customer, your concurrent structures will look like this:

```
             ┌ LOGICAL   { COMPANY  { CUSTOMER
             │                        (1,C)
JUNK MAIL  { + 
             │ PHYSICAL  { REPORT   { PAGE
             └                        (1,P)
```

The brackets in the two structures correspond exactly; the report covers the company and each page is for exactly one customer. In such a case you just turn the logical structure into your process structure; then you handle page breaks, for example, at CUSTOMER-BEGIN:

```
                              ┌ .BEGIN   { PRODUCE PAGE-HEADER
                              │
COMPANY  { CUSTOMER  {  PRINT CUSTOMER-INFO
           (1,C)              │
                              └ .END     { whatever
```

You will even be okay if each customer's outstanding invoices are listed in the letter, as long as it is guaranteed that the page will never overflow. Suppose your company doesn't allow a customer more than 5 outstanding invoices, and 5 will fit nicely on a page:

```
             ┌ LOGICAL   { COMPANY  { CUSTOMER  ┌ INTRO
             │                        (1,C)     │ INVOICE
             │                                  │ (1,5)
JUNK MAIL  { +                                  └ CLOSE
             │ PHYSICAL  { REPORT   { PAGE
             └                        (1,P)
```

There is still no problem melding physical into logical; page breaks are right at home in CUSTOMER-BEGIN:

```
                                      ⎧ .BEGIN   ⎧ PRODUCE PAGE-HEADER
                                      ⎪          ⎩ PRINT INTRO
                                      ⎪
COMPANY   ⎰ CUSTOMER  ⎰ INVOICE       ⎨ INVOICE  ⎰ PRINT INVOICE
          ⎱ (1,C)     ⎱ (1,5)         ⎪          ⎱
                                      ⎪
                                      ⎩ .END     ⎰ PRINT CLOSING
                                                 ⎱
```

So the first option for concurrent structures is: *if a structure is in one-to-one correspondence with the leftmost brackets of a concurrent structure, the structures can be melded.*

10.3 STRUCTURE CLASHES AND COROUTINES

Suppose no meld is possible in the project report. That is, assume that PAGE doesn't correspond exactly with DEPT:

```
                  ⎧ LOGICAL  ⎰ COMPANY  ⎰ DEPT    ⎰ PROJECT  ⎰ LINE  ⎰
                  ⎪          ⎱          ⎱ (1,D)   ⎱ (1,PR)   ⎱       ⎱
PROJECT   ⎰        ⎪
REPORT    ⎱        ⎨ +
                  ⎪
                  ⎩ PHYSICAL ⎰ REPORT   ⎰ PAGE    ⎰ LINE    ⎰
                             ⎱          ⎱ (1,PA)  ⎱ (1,L)   ⎱
```

(We have drawn in the shared LINE universal on each structure: each project has one line, and each page consists of a number of lines. We've mentioned several times that when two concurrent structures have common universals on the right, the processing will be affected. We will see why in a moment.)

Now we have what Jackson calls a **structure clash**. In fact, it's a particular type of structure clash, which he terms a boundary clash. The boundaries of pages and departments, for example, don't coincide. A department can take several pages, or part of one page, or parts of two pages, and so on. Another example of a boundary clash is the school bus problem we saw earlier: the grade boundaries didn't coincide with the bus boundaries.

How shall we produce an output that contains a boundary clash?

Our basic rule throughout the book has been that data structure yields process structure. So far we have applied the rule with excellent results to the three basic structures: sequence, alternation, and repetition. How shall we apply it to concurrency?

If the rule is any good, then it ought to mean the above two concurrent structures need **two concurrent routines**.

Continuing to turn the crank, we infer that one of the routines must be based on the **logical** data structure, while the second concurrent routine will be based on the **physical** data structure. And they should run something like this:

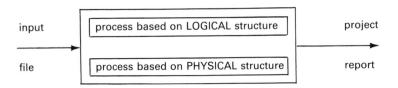

So we apparently need a process based on the logical structure running concurrently with a process based on the physical structure. Let's deal with a few of the questions this raises.

What will the top process be? The diagram shows that the upper process is to be based on the logical structure of the output. So this process will obviously be the LOM, which we derived from the LOS back in Chapter 7.

What will the bottom process be? The LOM produces print lines. It will be the job of the lower routine in the diagram—the one based on the **physical** structure—to take these print lines and impose the report's physical structure on them. This process is called the physical output mapping, or POM. In the next section we will work out the details of the POM.

What will pass between the two processes? As we just noted, what passes between the two routines is a file of print lines: namely, the LOS. The POM then takes this file of print lines and decides when to insert page headings or footings or whatever. This is why it is so important to identify when there is a common universal (like LINE) in two concurrent structures: if there is, the process structures will have to communicate with each other to pass the common universal.

So we want two processes—LOM and POM—running concurrently. And they have to communicate with each other so they can pass the print lines. Here is one view of what this means practically:

1. The LOM and POM should start simultaneously.
2. Whenever the LOM produces a print line, the line goes into a "pipe" between the two routines. During the run, this pipe will receive the entire LOS:

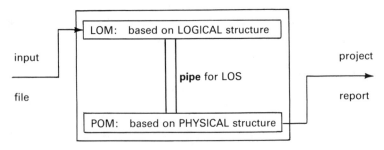

3. Whenever the POM needs a record, it gets the next one from the pipe. If the pipe is empty, the POM waits until the next record is available.
4. The run stops when both routines are finished.

In a few pages we will examine our options for making these routines run concurrently. But first we should tie up a loose end: the details of the POM.

10.4 THE STRUCTURE OF THE POM

It's easy to structure the POM from the physical output structure: we apply the looping rules we developed in Chapter 9. The framework will look like this:

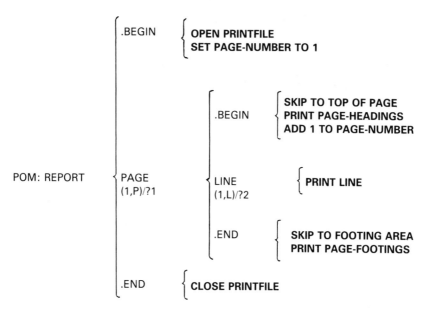

And it's easy to add the logic to produce correctly numbered page headings and footings, and to print the detail lines:

Next, the routine needs some input. We've already noted that the LOM will be producing print lines for its use. It can pick them up via the usual read-once-to-begin-again-when-consumed rule:

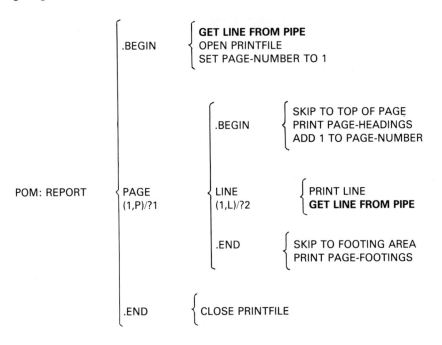

It remains only to add footnotes. As usual, ?1 will be:

```
?1/  UNTIL LINE-EOF = "YES"
```

where we assume that LINE-EOF will be set to "YES" when GET LINE FROM PIPE goes past the last line in the pipe. To work out the second footnote and supporting logic, suppose that we are to have, at most, 54 body lines per page. (A body line is any line other than a page header or page footer.) Then the following insertions will do the job:

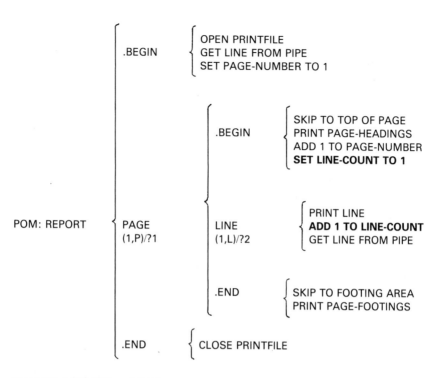

?1/ UNTIL LINE-EOF = "YES"
?2/ UNTIL (LINE-EOF = "YES") OR (LINE-COUNT > 54)

This completes the digression to work out the second of the two concurrent routines, the physical output mapping.

10.5 HOW SHALL WE IMPLEMENT COROUTINES?

Now, what shall we do with the LOM and POM? Recall that we said we wanted something like this:

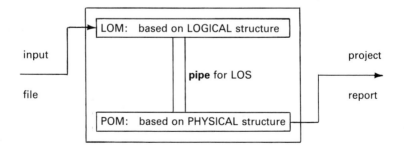

We refer to such concurrent routines as "coroutines."

If you're familiar with the UNIX operating system, you will know that it provides exactly the facility we have described, pipes and all.

If you don't have UNIX, a possible approach would be to run the two programs consecutively, with the LOM creating a temporary file that gets read by the POM:

We can think of this as the case of the infinite pipe: the LOM runs to end of job before the POM gets initiated, and the TEMP FILE is the pipe between them. The drawback to this approach is that it creates a lot of extra file access and slows things down considerably.

Another approach is to go to the other extreme: instead of an infinite pipe, have a vanishing one. The two routines run at the same time. When one needs data or services from the other, it signals the other to take over; then it waits for a signal back before it recommences. There are many systems that will support this wait/signal arrangement. But unfortunately, the systems in which most code gets written—arguably IBM COBOL and various BASICs—don't allow this sort of thing.

So what can we do?

If we want a reasonably efficient program, we're going to have to squeeze our **co**routines into a **sub**routine mold. The LOM will have to CALL or PERFORM the POM, passing it the LOS: a new print line on each invocation:

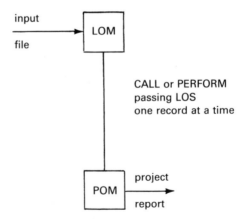

It's a Procrustean bed, but we have to lie in it. In Chapter 21 we will see Michael Jackson's approach to turning a coroutine into a subroutine. He manages to make the POM run as a subroutine of the LOM and keep the data structured design we derived above. But the result can be confusing for a maintainer meeting it for the first time, and some implementations are nearly indecipherable.

If we shun Jackson's technique, what do we do? We carefully data structured the POM, but found that the result doesn't work as a subroutine. Must we abandon the principle that process structure comes from data structure?

For a large class of problems, the answer is, no, we don't have to abandon the principle. If we are to derive the subroutine structure from the data structure, we will simply have to take another view of the data structure. The technique for deriving this other view is called hierarchy inversion. We turn our attention to it in Chapter 11.

10.6 SUMMARY

In this chapter we admitted that outputs have physical structures, which often clash with the logical ones. The typical picture is this:

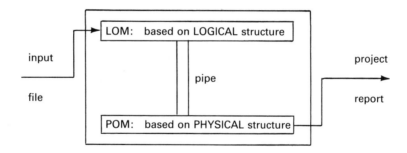

If the concurrent structures match, they can be melded to form a single process structure. But if they clash, we must create two concurrent processes:

It is easy to work out the two process structures based on the two data structures, but, unfortunately, the most common languages and operating systems don't support two concurrent processes communicating with each other like this.

To get acceptable performance we usually have to run the routines as a main-line/subroutine pair; normally, the POM is turned into a subroutine. This means that the data structured process logic we worked out for the POM isn't going to work.

Rather than abandon the principle that data structure yields process structure, we will redraw the physical output structure so we can create a subroutine from it. That is the topic of the next chapter.

10.7 EXERCISES

1. What revisions would the POM need to support the possibility of some lines overlaying each other—that is, having 0-line spacing?

2. Find out whether any system available to you supports communicating simultaneous processes like the LOM and the POM in this chapter. If one is available, implement the POM along with a simple LOM and run them together.

FURTHER READING

For a different slant on coroutines, see Section 14.2 in *The Art of Computer Programming*, Volume 1, by D. E. Knuth.

"Communicating Sequential Processes" by Hoare proposes language constructs to support concurrent routines that communicate with each other. "In parallel programming coroutines appear as a more fundamental program structure than subroutines. . . ."

For a description of the UNIX operating system, see *User Guide to the UNIX System*, by Yates and Thomas.

11

Inversion

In the previous chapter we saw that concurrent data structures are easy to handle if one of them matches the left end of the other. We just have to meld them.

When there is no match, we are driven to coroutines, one based on each of the concurrent data structures. Chapter 10 described how to use coroutines in adding the physical structure to the output. If you work with a language and operating system that make coroutines possible and practical, you are home free. The current chapter is of no interest to you, and you should move directly to chapter 12.

If you're still reading, it's presumably because you don't have coroutines at your disposal. In that case you will have to master inversion. But not yet. Many people find inversion heavy going; so *I recommend that on first reading you read only the summary (Section 11.9), skipping the rest of the chapter.* Return to it once you have mastered the main flow of Parts II and III.

11.1 THE BEGINNINGS OF INVERSION

Hierarchy inversion is Orr's technique for redrawing a data structure so we can code a subroutine from it. The first three sections of this chapter develop hierarchy inversion in a completely new context. Then in the last half of the chapter we apply the concepts to our report printing problem.

Suppose we are to produce a payroll system for an American company. We'll draw a Warnier/Orr diagram showing all the outputs of the complete system: not their details, just their names and when they're produced. We can use the LFUD technique we mastered for LOS in Chapter 6: List, Frequency, Universals, Diagram.

First we list all the atoms—that is, the reports:

OUTPUT
W2
941A
FICA
paychecks
check register

Then we show the frequency with which each is to appear:

OUTPUT	FREQUENCY
W2	1/YEAR (E)
941A	1/QUARTER (E)
FICA	1/MONTH (E)
paychecks	1/WEEK (E)
check register	1/WEEK (E)

The notation is the same as for LOSs: 1/YEAR (E) means "appears once per year, at YEAR-END."

Now we can do the universal analysis, step 3 of LFUD. We always need a universal that occurs exactly once; it becomes the leftmost bracket of the diagram. In this case nothing in the FREQUENCY column fills the bill, since we hope the payroll system will run for more than one year. But there is an answer: "payroll system" occurs exactly once in the life of the system. Starting with it, the universal analysis proceeds smoothly for several lines:

```
UNIVERSAL           OCCURS

PAYROLL SYSTEM      1
YEAR                1,Y/PAYROLL SYSTEM
QUARTER             4/YEAR
MONTH               3/QUARTER
```

So far, so good. Nobody doubts that a year has four quarters of three months each.

The last quantity left in the frequency column is WEEK. Where does it fit in the universal analysis? How many weeks in (a) a month, (b) a quarter, or (c) a year? Unfortunately, the answers turn out to be:

(a) 4 to 4.4 weeks in a month,

(b) 12.9 to 13.1 weeks in a quarter,

(c) 52.1 to 52.3 weeks in a year.

This is discouraging: Warnier/Orr diagrams have no provision for things happening a fractional number of times. So we can't nest WEEK in any other time unit. We have to go to the great granddaddy of universals, the payroll system itself. We get:

```
UNIVERSAL          OCCURS

PAYROLL SYSTEM     1
YEAR               1,Y/PAYROLL SYSTEM
QUARTER            4/YEAR
MONTH              3/QUARTER
WEEK               1,W/PAYROLL SYSTEM
```

Now we can finish LFUD by drawing the diagram. Because years and weeks both fall within the same bracket (payroll system) and go on simultaneously, we need the concurrence symbol:

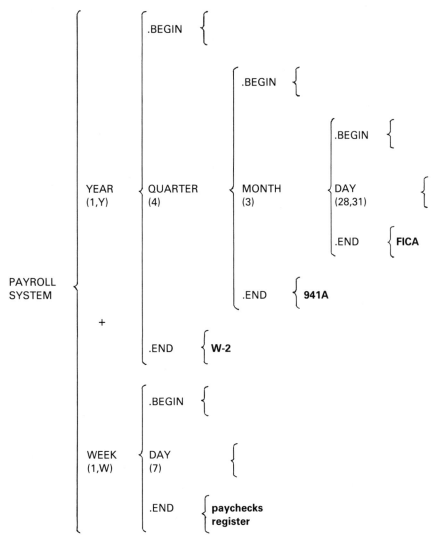

And of course the structures clash, as we found when we tried to relate weeks to years: there is no fit. This gives us a chance to use the technique of hierarchy inversion, as promised.

11.2 RESOLVING THE CLASH WITH HIERARCHY INVERSION

The key to solving structure clashes by inversion is: find a common universal. Looking at the diagram, you can see that the two hierarchies do indeed have a common universal, namely DAY. We quietly slipped DAY into the diagram, even though it didn't appear in the universal analysis, so that the MONTH-END and WEEK-END brackets could have something to follow.

If we hadn't done that, we would insert DAY now in order to get our common universal. Of course, we could equally well use HOUR or MINUTE or MICRO-SECOND; any of these fits neatly into both MONTH and WEEK, but we pick DAY because it is the *largest* common unit.

So we have either spotted or introduced a common universal. Now what?

Now we invert one of the hierarchies: we turn it inside out by pulling the rightmost universal through to the left. For example, if we start with:

WEEK
- .BEGIN
- DAY (7) — daily process
- .END

and invert it, we get:

DAY
- WEEK-BEGIN (0,1)/?1
- daily process
- WEEK-END (0,1)/?2

?1/ IF DAY = 1
?2/ IF DAY = 7

It may be worth a brief digression to prove these two structures are equivalent for our purposes. Number the processes in the *original* diagram like this:

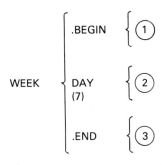

WEEK
- .BEGIN ⟨ ①
- DAY (7) ⟨ ②
- .END ⟨ ③

So any start-of-week processing goes in (1); regular daily processing goes in (2); and end-of-week processing (like printing checks) goes in (3).

Now let's watch the processing. Clearly:

```
PROCESS 1 RUNS AT THE BEGINNING OF THE WEEK; THEN
PROCESS 2 RUNS 7 TIMES
          2
          2
          2
          2
          2
          2; THEN
PROCESS 3 RUNS AT THE END OF THE WEEK.
```

Now here is the processing with the *inverted* version:

DAY
- WEEK-BEGIN (0,1)/?1 ⟨ ①
- daily process ⟨ ②
- WEEK-END (0,1)/?2 ⟨ ③

?1/ IF DAY = 1
?2/ IF DAY = 7

This, of course, means that a day's work is: "If it's the start of a week, do process 1. Always do process 2. Then, if it's the end of a week, do process 3." So if we watch the days of a week go by, we see:

```
FIRST DAY:    PROCESS 1
              PROCESS 2
SECOND DAY:          2
THIRD               2
FOURTH              2
FIFTH               2
SIXTH               2
SEVENTH             2
                    3
```

And the cycle repeats itself. The two diagrams, then, are equivalent: they result in the same processes being run in the same order.

That means we can redraw the payroll system like this:

But now, at last, we can eliminate the clash—because the bottom universal, DAY, fits neatly into the upper structure. The merged diagram looks like this:

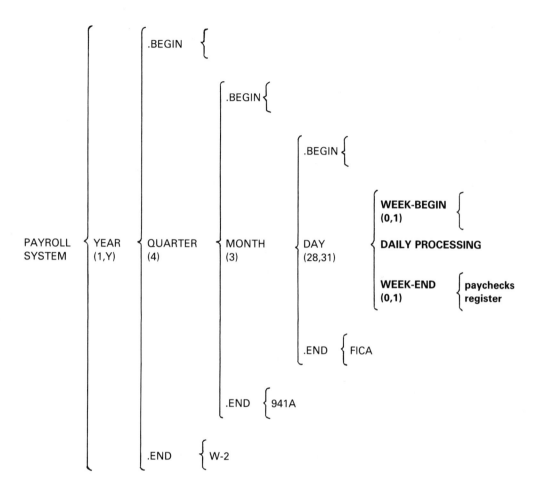

That is how inversion resolves boundary clashes. It lets us invert a structure and nest it in another, yielding a structure we have handled successfully many times before.

11.3 *VARIATIONS ON THE THEME*

We started with the bottom (WEEK) hierarchy and inverted it. We could instead have inverted the upper hierarchy and stuck it onto the lower, to get:

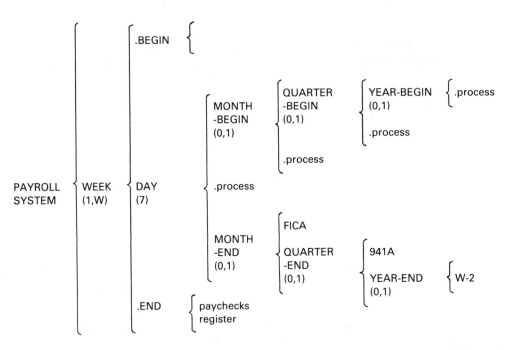

Once you get started inverting, you can have a field day. For example instead of pulling a hierarchy inside out to get the C-shaped inversion above, we could show some moderation and just flatten it:

DAY
- YEAR-BEGIN (0,1)
- QUARTER-BEGIN (0,1)
- MONTH-BEGIN (0,1)
- DAILY PROCESSING
- MONTH-END (0,1)
  - FICA
- QUARTER-END (0,1)
  - 941A
- YEAR-END (0,1)
  - W-2

We could then stick this onto DAY in the WEEK hierarchy.

Or we could flatten WEEK as well, then merge the two flattened hierarchies:

```
                                    ┌ YEAR-BEGIN      {
                                    │   (0,1)          {
                                    │
                                    │   QUARTER-BEGIN  {
                                    │   (0,1)
                                    │
                                    │   MONTH-BEGIN    {
                                    │   (0,1)
                                    │
                                    │   WEEK-BEGIN     {
                                    │   (0,1)
                                    │
PAYROLL   {  DAY    {  DAILY PROCESSING  {
SYSTEM       (1,D)  │
                                    │   WEEK-END       { paychecks
                                    │   (0,1)          { register
                                    │
                                    │   MONTH-END      { FICA
                                    │   (0,1)
                                    │
                                    │   QUARTER-END    { 941A
                                    │   (0,1)
                                    │
                                    └ YEAR-END         { W-2
                                        (0,1)
```

The possibilities are endless. And note that we're not just indulging in geometric acrobatics. For the programming languages and operating systems that most of us use, hierarchy inversion is vital.

For example, consider the flattened payroll system diagram we just created. It's less informative than the original diagram, which showed concurrence and nested time units. But it's almost certainly the view of the payroll system taken by the scheduler in computer operations. He (if a man) or she (if a woman) or it (if a program) decides each day whether end-of-week, end-of-month, or end-of-whatever has arrived and schedules the computer jobs accordingly.

In general, the most challenging thing about inversion is getting the footnotes right. We will have a more formal treatment of this matter in Part III.

So much for the payroll system. Our purpose in discussing it, you'll recall, was to develop the concept of hierarchy inversion. That done, we can return to the project report we were dealing with in Chapter 10 and apply hierarchy inversion to it.

Recall from the payroll example that the first step in inversion is to find a common universal. Luckily, the project report has one: LINE.

```
                  ⎧ LOGICAL  ⎧ COMPANY  ⎧ DEPT     ⎧ PROJECT  ⎧ LINE  ⎧
                  ⎪          ⎨          ⎨ (1,D)    ⎨ (1,PR)   ⎨       ⎨
                  ⎪          ⎩          ⎩          ⎩          ⎩       ⎩
PROJECT          ⎨
REPORT           ⎪    +
                  ⎪
                  ⎪ PHYSICAL ⎧ REPORT   ⎧ PAGE     ⎧ LINE  ⎧
                  ⎩          ⎨          ⎨ (1,PA)   ⎨ (1,L) ⎨
                             ⎩          ⎩          ⎩       ⎩
```

This, of course, is the same common universal that was passed down the pipe between the LOS and the POM in our Chapter 10 coroutine discussion.

Our report structure now looks a lot like the diagram for the payroll system, with LINE filling the role of DAY. We can invert the bottom hierarchy to:

```
            ⎧ PAGE-BEGIN   ⎧
            ⎪ (0,1)        ⎨
            ⎪              ⎩
            ⎪
LINE       ⎨ .PROCESSING  ⎧
            ⎪              ⎨
            ⎪              ⎩
            ⎪ PAGE-END     ⎧
            ⎪ (0,1)        ⎨
            ⎩              ⎩
```

(Notice that we haven't fully inverted: there are no REPORT-BEGIN or REPORT-END brackets. We'll discuss this later.)

Now we can eliminate the physical structure altogether by sticking its inversion wherever there is a LINE in the logical structure. In fact there are more lines than we've shown: COMPANY-TOTAL and DEPT-TOTAL both need lines. The inverted hierarchy can be stuck as many places as required. Here is the revised diagram, with the inverted hierarchy inserted in four places, marked by asterisks (***):

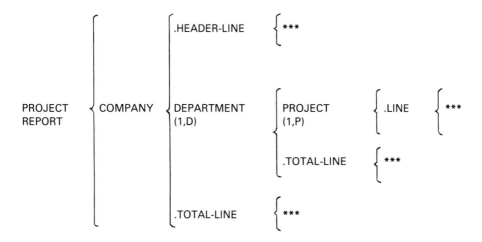

Our overriding goal has been to design the program that will produce this report, complete with page breaks. We can now satisfy ourselves that this is possible, by going as far as COBOL code.

The LINE processing is needed in several places—four to be exact—so it will be a subroutine. (As we've said several times, the subroutine is emulating a coroutine. We won't say it any more.) The subroutine's process structure will be the inverted hierarchy we derived above; let's insert the detailed instructions. They are the same ones we came up with in Chapter 10 for the original noninverted form:

```
                               ⎧ SKIP TO TOP OF PAGE
              PAGE-BEGIN        ⎨ PRINT PAGE-HEADINGS
              (0,1)/?X1         ⎩ ADD 1 TO PAGE-NUMBER
                                  SET LINE-COUNT TO 1

                               ⎧ PRINT LINE
PRINT A LINE   LINE PROCESSING  ⎨ ADD 1 TO LINE-COUNT
                               ⎩ (get line from pipe)

              PAGE-END          ⎧ SKIP TO FOOTING AREA
              (0,1)/?X2         ⎨ PRINT PAGE-FOOTINGS
```

Notice that the footnotes are ?X1 and ?X2. From now on we will use X to distinguish footnotes on the inverted structure from those on the uninverted version.

We have left the "get line from pipe" instruction in as a comment and reminder. Naturally there is no actual "getting" done; the print line is passed as a parameter. But you can see that we're going to have trouble: the PRINT A LINE subroutine is going to want a brand new print line in the middle of processing.

We have to figure out the footnotes. The easiest way to do this for an inversion is to look at the uninverted form. From Section 10.4 we see that this is as follows, with most details omitted:

POM: COMPANY
- .BEGIN { get line
- PAGE (1,P)/?1
  - .BEGIN {
  - LINE (1,L)/?2 { get line
  - .END {
- .END {

?1/ UNTIL LINE-EOF = "YES"
?2/ UNTIL (LINE-EOF = "YES") OR (LINE-COUNT > 54)

We will start with ?X2, the condition on the inverted PAGE-END. Clearly, PAGE-END is executed after all lines on the page are produced. And the above diagram shows that this happens when LINE-EOF = "YES" or LINE-COUNT > 54. So the inverted structure contains the following PAGE-END footnote:

```
?X2/ IF (LINE-EOF = "YES") OR (LINE-COUNT > 54)
```

Now we have a problem. PRINT A LINE will find out that LINE-EOF = "YES" when it tries to do the (get line) inside LINE processing; but of course it can't do such a "get" since the line is passed as a parameter.

There are two possible solutions. One is to have the LOM pass an additional parameter called LAST-LINE-SW or something of the sort, which is usually "NO" but is "YES" when it *accompanies* the last line. Then we can write:

```
?X2/ IF (LAST-LINE-SW = "YES") OR (LINE-COUNT > 54)
```

We have just delegated upward the problem of identifying the last line; but as long as the LOM has COMPANY-TOTAL to write, it should know which line is the last.

The other solution is more general, elegant, and difficult. It is suggested in the exercises at the end of the chapter.

Now, how about ?X1, the footnote on PAGE-BEGIN? The uninverted form shows that control gets to PAGE-BEGIN in one of two ways:

(a) Just after REPORT-BEGIN—that is, at the start of the run. For brevity we will use the expression ON 1 to denote a first-time condition.

(b) Just after PAGE-END—when control cycles around for the next page. Thus the condition here is the same as for PAGE-END, namely, IF LINE-COUNT > 54. (Why can we ignore the LINE-EOF = "YES" part of the condition?)

Putting these together, we get the inversion footnote on PAGE-BEGIN:

```
?X1/ (ON 1) OR (IF LINE-COUNT > 54)
```

See Section 11.6 for a further discussion of ON 1 and its implementation.

11.5 PUTTING IT INTO COBOL

You might render the result into COBOL as follows if your version of Cobol supports ON 1:

```
PRINT-A-LINE SECTION.
        ON 1                PERFORM PAGE-BEGIN
      ELSE IF LINE-COUNT > 54 PERFORM PAGE-BEGIN.

      PERFORM LINE-PROCESSING.

      IF (LAST-LINE-SW = "YES") OR (LINE-COUNT > 54)
          PERFORM PAGE-END.

      GO TO EXIT-SECTION.

PAGE-BEGIN.
      WRITE OUT-LINE FROM HEADING-LINE
          AFTER ADVANCING TO-TOP-OF-PAGE.
      ADD 1 TO PAGE-NO.
      MOVE 1 TO LINE-COUNT.

LINE-PROCESSING.
      WRITE OUT-LINE FROM BODY-LINE.
      ADD 1 TO LINE-COUNT.

PAGE-END.
      WRITE OUT-LINE FROM FOOTING-LINE AFTER ADVANCING TO-FOOTER.

EXIT-SECTION.
      EXIT.
```

Here PRINT-A-LINE has been made into a section. This is unnecessary, but if you do it, notice the required GO TO EXIT-SECTION.

11.6 VARIATIONS

We did not completely invert the REPORT structure; we left the REPORT-BEGIN logic to be handled by COMPANY-BEGIN, and the REPORT-END logic for COMPANY-END.

If you prefer to put all the REPORT logic together, then you will want to use a full inversion. You would be forced to do this if you made the POM a CALLed routine, rather than a PERFORMed one; the LOM would then be unable to do any file opening and closing for it.

Here is one way of structuring a full inversion:

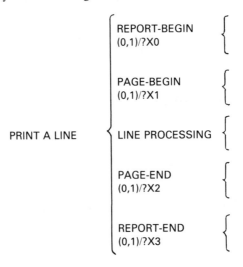

After our previous discussion, the footnotes are straightforward:

```
?X0/  ON 1
?X1/  (ON 1)                      OR (IF LINE-COUNT > 54)
?X2/  IF (LAST-LINE-SW = "YES") OR    (LINE-COUNT > 54)
?X3/  IF  LAST-LINE-SW = "YES"
```

Here is a second item that warrants discussion. We have used ON 1 as a first-time switch for simplicity, but most COBOLs don't support it. There are several alternatives:

1. Set up a REPORT-BEGIN-SW in Working-Storage, initialized to "YES" with a VALUE clause, and reset by the LINE-PROCESSING routine. (Why can't you reset it in REPORT-BEGIN with the full inversion we just saw?)

   This shares with ON 1 the problems that the routine cannot be restarted during the same run (to produce a second report when the first is finished) and that the routine may not work properly if run on-line or in overlay with some operating systems.

2. Use the REPORT-BEGIN-SW mentioned above, but initialize it in COM-PANY-BEGIN. This avoids the problems in (1) at the expense of an extra parameter.

3. Initialize LINE-COUNT to 99 or some other value exceeding 54. Then the PRINT-A-LINE test for PAGE-BEGIN is simply IF LINE-COUNT > 54.

Finally, note that once you have created a POM you will use it whenever you can. There are no prizes for starting from scratch with each report.

11.7 PUTTING IT ALL TOGETHER

What effect does all this have on the LOM? The following:

1. Before the first output statement
   - move "YES" to REPORT-BEGIN-SW (if used)
   - move "NO" to LAST-LINE-SW (if used)
2. For every OUTPUT statement:
   - build the line to be printed, doing any required display formatting
   - move the line to BODY-LINE, where PRINT-A-LINE will find it
   - PERFORM PRINT-A-LINE
3. For the last OUTPUT statement
   - move "YES" to LAST-LINE-SW before PERFORMing PRINT-A-LINE
4. If your PRINT-A-LINE contains PAGE and LINE logic only:
   - put REPORT-BEGIN logic into COMPANY-BEGIN
   - put REPORT-END logic into COMPANY-END

11.8 ON SUBROUTINES AND COROUTINES

Right. Talk about using a sledgehammer to crack a nut: it's taken us two chapters to write a routine that will handle page breaks. So it's good to recall the point of the exercise: to master a general approach to handling concurrent data structures.

Here is one practical consequence of this development:

Some subroutines are really coroutines.

You may have read that a subroutine should be completely predictable: what it passes back should depend only on what is passed to it on this particular invocation.

The problem is that you often have to write "subroutines" that require memory—i.e., that must maintain the value of one or more variables from one call to the next. Input and output routines (like the POM) are the classic examples: what they do on this call depends on what state they were in after the last one. This is not a matter for despair. If it happens, you don't have a bad subroutine; you have a good coroutine.

Such a subroutine/coroutine is just a program that writes or reads a parameter file to or from the module that calls it:

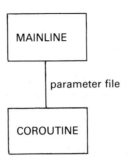

Remember the POM: its parameter file was the LOS.

If the parameter file has any interesting structure, that structure can contribute to the structure of the "subroutine." You may, for example, want to first work out a "pure" coroutine in uninverted form, then invert its hierarchy to get your subroutine.

On the other hand, if each call is just like the next—that is, if the subroutine never has to remember anything from one call to the next—then it is a true subroutine. In this case the parameter file will be no help in structuring it.

The point is this: A subroutine that needs to remember things from one call to the next is *really* a coroutine. And if it is a coroutine, the parameter file can help you structure it.

11.9 SUMMARY

"Hierarchy inversion" is a technique for making a coroutine run as a subroutine. It consists of transforming the structure of the coroutine:

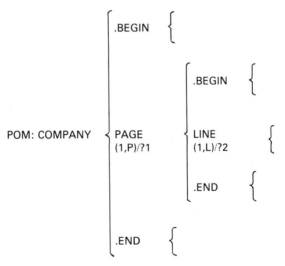

?1/ UNTIL LINE-EOF = "YES"
?2/ UNTIL (LINE-EOF = "YES") OR (LINE-COUNT > 54)

to get something that will run as a subroutine:

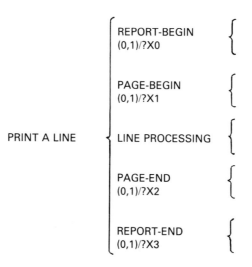

PRINT A LINE

REPORT-BEGIN
(0,1)/?X0

PAGE-BEGIN
(0,1)/?X1

LINE PROCESSING

PAGE-END
(0,1)/?X2

REPORT-END
(0,1)/?X3

?X0/ ON 1
?X1/ (ON 1)   OR (IF LINE-COUNT > 54)
?X2/ IF (LAST-LINE-SW = "YES") OR   (LINE-COUNT > 54)
?X3/ IF LAST-LINE-SW = "YES"

Normally, the challenging part is working out the footnotes. We identify the footnotes of the inverted structure with Xs—?X1, ?X2, etc.—to avoid confusion with the footnotes on the uninverted structure.

11.10 EXERCISES

1. For the project report, combine the LOM of Chapter 7, the input and control break logic of Chapter 9, and the output logic of this chapter to get a process structure you could code from. (Don't forget to clear the project data line after printing it, so DEPT-NUM will appear only on the first line of the department.)

2. Code an alternative version of PRINT-A-LINE using absorption (see Chapter 8) and a REPORT-BEGIN-SW.

3. Code a fully inverted version of PRINT-A-LINE—i.e., one with REPORT-BEGIN and REPORT-END logic—that can be CALLed.

4. The summary (Section 11.9) presents a "flat" inversion of the POM structure. Alternatively, we could have used a "C-shaped" inversion:

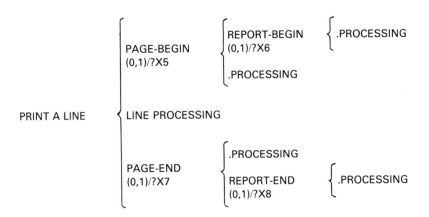

PRINT A LINE
{
PAGE-BEGIN (0,1)/?X5
{
REPORT-BEGIN (0,1)/?X6 { .PROCESSING

.PROCESSING
}

LINE PROCESSING

PAGE-END (0,1)/?X7
{
.PROCESSING

REPORT-END (0,1)/?X8 { .PROCESSING
}
}

Work out the conditions on the footnotes ?X5, ?X6, ?X7, and ?X8.

5. We said that the POM would be passed a LAST-LINE-SW value of "YES" with the last line it had to print. This would let it detect end-of-file when it tried to "get" another record in the middle of processing. We also mentioned that this wasn't entirely satisfactory. Here is a way to get rid of LAST-LINE-SW.

Design a coroutine to run between the LOM and the POM. Its job is to pass the POM two records—current and next—so the POM can "get" another line when it wants one:

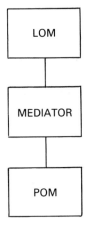

Assume the LOM will make one end-of-file call *after* it sends down the last record. Pay attention to such details as what happens if the first call is the end-of-file call.

12

Complex Calculations

Up to now the most complex calculation we've seen has been working out a total. Typically, this looked like:

$$
\text{COMPANY} \begin{cases} \text{.BEGIN} & \begin{cases} \text{SET COMPANY-TOTAL TO 0} \end{cases} \\[2em] \begin{matrix} \text{DEPARTMENT} \\ (1,D) \end{matrix} & \begin{cases} \text{ADD DEPARTMENT-AMOUNT TO COMPANY-TOTAL} \end{cases} \end{cases}
$$

Life offers more challenging computations than this. How are we to deal with them?

12.1 CALCULATION DIAGRAMS

It turns out that structuring a calculation is a snap if the calculation has been defined in the right way. So we will once again turn to the subject of requirements definition and describe the use of Warnier/Orr diagrams for defining calculations.

The basic idea is: put arithmetic operators in boxes. Plus is ⊞; minus is ⊟; and so on. Thus, if we want to calculate TOTAL-PAYABLE as INVOICE-TOTAL plus SHIPPING minus DISCOUNT, we can write:

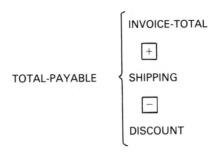

All we've done is write the computation vertically. But this brings the same advantages as other Warnier/Orr diagrams: we can provide increasing levels of details as part of the same picture, while leaving the high-level view intact. For example, we can look further into the computation of INVOICE-TOTAL. It is the sum of ITEM-COST for all items on the invoice. We could write this as:

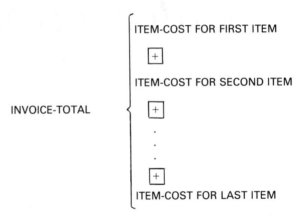

But this is unwieldy, so Warnier/Orr diagrams provide a notation for applying an operation to all members of a repetitive set:

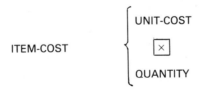

Writing the operator in front of the repeated item means to apply the operation between all occurrences. APL fans will be right at home with this.

Now suppose that the ITEM-COST for each item is equal to its UNIT-COST times the quantity. We would write:

```
              ┌ UNIT-COST
              │
ITEM-COST    ⟨   ×
              │
              └ QUANTITY
```

So far, then, we have:

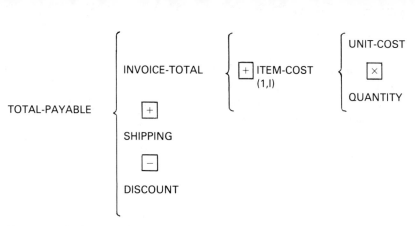

Now we ask the user how to compute the shipping charge. Suppose he says, "Shipping cost? Well, that depends on whether the destination is local or not. Local means less than 20 miles. On local shipments we use trucks and charge a flat $5. For nonlocal destinations we have to ship by air, which is a pain, so we charge $1,000 to discourage people."

That was a lot of information:

ADDRESS	DISTANCE	MEDIUM	CHARGE
local	< 20 miles	truck	$5
nonlocal	>= 20 miles	air	$1000

It's a shame to omit any of it from the diagram we work out with the user. If, for example, we write:

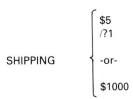

we'll have thrown out so much that nobody will know when to charge which amount. (Incidentally, people often confuse ⊞, meaning plus, with ⊕, meaning or; so it's advisable to use -or- for the exclusive or in these computation diagrams. Also, the (0,1) is often omitted in diagramming processes for users.)

Back to the SHIPPING diagram. It needs additional information to be usable at all. Perhaps:

$$
\text{SHIPPING} \left\{
\begin{array}{l}
\$5 \\
/?1 \\
\text{-or-} \\
\$1000
\end{array}
\right.
$$

?1/ IF DISTANCE < 20 MILES

But we've still omitted the fact that DISTANCE < 20 miles is the user's definition of local, as well as the fact that one shipment is by truck, the other by air. This is reminiscent of the discussion of regular Warnier/Orr diagrams in Chapter 3. Recall the diagram:

$$
\text{MESSAGE 2} \left\{ \begin{array}{l} \text{"GOOD MORNING"} \\ (0,1)/?1 \\[1em] \oplus \\[1em] \text{"GOOD DAY"} \\ (0,1) \end{array} \right.
$$

?1/ IF HOUR < 12

We said that if you wanted to emphasize the conditions, you could write:

$$
\text{MESSAGE 2} \left\{ \begin{array}{ll} \textbf{MORNING} & \left\{ \text{"GOOD MORNING"} \right. \\ (0,1)/?1 & \\[1em] \oplus & \\[1em] \overline{\textbf{MORNING}} & \left\{ \text{"GOOD DAY"} \right. \\ (0,1) & \end{array} \right.
$$

?1/ IF HOUR < 12

This formed a condition sandwich: a condition (MORNING) between two layers of data (MESSAGE 2 and "GOOD MORNING"). We can just as easily make a condition sandwich with our computation diagram:

$$
\text{SHIPPING} \left\{ \begin{array}{ll} \textbf{IF LOCAL} & \left\{ \$5 \right. \\ /?1 & \\[1em] \text{-or-} & \\[1em] \textbf{IF } \overline{\textbf{LOCAL}} & \left\{ \$1000 \right. \end{array} \right.
$$

?1/ IF DISTANCE < 20 MILES

We've inserted the word "IF" so the users don't choke on the condition. The INVOICE-TOTAL calculation was pure data and operations; we want to bring it clearly to their attention that LOCAL is not a data item.

Another way to record all the information is like this:

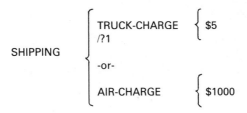

SHIPPING
{
  TRUCK-CHARGE /?1 { $5
  -or-
  AIR-CHARGE { $1000
}

?1/ LOCAL: DISTANCE < 20 MILES

Here we have put the condition name (LOCAL) and the condition test (DISTANCE < 20) into a footnote and named the charges (TRUCK-CHARGE, AIR-CHARGE). This will be especially useful if, for example, the truck charge is changed to $.40 times distance:

SHIPPING
{
  TRUCK-CHARGE /?1 {
    $.40
    ×
    DISTANCE
  }
  -or-
  AIR-CHARGE { $1000
}

?1/ LOCAL: DISTANCE < 20 MILES

So there are a lot of ways to deal with conditions; find one that is clear to your user.

Finally, consider DISCOUNT. Suppose there is no discount for INVOICE-TOTAL up to $100; 1 percent from there to $250; 3 percent from there to $1,000; and 5 percent if $1,000 or more. We can write:

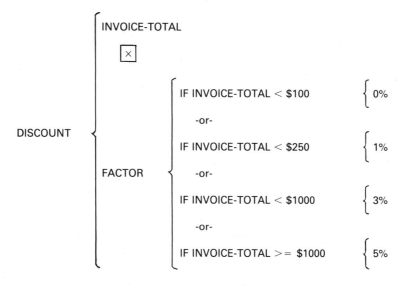

DISCOUNT
{
  INVOICE-TOTAL
  ×
  FACTOR
  {
    IF INVOICE-TOTAL < $100 { 0%
    -or-
    IF INVOICE-TOTAL < $250 { 1%
    -or-
    IF INVOICE-TOTAL < $1000 { 3%
    -or-
    IF INVOICE-TOTAL >= $1000 { 5%
  }
}

This is irregular, since it relies on the tests being made in the order listed; but it is perfectly clear and not really susceptible to misinterpretation.

We can now combine the calculation fragments to get the complete calculation of TOTAL-PAYABLE:

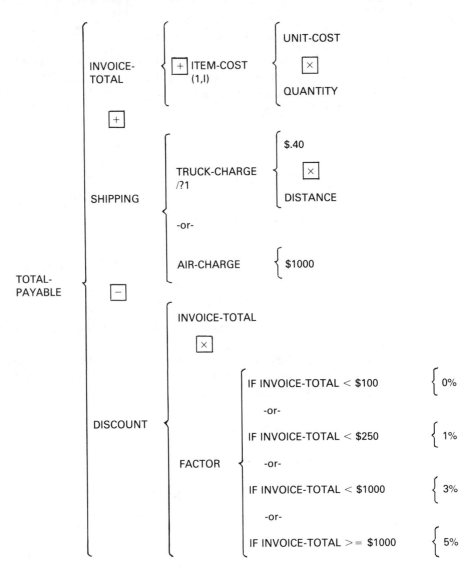

?1/ LOCAL: DISTANCE < 20 MILES

These diagrams are excellent for user communication. I know one analyst who used them to document the calculation of an intricate insurance premium. The rules were extremely complex: the final diagram contained several hundred brackets and took dozens of pages. He thought he had the users' requirements down pat; but when he walked through the calculation diagrams with them, they found *sixty* errors.

Of course he was able to correct the errors for the price of redrawing a few brackets. A device that lets users find so many errors so easily is going to save a lot of money by reducing testing, reprogramming, and maintenance.

Incidentally, there's no reason to restrict these charts to add, subtract, multiply, and divide. For example, suppose the TRUCK-CHARGE had a minimum of $2. You would write:

```
                              ┌                           ┌ $.40
                              │  DISTANCE-CHARGE  ┌        │
                              │                   ┤  ┌─┐   │ ×
        TRUCK-CHARGE  ┤       │  ┌─────┐          └  └─┘   └
                              │  │ MIN │                     DISTANCE
                              │  └─────┘
                              │
                              └  $2
```

Any operation or function that produces one answer from two data elements can be handled nicely.

12.2 COMPLEX CONDITIONS

Sometimes it's not the arithmetic of a situation that's difficult; what's hard is determining *when* to make a particular calculation. We're not talking just about Dagwood condition sandwiches, with several layers of conditions; we're talking about situations where you have to do a fair bit of work before you have any conditions to test.

Suppose you have to calculate a Christmas bonus. Some employees get $20 times the number of children they have; others get a flat $30:

```
                                 ┌                         ┌ NUMBER-OF-CHILDREN
                                 │  KID-AMOUNT     ┌        │
                                 │  (0,1)/?1       ┤  ┌─┐   │ ×
                                 │                 └  └─┘   └
       CHRISTMAS-BONUS  ┤        │                           $20
                                 │
                                 │  -or-
                                 │
                                 │  FLAT-RATE      ┤ $30
                                 └  (0,1)          └
```

To find which bonus an employee gets, calculate "points" as follows. Full-time employees get 5 points for every year of service; part-time employees get 2 points per year. Anyone with 40 points or more is entitled to 10 extra points.

You get the KID-AMOUNT bonus if your points exceed 3 times your age; otherwise, you get the flat rate.

This would obviously make an impossibly complicated footnote. You can't even make a condition sandwich of it, because the condition itself contains calculations.

Now, you can certainly write a regular Warnier/Orr process diagram—sequence, alternation, and repetition—to do the whole Christmas bonus routine.

But here is an alternative approach that has been used successfully, and with good user understanding. (It's not kosher Warnier/Orr.) The approach is to **diagram the footnote**. A footnote is a condition: its job is to make a test and determine if the condition is true or false. There's no reason we can't have Warnier/Orr operators like "is less than" or "equals." For example:

$$
?1 \left\{ \begin{array}{l} \text{POINTS} \\[4pt] \boxed{>} \\[4pt] \text{TRIPLE-AGE} \end{array} \right.
$$

This says: condition-1 holds if POINTS is greater than TRIPLE-AGE. We can elaborate:

$$
?1 \left\{ \begin{array}{l} \text{POINTS} \left\{ \begin{array}{l} \text{POINTS/YEAR} \left\{ \begin{array}{l} \text{IF FULL-TIME} \left\{ 5 \right. \\[4pt] \text{-or-} \\[4pt] \text{IF PART-TIME} \left\{ 2 \right. \end{array} \right. \\[4pt] \boxed{\times} \\[4pt] \text{YEARS-OF-SERVICE} \end{array} \right. \\[16pt] \boxed{>} \\[16pt] \text{TRIPLE-AGE} \left\{ \begin{array}{l} \text{AGE} \\[4pt] \boxed{\times} \\[4pt] 3 \end{array} \right. \end{array} \right.
$$

12.3 *PROGRAM DESIGN AND CODING*

This chapter is about how to structure the programming of a complex calculation. We digressed into requirements definition to look at features of Warnier/Orr diagrams that make them suitable for documenting complex calculations. We stressed how useful the diagrams are in user communications.

But there is more to like about them: they can practically program themselves. We can use the coding rules we have already developed, though with some minor enhancements. Notice how we handle the computation of

$$\text{INVOICE-TOTAL} \left\{ \boxed{+} \begin{array}{l} \text{ITEM-COST} \\ (1,\text{I}) \end{array} \right.$$

in the following code:

```
COMPUTE-TOTAL-PAYABLE.
    PERFORM COMPUTE-INVOICE-TOTAL.
    PERFORM COMPUTE-SHIPPING.
    PERFORM COMPUTE-DISCOUNT.
    COMPUTE TOTAL-PAYABLE =
                    INVOICE-TOTAL + SHIPPING - DISCOUNT.

*----------------------------------------------------------------

COMPUTE-INVOICE-TOTAL.
    MOVE ZERO TO INVOICE-TOTAL.
    PERFORM ADD-ITEM-COST
        VARYING ITEM-NO FROM 1 BY 1 UNTIL ITEM-NO > I.

ADD-ITEM-COST.
    PERFORM COMPUTE-ITEM-COST.
    ADD ITEM-COST TO INVOICE-TOTAL.

COMPUTE-ITEM-COST.
    COMPUTE ITEM-COST = UNIT-COST (ITEM-NO)
                    * QUANTITY (ITEM-NO).

*----------------------------------------------------------------

COMPUTE-SHIPPING.
    IF DISTANCE < 20
*                           (LOCAL)
        PERFORM COMPUTE-TRUCK-CHARGE
        MOVE TRUCK-CHARGE TO SHIPPING
    ELSE
        PERFORM COMPUTE-AIR-CHARGE
        MOVE AIR-CHARGE TO SHIPPING.

COMPUTE-TRUCK-CHARGE.
    COMPUTE TRUCK-CHARGE = .40 * DISTANCE.

COMPUTE-AIR-CHARGE.
    COMPUTE AIR-CHARGE = 1000.

*----------------------------------------------------------------

COMPUTE-DISCOUNT.
    PERFORM FIND-DISCOUNT-FACTOR.
    COMPUTE DISCOUNT = INVOICE-TOTAL * DISCOUNT-FACTOR.

FIND-DISCOUNT-FACTOR.
        IF INVOICE-TOTAL < 100    MOVE 0   TO DISCOUNT-FACTOR
    ELSE IF INVOICE-TOTAL < 250   MOVE .01 TO DISCOUNT-FACTOR
    ELSE IF INVOICE-TOTAL < 1000  MOVE .03 TO DISCOUNT-FACTOR
    ELSE                          MOVE .05 TO DISCOUNT-FACTOR.
```

Notice the layout of FIND-DISCOUNT-FACTOR. It would be misleading to lay it out as a set of successively indented nested IFs. It is implementing a table; the more it looks like one, the clearer it is.

Notice also that the code has been divided into clusters separated by rows of hyphens. Each cluster might well get a page to itself.

This code contains a lot of very short paragraphs. They make it easy to correlate the code and the diagram. On the other hand, the code itself is harder to follow than it might be. You can simplify it by using absorption (see Chapter 8): instead of performing a short paragraph, replace the PERFORM with the actual lines of the paragraph. Of course this doesn't work with PERFORM . . . UNTIL.

And naturally you can also use sections and modules, as described in Chapter 8, when programming from a calculation diagram.

12.4 GENERAL COMMENTS

The charts we just discussed are the preferred way to document calculations. Their clarity is, I think, due partly to the fact that they focus on the **output** of the calculation: the INVOICE-TOTAL in the above example.

There is another way of handling calculations. You should use it when you can't see how to use the type we just described. For example, suppose the user is describing a process that calculates several needed data elements at different points along the way. Your first step would be to document the process with regular Warnier/Orr process diagrams, as described in Chapter 3.

Having thus understood the process, you could then try creating a calculation diagrams (of the sort we have been describing) for each data item.

Incidentally, it isn't always clear what to do with these calculation diagrams once you draw them. The worksheet (see Chapters 6 and 7) will refer to them, of course. I know one analyst who regularly drew calculation diagrams of each calculated field right onto his LOS. His user, who had never dealt with data processing before, found the result very clear.

12.5 SUMMARY

To document a calculation, focus on its result. Back off the result to the appropriate inputs by using Warnier/Orr calculation diagrams, which show arithmetic operators in boxes. The calculation "A = B + C" is diagrammed as:

$$A \begin{cases} B \\ \boxed{+} \\ C \end{cases}$$

You can also, if you are feeling frisky, document footnotes with such diagrams. The footnote ?1/ X > Y could be shown:

Users understand calculation diagrams easily, and programming from them can be almost mechanical.

12.6 EXERCISES

1. Diagram the following calculation:
    Regular pay is computed as follows. Managers are paid the amount in the SAL-ARY field. Others employees get an HOURLY-AMOUNT times imputed hours (imputed hours = REGULAR-HOURS plus 1.5 times OVERTIME-HOURS). A manager is anyone with more than 500 JOB-POINTS. All employees with more than 5 YEARS-OF-SERVICE are eligible for bonuses. Those whose AGE exceeds 40 get 10% of regular pay; those 40 and under get 5%. Total pay equals regular pay plus bonus.

2. Recall a complicated calculation you have had to define or program. Try diagramming it with the calculation diagrams. What problems do you run into? Is the result better or worse than the way the calculation was defined originally? Which would you rather program from? What improvements or additional features would make the calculation diagrams more useful?

FURTHER READING

The INVOICE-TOTAL problem given in this chapter is modified from an example in *Structured Systems Analysis* by Chris Gane and Trish Sarson. For other approaches to the problem, see Section 5.4 of that book.

Part III

INPUT

We have been indulging in the pleasant fantasy that input files always have the same structure as output files. It is now time to meet the real world. In this part of the book we look carefully at the ways of getting data into the program.

We began in Chapters 5 and 6 by fully describing the output. Then in Chapter 7 we identified which data items on the output were "required": that is, which of them needed to be supplied as input. We diagrammed the logical input file to show the order in which this data had to be supplied. Since then we have assumed that a suitable routine will return exactly the right data in the right order whenever the LOM says "GET LOGICAL RECORD".

In Part III we'll discuss the writing of the input logic to provide the required data to the LOM.

There are few new principles here. But a couple of issues will arise more than once:

1. *Should the input be handled in a separate routine?* Some people prefer a separate read routine even when it's not logically necessary; we'll outline the pros and cons.
2. *Should the input routine be inverted* if it exists? Here the answer is unanimous: only invert if your system makes coroutines impossible or impractical.

The material on inversion has been segregated at the end of each chapter to make it easy to skip. Even if you need inversion because of the limitations of your system, you'll find the exposition easier to follow if you skip the inversion material on first reading.

13

Physical Input Mapping

In this chapter we will work out the general form of a physical input mapping (PIM) to pass data to the LOM. In subsequent chapters we will adapt it to more complex cases. Throughout Part III we will use the terms "PIM," "input mapping," and "read routine" interchangeably.

13.1 *WHERE THE PHYSICAL INPUT MAPPING FITS IN*

In Chapter 10 ("Concurrency") we observed that the task of turning an input file into a project report could be diagrammed like this:

We observed that the output had two *concurrent* structures:

```
                      ⎧ LOGICAL  ⎧ COMPANY ⎧ DEPT      ⎧ PROJECT
                      ⎪          ⎨         ⎨ (1,D)     ⎨ (1,PR)
  PROJECT   ⎧         ⎪          ⎩         ⎩           ⎩
  REPORT    ⎨         ⎪     +
            ⎩         ⎪          ⎧ REPORT  ⎧ PAGE
                      ⎩ PHYSICAL ⎨         ⎨ (1,PA)
                                 ⎩         ⎩
```

Data structure yields process structure, so we needed two concurrent routines:

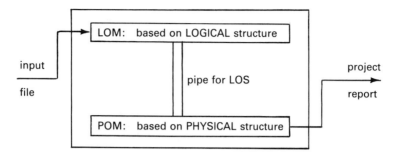

The "pipe" was a channel along which the LOM passed lines to the POM (physical output mapping) for printing.

Now the time has come to admit that the process has more than just *output* data structures to deal with; it also has inputs. And it must deal with them at the same time it produces the outputs; that is, the two data structures are concurrent from the point of view of the process. So the total data structure for the process is:

$$\text{COMPLETE DATA STRUCTURE} \begin{cases} \text{INPUT structure} \\ + \\ \text{OUTPUT structure} \end{cases}$$

And each of these two structures has both a logical and a physical nature concurrently:

$$\text{COMPLETE DATA STRUCTURE} \begin{cases} \text{INPUT} \begin{cases} \text{PHYSICAL INPUT} \\ + \\ \text{LOGICAL INPUT} \end{cases} \\ + \\ \text{OUTPUT} \begin{cases} \text{LOGICAL OUTPUT} \\ + \\ \text{PHYSICAL OUTPUT} \end{cases} \end{cases}$$

So by analogy to our work in Chapter 10, we conclude that the complete set of processes we need to do the job will be as follows:

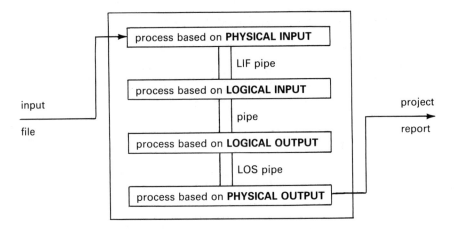

We have four concurrent processes and three pipes.

But the picture can be simplified. In Chapter 7 we saw that the logical input (LIF) always has the same structure as the logical output; thus, the two middle processes have the same structure and can be combined into one. Combining them, and naming the surviving routines, we get:

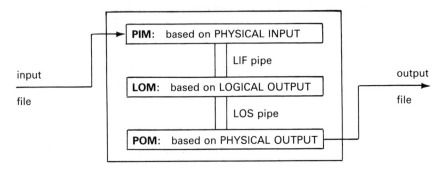

The topmost process is the input mapping or read routine we have so long awaited. We'll normally call it the physical input mapping, or PIM.

We combined the middle routines—the ones based on LIF and LOS—because they had the same structure. Sometimes we can go further with the combining. As we saw in Section 10.2, it occasionally happens that the physical output structure matches the logical output structure. When this happens, we can meld the two structures and create a common routine to do the work of both LOM and POM.

And such melding is far more commonly possible on the input side. If you find that the physical files available to you match the structure and sequence of the LOS, then you have a choice. You can create a PIM anyway, for the sake of uniformity; or you can meld the input processing into the LOM and eliminate the physical input mapping entirely.

Since there are sometimes clashes between physical and logical input, and since these cases definitely require input mappings (or read routines, to use the more homely term), we will discuss input mappings extensively. You can then make your own decision about whether to create one in cases where there is no input structure clash.

13.2 PHYSICAL INPUT MAPPING: OPTIONS AND STRATEGY

This chapter is about how to implement the PIM. We will be piggybacking on the work we did in Chapters 10 and 11.

Recall Chapter 10. We first designed the concurrent LOM and POM as pure "coroutines"—that is, as communicating parallel processes. We observed that some systems—UNIX for example—make it easy to implement coroutines directly; but usually no such system is available.

One alternative is to create stand-alone programs passing a temporary file, but that arrangement can be expensive to run. We were eventually driven to implement the POM coroutine as a subroutine, using hierarchy inversion.

Our strategy for the physical input mapping in this chapter will be the same.

- We will first construct the LOM and PIM as pure coroutines. The PIM will be based on the physical input file structure (section 13.3).

- Then we will apply hierarchy inversion to derive a PIM subroutine (sections 13.5–13.7).

Lest we lose the forest in the trees, note that a program with Chapter 11's POM subroutine *and* this chapter's PIM subroutine would have the following module structure:

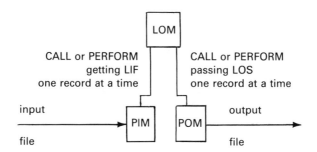

To keep things simple, in this chapter we will ignore the POM half of the diagram.

Our tactic will be to work out the PIM structures—coroutine and subroutine—for the simplest possible input file: one that already has the same structure as the logical output. The result will be practically useless in itself but will provide a foundation for subsequent chapters. We begin with the pure coroutine structure.

13.3 PURE COROUTINES

Recall the employee loan list of Chapter 4:

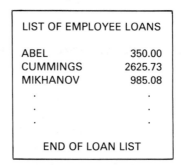

```
LIST OF EMPLOYEE LOANS

ABEL                 350.00
CUMMINGS            2625.73
MIKHANOV             985.08
      .                 .
      .                 .
      .                 .

     END OF LOAN LIST
```

We will assume that the input file is already in the right order and will create these two coroutines:

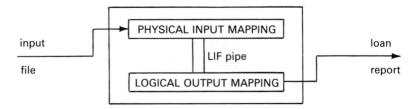

We start with the input mapping. It has to read the LOAN file and produce the logical input file for the LOS; so it is essentially the same as the loan program we created in Chapter 4, except that:

1. Instead of displaying a line for an input record, it writes a logical record to the LOM; and
2. It has to write an explicit end-of-file indicator at COMPANY-END. (Remember, the LOM finds end-of-file by reading one *past* the last record.)

Copying the structure from Chapter 4, we get:

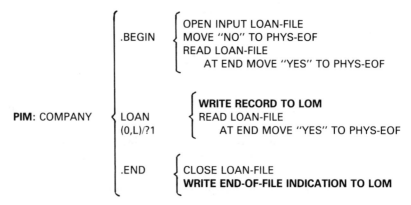

```
                                    ┌ OPEN INPUT LOAN-FILE
                        .BEGIN     ┤ MOVE "NO" TO PHYS-EOF
                                    │ READ LOAN-FILE
                                    └    AT END MOVE "YES" TO PHYS-EOF

                                    ┌ WRITE RECORD TO LOM
        PIM: COMPANY    LOAN        ┤ READ LOAN-FILE
                        (0,L)/?1    └    AT END MOVE "YES" TO PHYS-EOF

                        .END        ┤ CLOSE LOAN-FILE
                                    └ WRITE END-OF-FILE INDICATION TO LOM
```

?1/ UNTIL PHYS-EOF = "YES"

Notice that the end-of-file indicator for the physical input file has been christened PHYS-EOF.

So much for the PIM. The structure of the other coroutine, the LOM, is even simpler to derive. Clearly it is:

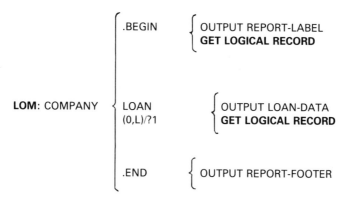

?1/ UNTIL END OF LOGICAL INPUT

We now have the pure coroutine forms of our two processes.

13.4 WHAT'S THE POINT IN AN INPUT MAPPING?

We have gone to some lengths to separate the input logic into its own routine. We'll briefly look at some of the arguments for and against doing so, starting with the arguments in favor.

Structure clash: Everyone agrees on this one: when there is a structure clash between the physical input and the logical output, a separate input mapping is a necessity. No melding of routines is possible; that's what structure clash means. Recall that in Chapter 10 the thing that forced us to have separate LOM and POM mappings was a structure clash between logical and physical output. Of course in the case of the LOAN file we just discussed, there is no structure clash.

Data independence: The separate-mapping enthusiasts can argue that burying the physical input instructions in a separate routine makes your program more independent of the physical structure of the data. If somebody changes the file structure or converts to a data base management system, the main line of your program doesn't have to be changed. Of course your physical read routine (input mapping) still needs changing. The saving only arises if several outputs need essentially the same information and can share a common read routine.

Consistency: The final reason for having a separate read routine is for consistency of system structure. Some developers find that by giving every part of their system the same input-process-output routine structure, they end up with a system that is easier to maintain because it's easier to predict where to look for specific logic.

On the other side of the fence are those who believe that a separate routine should be created only when absolutely necessary: that is, only when there is a structure clash to resolve. Their arguments boil down to one:

Simplicity: The fewer parts there are to a system, they say, the easier it will be to understand. What is the point of creating separate routines when there is no logical need to do so? You increase your filing burden, you have twice as many places to look when things go wrong, and you mask the special needs of structure clashes by making their code look physically like all the other components of the system.

Those are the main arguments on both sides. If you aren't totally persuaded by either position, you may want to experiment with both approaches to find which you prefer.

If you are not studying inversion, please skip to section 13.8.

13.5 STARTING THE INVERSION: CHANGING THE LOM

Now, for those who are still reading, we will see how to create a **sub**routine structure for the LOAN input:

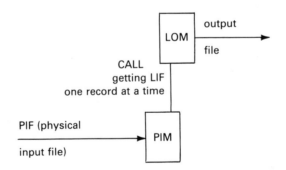

Note that the LOM is now on top. In this arrangement we will occasionally refer to the LOM as the main line and to the PIM as the subroutine. We choose to implement the input mapping as a CALLed subroutine (rather than a PERFORMed one); in the terminology of Chapter 8, we will make it a separate module.

Converting the LOM to this calling structure is easy. It becomes:

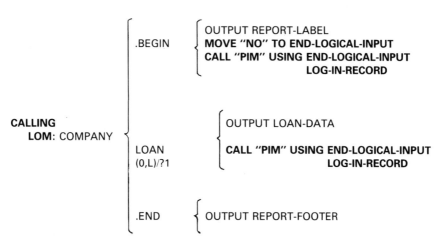

CALLING
LOM: COMPANY

.BEGIN
OUTPUT REPORT-LABEL
MOVE "NO" TO END-LOGICAL-INPUT
CALL "PIM" USING END-LOGICAL-INPUT
LOG-IN-RECORD

LOAN
(0,L)/?1
OUTPUT LOAN-DATA
CALL "PIM" USING END-LOGICAL-INPUT
LOG-IN-RECORD

.END
OUTPUT REPORT-FOOTER

?1/ UNTIL END-LOGICAL-INPUT = "YES"

Notice the two parameters on the CALL. One is the logical loan record, of course; the PIM exists to supply such records to the LOM.

The other parameter, called END-LOGICAL-INPUT, is to let the PIM signal end of file. The LOM sets END-LOGICAL-INPUT to "NO" at COMPANY-BEGIN; the input mapping must set it to "YES" on the call *after* the one in which it passes back the last logical record. It will thus be offering the LOM exactly the same services as a COBOL READ, which triggers AT END on the READ after the last record.

13.6 COMPLETING THE INVERSION: THE PIM

Now, what shall we do to make a subroutine out of the input mapping?

When your only tool is a hammer, everything looks like a nail. Our tool is hierarchy inversion. Recall how in Chapter 11 we inverted:

PAGE
.BEGIN

LINE
(L)

.END

to get:

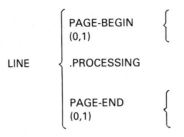

LINE
- PAGE-BEGIN (0,1)
- .PROCESSING
- PAGE-END (0,1)

Similarly, we are tempted to invert the PIM hierarchy:

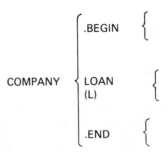

COMPANY
- .BEGIN
- LOAN (L)
- .END

to get:

LOAN
- COMPANY-BEGIN (0,1)
- LOAN PROCESSING
- COMPANY-END (0,1)

But we have to allow for the fact that each call will get *either* a LOAN *or* an end-of-file indication. So the structure will be:

PIM'
- COMPANY-BEGIN (0,1)/?X1
- LOAN (0,1)/?X2 { ...
- ⊕
- COMPANY-END (0,1) { ...

?X1/ IF FIRST TIME THROUGH
?X2/ IF NOT AT END OF PHYSICAL INPUT

That is, the LOAN and COMPANY-END brackets are mutually exclusive. (Note that we have used the prime symbol ['] to indicate the subroutine version of the PIM. And, as in Chapter 11, we have distinguished inversion footnotes by X: ?X1, ?X2.)

If we now insert the logic we derived previously, the result is:

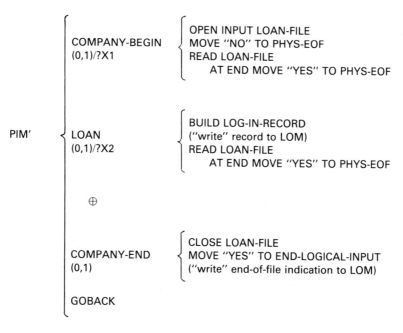

PIM'

COMPANY-BEGIN
(0,1)/?X1

OPEN INPUT LOAN-FILE
MOVE "NO" TO PHYS-EOF
READ LOAN-FILE
    AT END MOVE "YES" TO PHYS-EOF

LOAN
(0,1)/?X2

BUILD LOG-IN-RECORD
("write" record to LOM)
READ LOAN-FILE
    AT END MOVE "YES" TO PHYS-EOF

⊕

COMPANY-END
(0,1)

CLOSE LOAN-FILE
MOVE "YES" TO END-LOGICAL-INPUT
("write" end-of-file indication to LOM)

GOBACK

?X1/ ON 1
?X2/ IF PHYS-EOF = "NO"

The WRITE instructions have been left in as comments, but of course no physical writing takes place. The record, or the end-of-file indication, is passed back to the LOM automatically when the GOBACK is executed.

This gives the following COBOL:

```
PROCEDURE DIVISION USING END-LOGICAL-INPUT
                       LOG-IN-RECORD.

COMPANY.
    ON 1 PERFORM COMPANY-BEGIN.
    IF PHYS-EOF = "NO"
        PERFORM LOAN
    ELSE
        PERFORM COMPANY-END.
    GOBACK.

COMPANY-BEGIN.
    OPEN INPUT LOAN-FILE.
    MOVE "NO" TO PHYS-EOF.
    READ LOAN-FILE
        AT END MOVE "YES" TO PHYS-EOF.

LOAN.
    MOVE IN-EE-NAME      TO LOG-IN-EE-NAME.
    MOVE IN-LOAN-AMOUNT TO LOG-IN-LOAN-AMOUNT.
    READ LOAN-FILE
        AT END MOVE "YES" TO PHYS-EOF.

COMPANY-END.
    CLOSE LOAN-FILE.
    MOVE "YES" TO END-LOGICAL-INPUT.
```

13.7 INVERSION VARIATIONS

In the interest of brevity, we have been expressing the first-time condition as:

```
?1/ ON 1
```

But, as we mentioned in Chapter 11, ON 1 can be dicey with on-line systems and with overlay; and it suffers from the further drawback of not existing in most COBOLs. One way to avoid it is to have the LOM invoke COMPANY-BEGIN logic directly, presumably with separate entry point in the input mapping.

If you can live with multiple entry points, you have another option:

- ENTRY1 is GET FIRST RECORD: it does COMPANY-BEGIN, then continues through the remainder of the input mapping logic.
- ENTRY2 is GET NEXT RECORD: it always skips the processing for COMPANY-BEGIN.

Naturally, the main-line LOM will call ENTRY1 to start, and ENTRY2 when a record is consumed.

If you reject multiple entry points, you can administer your own switch to replace ON 1. You add a linkage field called FIRST-CALL-SW or COMPANY-BEGIN-SW or something of the sort. The main line LOM initializes FIRST-

CALL-SW to "YES" at start-of-job; the input mapping LOAN logic sets it to "NO". Then footnote 1 is:

```
?1/ IF FIRST-CALL-SW = "YES"
```

To keep things brief we will normally write ON 1. You can think of it as shorthand for the above paragraphs.

13.8 SUMMARY

The basic form of the trivial physical input mapping (PIM) is

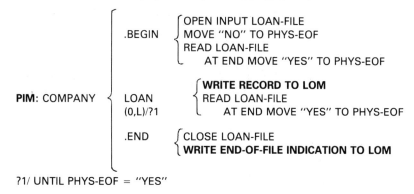

When inverted this has the following structure:

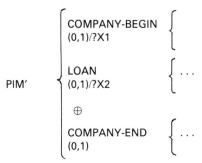

?X1/ IF FIRST TIME THROUGH
?X2/ IF NOT AT END OF PHYSICAL INPUT

13.9 EXERCISES

1. Suppose there are 100 records on the physical input file:
   (a) How many times will the PIM be called?
   (b) On which call will PHYS-EOF be set to "YES"?
   (c) On which call will END-LOGICAL-INPUT be set to "YES"?
2. Now suppose the input file has no records—i.e., is empty. What are the answers to (a), (b), and (c) above? What if the input file has one record?
3. Rework the model so the LOM and PIM contain logical OPEN and CLOSE statements. They can be thought of as dealing with header and trailer records on the file. What does the inverted PIM look like now?

14

Driver Files and the LDS

In the previous chapter we worked out the general form of the physical input mapping for a trivial input file, and showed how to invert it. In this chapter we begin to look at more interesting inputs, but we continue to assume there is at least one input file with the same structure as the output. Much of the discussion will center on ways to use the fields on such a "driver file" as keys to retrieve information from other files.

We also introduce the concept of Logical Data Structure. The LDS represents the minimum input data required by an output. It is useful as a sort of input shopping list, and it provides an efficient structure for the input processing.

14.1 WHAT IS A DRIVER FILE?

An input file with the same structure and sequencing as the required output is called a **driver file**. We've seen nothing but driver files so far in this book, since throughout Part II we assumed that there was a physical input file we could read sequentially.

Why make up a name for such a trivial concept? The main reason is that Orr's data base design techniques—which we do not discuss in this book—lead to the creation of driver files, or things that can be sorted to get driver files. A secondary consideration is that because they are not very complicated, driver files provide a good vehicle for introducing a number of supporting ideas.

Here is a more intricate example of a driver file. It is a variant on the project report we have been using throughout the book.

Suppose the company for whom the report is prepared has plants in several cities. It wants the report broken down by city, then department and project. The LOS looks basically like this, where individual data items are not shown:

$$\text{COMPANY} \left\{ \begin{array}{l} \text{CITY} \\ \text{(1,C)} \end{array} \right. \left\{ \begin{array}{l} \text{DEPT} \\ \text{(1,D)} \end{array} \right. \left\{ \begin{array}{l} \text{PROJECT} \\ \text{(1,P)} \end{array} \right.$$

We will assume there is a driver file: a physical file with the same structure as this output. For the moment, we will also assume that this driver file contains all the required data elements. The stand-alone structure of the input mapping will be the multilevel-control break structure we worked out in Chapter 9:

```
                .BEGIN  { OPEN INPUT PROJ-FILE
                          MOVE "NO" TO PHYS-EOF
                          READ PROJ-FILE
                              AT END MOVE "YES" TO PHYS-EOF

                        .BEGIN  { MOVE IN-CITY# TO CURR-CITY#
                                  MOVE CITY DATA INTO LOG-IN-RECORD

                                .BEGIN  { MOVE IN-DEPT# TO CURR-DEPT#
                                          MOVE DEPT DATA INTO LOG-IN-RECORD

COMPANY { CITY    { DEPT    { PROJECT   { MOVE PROJ DATA INTO LOG-IN-RECORD
          (1,C)/?1  (1,D)/?2  (1,P)/?3    WRITE LOGICAL RECORD
                                          READ PROJ-FILE
                                              AT END MOVE "YES" TO PHYS-EOF

                                .END  {

                        .END  {

                .END  { CLOSE SALES-FILE
                        MOVE "YES" TO END-LOGICAL-INPUT
                        WRITE END-OF-FILE INDICATION
```

?1/ UNTIL PHYS-EOF = "YES"
?2/ UNTIL (PHYS-EOF = "YES") OR (IN-CITY# > CURR-CITY#)
?3/ UNTIL (PHYS-EOF = "YES") OR (IN-CITY# > CURR-CITY#) OR (IN-DEPT# > CURR-DEPT#)

Notice that so far all operations are logical, not physical: the file is not opened or closed, the fictitious MOVE . . . INTO instruction is used, and so on. Specifically, the operations are not intended to be in COBOL or any other language. Also note that it is implicit in our approach that (for example) the CITY DATA doesn't change from one output record to the next unless it's reset; that's why it can be set up at CITY-BEGIN and be inherited by all projects for that city.

(If you would like to see an inverted version of this solution, please turn to sections 14.8 and 14.9.)

14.2 DIRECT ACCESS IS BORING

A driver file has the same **structure** as the main line, but it doesn't necessarily have all **information** required. We may well have to go to direct access files for such things as city name, department budget, and the like.

We have a new rule: *Only sequential files affect the program structure*. Direct access files don't. (Except for a possible found/not-found alternation). When you need a direct record, get it; the sequential file will tell you where to do it.

So to get city name and department budget and whatnot, we modify the stand-alone input mapping from Section 14.1 as follows:

```
          ┌          ┌ GET COMPANY DATA
          │          │ MOVE COMPANY-DATA INTO LOG-IN-RECORD
          │ .BEGIN   │ OPEN INPUT PROJ-FILE
          │          │ MOVE "NO" TO PHYS-EOF
          │          │ READ PROJ-FILE
          │          └      AT END MOVE "YES" TO PHYS-EOF
```

```
                                ┌         ┌ MOVE IN-CITY# TO CURR-CITY#
                                │ .BEGIN  ┤ READ CITY-FILE WITH KEY IN-CITY#
                                │         └ MOVE CITY DATA INTO LOG-IN-RECORD
```

```
                                                      ┌         ┌ MOVE IN-DEPT# TO CURR-DEPT#
                                                      │ .BEGIN  ┤ READ DEPT-FILE WITH KEY IN-DEPT#
                                                      │         └ MOVE DEPT DATA INTO LOG-IN-RECORD
```

```
                                                                  ┌ MOVE PROJ DATA INTO LOG-IN-RECORD
                                                      PROJECT     │ WRITE LOGICAL RECORD
COMPANY ┤ CITY          ┤ DEPT          ┤ (1,P)/?3    ┤ READ PROJ-FILE
          (1,C)/?1          (1,D)/?2                   └      AT END MOVE "YES" TO PHYS-EOF
```

```
                                                      .END ┤
```

```
                                .END ┤
```

```
          ┌          ┌ CLOSE SALES-FILE
          │ .END     ┤ MOVE "YES" TO END-LOGICAL-INPUT
          │          └ WRITE END-OF-FILE INDICATION
```

?1/ UNTIL PHYS-EOF = "YES"
?2/ UNTIL (PHYS-EOF = "YES") OR (IN-CITY# > CURR-CITY#)
?3/ UNTIL (PHYS-EOF = "YES") OR (IN-CITY# > CURR-CITY#) OR (IN-DEPT# > CURR-DEPT#)

Notice that we have treated COMPANY-DATA as a direct access file. It is normally a sequential file with only one record: a date card or something of the sort. This is conceptually the same as direct access.

14.3 TABLE LOOKUP

We have been discussing the city and department files as ordinary direct-access files. But there are other types of files that are conceptually direct: they include sequential files sorted in the right order, and lookup tables. We will discuss tables first.

Suppose that instead of being on a direct-access file, DEPT details are in a sequential table with, say, 30 entries. The entries are in no particular order.

The basic structure of the input mapping will be just as before. The difference is the logic at DEPT-BEGIN. We're interested in the structure of the input file, since that is what the PIM is based on. The table structure is:

DEPARTMENTS PIF: COMPANY { DEPT (30) { .# .NAME

(PIF stands for physical input file.)

Another way to look at it is this:

DEPARTMENTS PIF: COMPANY {
PREVIOUS-DEPT (0,P) {
THIS-DEPT { .# .NAME
SUBSEQUENT-DEPT (0,S) {

Adding the logic and footnotes, and inserting this into the PIM structure, gives:

DEPT-BEGIN {
.BEGIN { LOAD DEPARTMENTS TABLE
MOVE 1 TO SUB
PREVIOUS-DEPT (0,P)/?6 { ADD 1 TO SUB
THIS-DEPT { MOVE DEPT-NAME (SUB) INTO LOG-IN-RECORD

?X6/ UNTIL DEPT# (SUB) = IN-DEPT#

The universal SUBSEQUENT-DEPT disappeared because it didn't need any processing.

Notice, incidentally, how similar this remaining logic is to our standard looping logic. Instead of **reading** once to begin and again when consumed, we are instead **incrementing** SUB (which conceptually starts at zero) once to begin, and again when an occurrence is consumed.

The operation LOAD DEPARTMENTS TABLE needn't be repeated for every department. We can improve performance by moving it to COMPANY-BEGIN.

14.4 SEQUENTIAL FILES AS DIRECT ACCESS

We have been discussing files that can be used to provide information that is missing from the driver file. We have already looked at genuine direct access files and at a table lookup.

Now we will look at another kind of supporting file that is basically direct access: a sequential file sorted in the right order. For example, suppose that in the example we've been using we have the following files:

CITY FILE: COMPANY $\left\{ \begin{array}{l} \text{CITY} \\ \text{(1,C)} \end{array} \right.$ $\left\{ \begin{array}{l} \text{.\#} \\ \text{city data} \end{array} \right.$

DEPT FILE: COMPANY $\left\{ \begin{array}{l} \text{CITY} \\ \text{(1,C)} \end{array} \right.$ $\left\{ \begin{array}{l} \text{DEPT} \\ \text{(1,D)} \end{array} \right.$ $\left\{ \begin{array}{l} \text{.CITY\#} \\ \text{.DEPT\#} \\ \text{dept data} \end{array} \right.$

These files can be treated as direct access files. Since they are in the same order as the project driver file, we can simply open and read them once at COM-PANY-BEGIN. Then for each project record we read until we get a hit. The situation is very much as it was for table lookup.

In fact we can basically copy over the result of the table-lookup analysis. For the CITY file, for example, the result is:

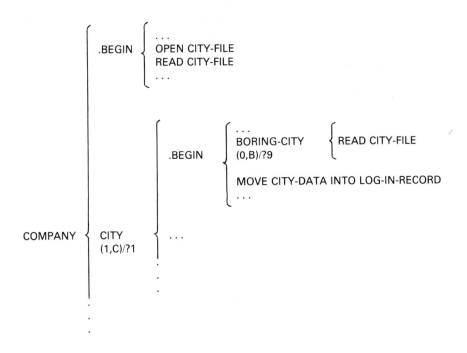

.BEGIN
 . . .
 OPEN CITY-FILE
 READ CITY-FILE
 . . .

.BEGIN
 . . .
 BORING-CITY READ CITY-FILE
 (0,B)/?9
 MOVE CITY-DATA INTO LOG-IN-RECORD
 . . .

COMPANY CITY . . .
  (1,C)/?1

?9/ UNTIL CITY# ON CITY-FILE = CITY# ON PROJECT-FILE

14.5 WHY PUT DIRECT ACCESS IN A PIM?

We have spent a fair bit of energy working out how to get the direct access into the input mapping when the driver file doesn't have all the needed information. But why not dispense with the input mapping altogether, and put the direct access logic directly into the main line LOM?

We will not revisit the independence-and-consistency-versus-simplicity argument of section 13.4. We merely note that putting the direct access logic into the LOM presents no logical difficulties: if something would go at CITY-BEGIN in a PIM, you can instead put the same logic at CITY-BEGIN in the LOM. The choice is yours. Orr himself doesn't seem to take a hard line on the subject, and his followers are split.

The next two sections (14.6 and 14.7) will discuss the introduction of hidden hierarchies into the input mapping, in the interests of efficiency. If you belong to the do-everything-in-the-LOM school, notice that you can introduce the same hidden hierarchies into the LOM instead.

In this chapter we have postulated a driver file—a physical input file with the same structure as the logical input file (LIF) and the LOS. Recall from Section 7.1 that the LIF always has the same structure as the LOS. We have based the input mapping on this common structure.

But the result is sometimes less efficient than it ought to be. In this section we will discuss changes to make the input mapping more efficient; in the next we will introduce a new data structure that can be used in creating this improved mapping.

The problem with basing the input mapping on the LOS/LIF structure is that things can get done more times than necessary. As a concrete example, recall the Expense Report, which we last saw in Section 7.5. It had the following layout:

```
              MONTHLY EXPENSE REPORT              PAGE   1
                    MAY   1987


EXPENSE CATEGORY
DATE          SUPPLIER      ITEM                   COST

OFFICE SUPPLIES

05-10-87      PRINTERS INC.  BUSINESS CARDS          50.00
05-10-87      PRINTERS INC.  LETTERHEAD              75.00
05-15-87      COMPUSTORE     DISKETTES               90.00

                            TOTAL FOR OFFICE SUPPLIES   215.00

   .             .             .                        .
   .             .             .                        .
   .             .             .                        .


TRAVEL EXPENSES

05-03-87      JENKINS        CARSON CITY, NV        525.00
05-03-87      STEVENSON      LANSING,MI             375.26
05-21-87      MILLBROOK      PRINCE ALBERT, SASK    400.18

                            TOTAL FOR TRAVEL EXPENSES  1,300.44
                                  .                        .
                                  .                        .
                                  .                        .
                            GRAND TOTAL            45,907.95
```

This resulted in the following LOS:

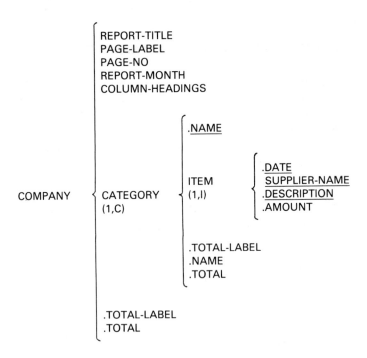

Notice the sequence indicated by the underlining. Categories are in order by name; items within the category are sequenced by date, then supplier name, then description.

Now suppose we were to generate an input mapping based on a driver file with the same structure:

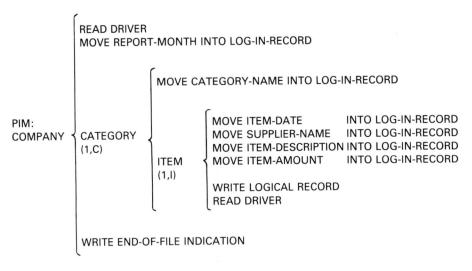

This is perfectly correct, but quite inefficient. The moving of the ITEM-DATE into the logical record happens on every item. But the sequencing of the LOS (and hence of the driver file) shows that within a category all the items for the same date are grouped together. It would make more sense if we move the date to the logical record only when it *changes*. (As before, we are assuming that each new output record starts with the previous output record's values.)

If we expose the hidden hierarchy caused by the ITEM-DATE sequencing, we get a perfect opportunity for this optimization. (See Section 6.4 if you could use a refresher on hidden hierarchies.)

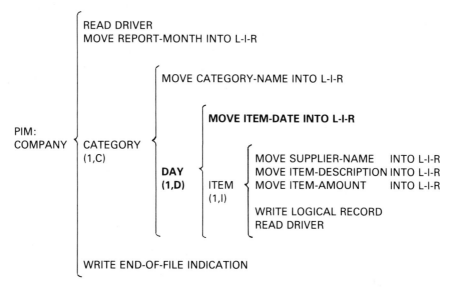

(Logical input record has been abbreviated to L-I-R.) And of course this still isn't the best we can do. The underlining in the LOS shows that the items for the same day are grouped by supplier. So we can expose another level of hidden hierarchy and write:

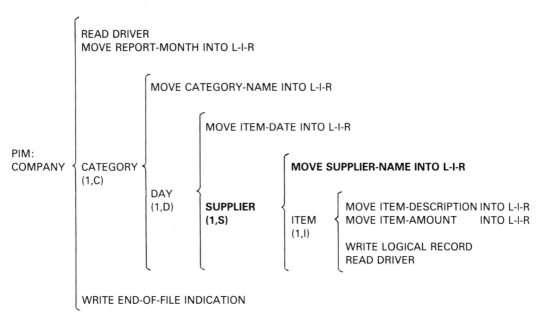

By taking account of the hidden hierarchies, and setting elements in the logical record only when they change, we are able to improve the efficiency of the input mapping. Saving moves may or may not be important; but if, for example, the SUPPLIER-NAME has to be read from a direct-access file, based on a key on the driver file, the gain in efficiency can be considerable.

So the most efficient structure for the input mapping is derived by:

1. Exposing all hidden hierarchies, and
2. Setting each required element on the logical record only when it changes.

These rules are normally straightforward to apply. But if you would like a more formal approach, you will find one in the next section.

14.7 *THE LOGICAL DATA STRUCTURE*

We have just seen that basing the input mapping on a driver structure drawn to match the LOS can lead to inefficiencies. That's because, as we saw in Section 6.4, the standard form of the LOS sometimes hides hierarchies.

Some people get around the problem by always showing the hidden hierarchies in the LOS. But a more common approach is to work out what's called the **logical data structure**, or LDS. The LDS represents the minimum data requirements to produce the output. So not only does it provide an efficient structure for the input mapping, it also serves as a sort of shopping list when you are considering possible physical input files.

Basically, the LDS is the LOS with:

1. Hidden hierarchies exposed;
2. Only Required elements (as opposed to Literal and Calculated) shown; and
3. Each element placed according to its frequency of change.

So for the Expense Report, for example, the LDS would be:

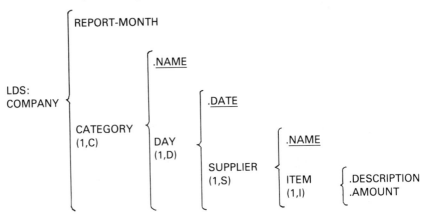

Recall the dot convention: e.g., .DESCRIPTION in the ITEM bracket means ITEM.DESCRIPTION.

Here is another example—the LDS for the Project List from Section 6.1:

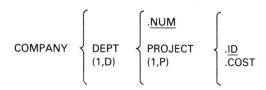

Here the LDS is simply the LOS minus literal and calculated items: there is no hidden hierarchy to expose.

When the required data are drawn in ths way, it is clear how to arrange the input mapping: a move-to-logical-record at the position corresponding to each element in the LDS.

So the question is: How do we derive the LDS? The simplest way is by inspection, as we just did. That is, apply the above three rules to the LOS: expose hidden hierarchies, show only required elements, and place each element according to its frequency of change.

But you can attack the logical data structure from a different angle. The LDS is a Warnier/Orr diagram, and any Warnier/Orr diagram can be derived by using the LFUD approach we introduced in Section 6.1. Here is how the four steps of LFUD—List, Frequency, Universal Analysis, Diagram—apply to creating an LDS:

1. LIST the atoms. As we saw above, the atomic elements of the LDS are the **required data elements** of the output.
2. Give the FREQUENCY of each atom. As our discussion in the previous section showed, the LDS should place each element according to its **frequency of change**. The whole point is to improve efficiency of the input mapping by only dealing with an item when it changes.
3. Do the UNIVERSAL ANALYSIS to find how the brackets identified in Step 2 relate to each other.
4. Draw the DIAGRAM.

As an example, we can quickly run through the LFUD of the Expense Report. First, list the *required elements*:

REQUIRED FIELD
REPORT-MONTH CATEGORY-NAME ITEM-DATE SUPPLIER-NAME ITEM-DESCRIPTION ITEM-AMOUNT

Then give the frequency with which each *changes*. To do this, you must know the output's sequencing. Then it is straightforward to write:

REQUIRED FIELD	CHANGES
REPORT-MONTH	1/COMPANY
CATEGORY-NAME	1/CATEGORY
ITEM-DATE	1/DAY
SUPPLIER-NAME	1/SUPPLIER
ITEM-DESCRIPTION	1/ITEM
ITEM-AMOUNT	1/ITEM

Now do the universal analysis, copying down the unique frequencies from the changes column and relating them to each other:

UNIVERSAL	OCCURS
COMPANY	1
CATEGORY	1,C/COMPANY
DAY	1,D/CATEGORY
SUPPLIER	1,S/DAY
ITEM	1,I/SUPPLIER

Finally, draw the diagram by setting up the indicated structure of brackets . . .

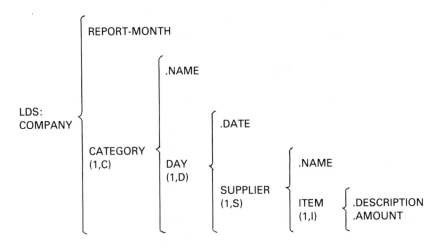

. . . and then inserting the elements:

This completes the development of the LDS using the LFUD process. Note that there is no need to start anew when listing the required elements and giving their frequencies of change. The worksheet we used in Chapters 6 and 7 to derive the LOS and LOM can simply be extended by one column:

DATA ELEMENT	APPEARS	t	DETAILS	EXECUTED	CHANGES
REPORT-TITLE	1/COMPANY	L	"MONTHLY EXPENSE REPORT"		
PAGE-LABEL	"	L	"PAGE"		
PAGE-NO		C	1.SET PAGE-NO TO 1 2.ADD 1 TO PAGE-NO		
REPORT-MONTH	"	*		1/COMPANY (B)	1/COMPANY
COLUMN-HEADINGS	"	L	"CATEGORY SUPPLIER " "DATE "	1/PAGE	
CATEGORY-NAME	1/CATEGORY	*			1/CATEGORY
ITEM-DATE	1/ITEM	*			1/DAY
SUPPLIER-NAME	"	*			1/SUPPLIER
ITEM-DESCRIPTION	"	*			1/ITEM
ITEM-AMOUNT	"	*			1/ITEM
CATEGORY-TOTAL-LABEL	1/CATEGORY	L	"TOTAL FOR"		
CATEGORY-NAME	"	R			
CATEGORY-TOTAL	"	C	1.SET CATEGORY-TOTAL TO 0 2.ADD ITEM-AMOUNT TO CATEGORY-TOTAL	1/CATEGORY (B) 1/ITEM	
COMPANY-TOTAL-LABEL	1/COMPANY	L	"GRAND TOTAL"		
COMPANY-TOTAL	"	C	1.SET COMPANY-TOTAL TO 0 2.ADD CATEGORY-TOTAL TO COMPANY-TOTAL	1/COMPANY (B) 1/CATEGORY (E)	

The required elements are already here: they are the ones with type *. We simply fill in the new column—for the required elements only, of course—and then use its contents as input to the LDS universal analysis. (If you've seen the "Output Definition Form" of Ken Orr & Associates, notice that the rightmost two columns are interchanged here.)

As we have remarked before, LFUD can be used to draw any Warnier/Orr diagram. The only questions you need answered before applying it to a new type of diagram are (1) what are the atoms, and (2) which frequency are we talking about? The following table shows the answers to these questions for the LOS and LDS:

	LOS	LDS
LIST:	ALL FIELDS	REQUIRED FIELDS
FREQUENCY:	APPEARANCE	CHANGE

This completes our development of the logical data structure. To recap, the LDS gives the minimum required data for an output. It does two things for you:

1. The LDS is a shopping list for input, to ensure you find files that can present all the required data in the required order. (If the input is not in the required order, you have what's called an **ordering clash**. See Chapter 16 for a discussion.)
2. The LDS shows all your hidden hierarchies and makes explicit where each element changes, so you can make your input processing as efficient as possible.

If you are not studying inversion, please skip to Section 14.10

14.8 THE STRUCTURE OF A PIM SUBROUTINE

Suppose you decide to have a separate input mapping routine. And suppose further that your system makes coroutines impractical, so that an input **sub**routine is called for. Let's look at how you can invert the structure from section 14.1 to create such a subroutine.

We use the same general inversion structure we worked out for the loan report PIM in the previous chapter. As you may recall, its structure was:

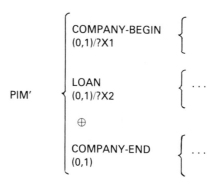

PIM'

COMPANY-BEGIN
(0,1)/?X1

LOAN
(0,1)/?X2

⊕

COMPANY-END
(0,1)

?X1/ ON 1
?X2/ IF PHYS-EOF = "NO"

We have eliminated the GOBACK; it's understood. Naturally you can't eliminate it from the COBOL.

Now we will adapt this structure to the city report. Basically, all action is in the center bracket; COMPANY-BEGIN and COMPANY-END brackets never change much. This time the main line LOM wants to hear about projects, not loans; so the structure will be:

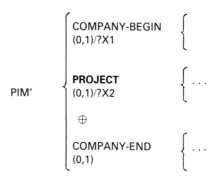

PIM'

COMPANY-BEGIN
(0,1)/?X1

PROJECT
(0,1)/?X2

⊕

COMPANY-END
(0,1)

?X1/ ON 1
?X2/ IF PHYS-EOF = "NO"

We have once again used the prime symbol (') to distinguish the subroutine PIM, and X to mark its footnotes.

To get the contents of the PROJECT bracket, we will create a C-shaped inversion of the CITY hierarchy shown in the previous section, just as we did with the payroll hierarchy in Chapter 11. The result is:

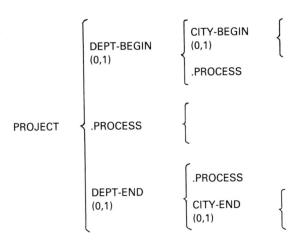

We have not put COMPANY-BEGIN and COMPANY-END on the structure; the reason will become clear in a minute.

This is equivalent to the original CITY-DEPT-PROJECT hierarchy, as we proved in Chapter 11. We can now paste it onto the basic PIM′ structure to get:

PIM′ {
  COMPANY-BEGIN (0,1)/?X1 {
  PROJECT (0,1)/?X2 {
    DEPT-BEGIN (0,1)/?X4 {
      CITY-BEGIN (0,1)/?X3 {
      .PROCESS
    }
    .PROCESS {
    }
    ⊕
    DEPT-END (0,1)/?X5 {
      .PROCESS
      CITY-END (0,1)/?X6 {
    }
  }
  COMPANY-END (0,1) {
}

Aside from transcribing the detailed instructions into these brackets from the uninverted form, there is only one step left: to work out the footnotes. This is the interesting part of inversion.

14.9 THE FOOTNOTES FOR THE PIM SUBROUTINE

We get the first two footnotes for free from the basic inverted PIM structure:

```
?X1/ ON 1
?X2/ IF PHYS-EOF = "NO"
```

Recall that the ON 1 is shorthand for a wide range of options, including the use of separate entry points.   Section 13.7 outlined the choices.

The other footnotes will take more attention.   You might try working them out for yourself first.   This process is prone to errors; doing it in two different ways and comparing the results is always a good idea.

We apply the following rule.   For each universal in the subroutine form:

1. Find the corresponding universal in the stand-alone form.
2. Figure out all the ways control can get there.
3. Join all these conditions by **or**.
4. Simplify.

This is just what we did for PAGE-END and PAGE-BEGIN in Chapter 11.

For example, consider CITY-END.   Here is a fragment of the stand-alone form:

```
                  ⎧  . . .
                  ⎪
      . . . CITY  ⎨  DEPT      {
                  ⎪  (1,D)/?2
                  ⎪
                  ⎩  .END      {
```

?2/ UNTIL (PHYS-EOF = "YES") OR (IN-CITY# > CURR-CITY#)

Obviously, control can get into CITY-END only when DEPT stops repeating, and the above footnote tells exactly when that can happen.   So the inverted structure footnote on CITY-END is:

```
?X6/ IF (PHYS-EOF = "YES") OR (IN-CITY# > CURR-CITY#)
```

Similarly, the condition for DEPT-END is derived from the uninverted footnote ?3:

```
?X5/ IF (PHYS-EOF = "YES") OR (IN-CITY# > CURR-CITY#) OR (IN-DEPT# > CURR-DEPT#)
```

Now let's look at the universal CITY-BEGIN. Here is a fragment of the original, stand-alone form:

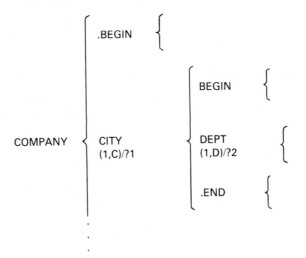

?1/ UNTIL PHYS-EOF = "YES"
?2/ UNTIL (PHYS-EOF = "YES") OR (IN-CITY# > CURR-CITY#)

There are two ways to get into CITY-BEGIN:

1. Control can fall through from COMPANY-BEGIN, which we have already concluded happens ON 1.
2. Control can return directly to CITY-BEGIN from CITY-END. This will only happen if IN-CITY# > CURR-CITY#.

Thus, the complete condition on CITY-BEGIN is:

?X3/ (ON 1) OR (IF IN-CITY# > CURR-CITY#)

Similarly, control gets to DEPT-BEGIN by either falling through from CITY-BEGIN (the condition we just worked out) or returning directly from DEPT-END (IN-DEPT# > CURR-DEPT#). Thus we have:

?X4/ (ON 1) OR (IF IN-CITY# > CURR-CITY#) OR (IF IN-DEPT# > CURR-DEPT#)

We now have the complete set of footnotes:

```
?X1/  ON 1
?X2/  IF  PHYS-EOF = "NO"
?X3/  (ON 1)              OR (IF IN-CITY# > CURR-CITY#)
?X4/  (ON 1)              OR (IF IN-CITY# > CURR-CITY#) OR (IF IN-DEPT# > CURR-DEPT#)
?X5/  IF (PHYS-EOF="YES") OR    (IN-CITY# > CURR-CITY#) OR    (IN-DEPT# > CURR-DEPT#)
?X6/  IF (PHYS-EOF="YES") OR    (IN-CITY# > CURR-CITY#)
```

The pattern is clear; adapting these footnotes to different hierarchical reports or to different numbers of levels should be straightforward. Notice in this particular case there is no processing at DEPT-END (?X5) and CITY-END (?X6). These footnotes are included here for reference in situations where some processing is required.

14.10 SUMMARY

A driver file is a file that has the same structure as the required output, but that may lack some of the information needed for the output. This additional information will normally be contained in direct-access files keyed off the driver file. (Direct access in this case includes table lookup and matched sequential files.) Direct access does not change the program structure, except for the possible inclusion of a found / not-found alternation on each attempted read.

Reading of the driver file and associated direct access files can be delegated to an input mapping, or melded into the mainline LOM, according to taste.

The logical data structure shows the minimum required data for an output. It is a yardstick with which to measure candidate input files, and it provides an efficient structure for input processing. Notice that the LDS is not restricted to situations in which a driver file exists. The LDS can be derived by performing Chapter 6's LFUD operation on the *required* elements, according to their frequency of *change*.

If you want to create an input subroutine when there is a driver file, do the following:

1. Derive the stand-alone (uninverted) structure of the input mapping from the structure of the input file. Expose hidden hierarchies, and move elements to the logical record only when they change.

2. Invert this structure into the basic PIM subroutine from the previous chapter:

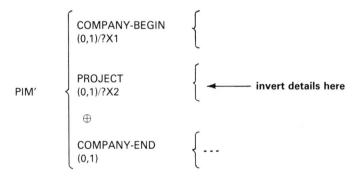

```
?X1/ ON 1
?X2/ IF PHYS-EOF = "NO"
```

3. Work out the footnote for each universal of this inverted structure by ORing all the conditions that let control reach it on the stand-alone structure.

14.11 EXERCISES

1. Code the input subroutine for the CITY-DEPT-PROJECT problem. Use the structure from Section 14.8, the footnotes from Section 14.9, and the detailed instructions from Section 14.1.

2. We have been ignoring the possibility that, for example, the required city might be missing from the CITY file. What will your user want you to do in such a case? How can you do it?

3. What are the pros and cons of creating an input mapping when there is a driver file?

4. Can you think of a way to make all the ON 1 conditions unnecessary in the footnotes to the inversion? (*Hint*: The logical record itself can be used as a switch.)

15

When There Isn't Any Driver

In Chapter 14 we examined the creation of the physical input mapping when there is a driver file—that is, when there is an input file in the same order as the output, with direct pointers to any additional information needed.

Now we move on to the more general case in which no driver exists.

15.1 OVERDETAILED DRIVERS

For this example we'll return to the original form of the project report, the one with no CITY level.   Its LOM looked like:

LOM: COMPANY
- .BEGIN { GET LOGICAL RECORD
- DEPT (1,D)
  - .BEGIN {
  - PROJECT (1,P) { GET LOGICAL RECORD
  - .END {
- .END {

where most of the atoms are omitted.

The logical input file is:

$$\text{LIF: COMPANY} \left\{ \begin{array}{l} \text{DEPT} \\ \text{(1,D)} \end{array} \right. \left\{ \begin{array}{l} \text{PROJECT} \\ \text{(1,P)} \end{array} \right. \left\{ \begin{array}{l} \underline{\text{DEPT-NUM}} \\ \text{.ID} \\ \text{.COST} \end{array} \right.$$

Now, suppose the input file looks like this:

$$\text{PIF: COMPANY} \left\{ \begin{array}{l} \text{DEPT} \\ \text{(1,D)} \end{array} \right. \left\{ \begin{array}{l} \text{PROJECT} \\ \text{(1,P)} \end{array} \right. \left\{ \begin{array}{l} \textbf{WORKER} \\ \textbf{(1,W)} \end{array} \right. \left\{ \begin{array}{l} \underline{\text{DEPT-NUM}} \\ \underline{\text{PROJECT-ID}} \\ \text{WORKER-COST} \end{array} \right.$$

It's almost a driver file. In fact, it's *more* than a driver file: it has an extra level of structure on the right, the WORKER level. This overdetailing will require changes from the simplified models we worked out in the previous chapter.

The cost of a project is the sum of the costs associated with all workers on the project. Using the input file to generate our structure, and applying the standard control break logic of Chapter 9, we get the following figure. Notice where the write of the logical record takes place:

An inverted version of this solution appears in Section 15.4.

```
            ┌         ┌ OPEN INPUT WORKER-FILE
            │ .BEGIN  │ MOVE "NO" TO PHYS-EOF
            │         │ READ WORKER-FILE
            │         └     AT END MOVE "YES" TO PHYS-EOF
            │
            │              ┌         ┌ MOVE IN-DEPT# TO CURR-DEPT#
            │              │ .BEGIN  │ MOVE IN-DEPT# INTO LOG-IN-RECORD
            │              │         └
            │              │
            │              │              ┌         ┌ MOVE IN-PROJ-ID TO CURR-PROJ-ID
            │              │              │ .BEGIN  │ MOVE IN-PROJ-ID INTO LOG-IN-RECORD
            │              │              │         └ SET PROJECT-COST TO 0
            │              │              │
PIM:        │              │              │              ┌ ADD WORKER-COST TO PROJECT-COST
COMPANY  { DEPT    { PROJECT   { WORKER  { READ WORKER-FILE
            │ (1,D)/?1      │ (0,1)/?2      │ (1,W)/?3     └     AT END MOVE "YES" TO PHYS-EOF
            │              │              │
            │              │              │ .END     ┌ MOVE PROJECT-COST INTO LOG-IN-RECORD
            │              │              │          └ WRITE LOGICAL RECORD
            │              │
            │              │ .END   { SKIP
            │
            │         ┌ CLOSE WORKER-FILE
            │ .END    │ MOVE "YES" TO END-LOGICAL-INPUT
            └         └ WRITE END-OF-FILE INDICATION
```

?1/ UNTIL PHYS-EOF = "YES"
?2/ UNTIL (PHYS-EOF = "YES") OR (IN-DEPT# > CURR-DEPT#)
?3/ UNTIL (PHYS-EOF = "YES") OR (IN-DEPT# > CURR-DEPT#) OR (IN-PROJ-ID > CURR-PROJ-ID)

15.2 SPLITTING INPUT RECORDS

We just saw one example that strained the simplified techniques of Chapter 14:
an input file with an extra level of structure beyond the rightmost universal on the
LOM.

Here is a second example with too many levels of structure. We are writing
a program to list all our customers. The LOS is:

LOS: COMPANY { CUSTOMER (C) {

Someone has set up the physical input file so each record contains 10 customers:

PIF: COMPANY { RECORD (1,R) { CUSTOMER (10) {

Of course, it's unrealistic to assume the number of customers will always be a multiple of 10; but it keeps the example's bookkeeping from obscuring the principle.

We want to pass these customers to the main line one at a time. The basic input mapping is:

```
PIM:
COMPANY
    .BEGIN
        OPEN INPUT WORKER-FILE
        MOVE "NO" TO PHYS-EOF
        READ WORKER-FILE
            AT END MOVE "YES" TO PHYS-EOF

    RECORD
    (1,R)/?1
        .BEGIN
            MOVE 1 TO SUB

        CUSTOMER
        (1,10)/?2
            MOVE CUST (SUB) TO LOG-IN-RECORD
            WRITE LOGICAL RECORD
            ADD 1 TO SUB

        .END
            READ CUST-FILE
                AT END MOVE "YES" TO PHYS-EOF

    .END
        CLOSE CUST-FILE
        MOVE "YES" TO END-LOGICAL-INPUT
        WRITE END-OF-FILE INDICATION
```

?1/ UNTIL PHYS-EOF = "YES"
?2/ UNTIL SUB > 10

Note that we have essentially used the read-once-to-begin-again-when-consumed rule twice: with READ for the records, and with SUB for the customers within a record.

If you are studying inversion, you may find inverting the above structure a useful exercise at this point; the process should be almost mechanical by now. Compare your result with the following:

PIM'
- COMPANY-BEGIN (0,1)/?X1
  - OPEN INPUT CUST-FILE
  - MOVE "NO" TO PHYS-EOF
  - READ CUST-FILE
    - AT END MOVE "YES" TO PHYS-EOF
- CUSTOMER (0,1)/?X2
  - RECORD-BEGIN (0,1)/?X3
    - MOVE 1 TO SUB
  - .PROCESS
    - MOVE CUST (SUB) TO LOG-IN-RECORD
    - ("write" logical record)
    - ADD 1 TO SUB
  - RECORD-END (0,1)/?X4 ⊕
    - READ CUST-FILE
      - AT END MOVE "YES" TO PHYS-EOF
- COMPANY-END (0,1)
  - CLOSE CUST-FILE
  - MOVE "YES" TO END-LOGICAL-INPUT
  - ("write" end-of-file indication)

?1/ ON 1
?2/ IF PHYS-EOF = "NO"
?3/ (ON 1) OR (IF SUB > 10)
?4/ IF SUB > 10

15.3 DATA BASE

Our next example uses an input that is becoming commonplace: a hierarchical data base. Suppose we are to produce an output with this logical input file:

LIF: COMPANY
- AGENT (1,A)
  - CUSTOMER (1,C)
    - SALE (1,S)

Now suppose the input data base contains this structure:

This diagram means that each agent record is linked to all its customer records. In our fictitious data base language you can GET records of a given type (e.g., AGENT) sequentially. And having gotten an AGENT, you can sequentially GET the CUSTOMERs belonging to that agent.

Try drawing a Warnier/Orr diagram of the above structure. Then check your solution against this:

$$
\text{PIF: COMPANY} \left\{ \begin{array}{l} \text{AGENT} \\ (1,A) \end{array} \left\{ \begin{array}{l} \textbf{AGENT-RECORD} \\ \\ \text{CUSTOMER} \\ (1,C) \end{array} \left\{ \textbf{CUSTOMER-RECORD} \right. \right. \right.
$$

That is, the collection of information about any given agent consists of an AGENT record, "followed" by some number of CUSTOMER records belonging to that agent.

If we add SALE records to the structure, we get:

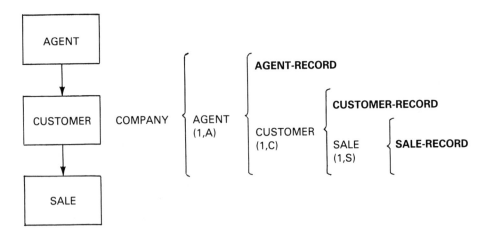

We will now work out the uninverted form of the physical input mapping for this data base. We will do it one level at a time for pedagogical reasons.

Suppose for some reason we only have to read AGENT records: say, the required output is a file giving the name and address of each agent. Then we can easily come up with the PIM using our basic rule of sequential processing: read once to begin, and again when a record is consumed. We have:

```
           ┌  .BEGIN        ┌  GET FIRST AGENT
           │                └
COMPANY   ─┤
           │                ┌  process agent
           │  AGENT         ┤
           └  (1,A)/?1       └  GET NEXT AGENT
```

?1/ UNTIL ALL AGENTS PROCESSED

In our fictitious data-base language the GET statement has an AT END just like the COBOL READ. So we will handle the "until all agents processed" this way:

```
                      ┌  MOVE "NO" TO ALL-AGENTS-DONE
           .BEGIN    ─┤  GET FIRST AGENT
                      └       AT END MOVE "YES" TO ALL-AGENTS-DONE

COMPANY   ─┤
                      ┌  process agent
           AGENT     ─┤  GET NEXT AGENT
           (1,A)/?1   └       AT END MOVE "YES" TO ALL-AGENTS-DONE
```

?1/ UNTIL ALL-AGENTS-DONE = "YES"

Of course if there is some COMPANY level data—like a date, for example—that has to appear on the output, the logic to obtain it will appear in COMPANY-BEGIN.

Now let's look at each CUSTOMER for each AGENT. The principle is exactly the same: read once to begin, and again when a record is consumed:

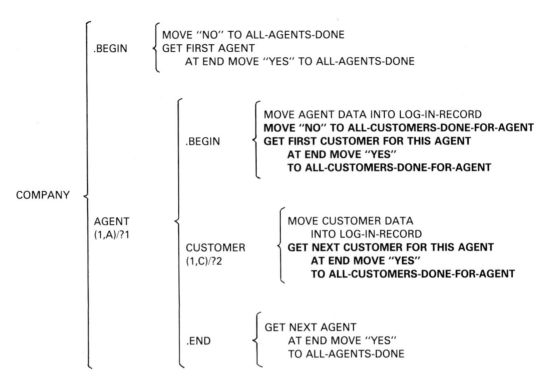

COMPANY
- .BEGIN
  - MOVE "NO" TO ALL-AGENTS-DONE
  - GET FIRST AGENT
    - AT END MOVE "YES" TO ALL-AGENTS-DONE
- AGENT (1,A)/?1
  - .BEGIN
    - MOVE AGENT DATA INTO LOG-IN-RECORD
    - **MOVE "NO" TO ALL-CUSTOMERS-DONE-FOR-AGENT**
    - **GET FIRST CUSTOMER FOR THIS AGENT**
      - **AT END MOVE "YES"**
      - **TO ALL-CUSTOMERS-DONE-FOR-AGENT**
  - CUSTOMER (1,C)/?2
    - MOVE CUSTOMER DATA INTO LOG-IN-RECORD
    - **GET NEXT CUSTOMER FOR THIS AGENT**
      - **AT END MOVE "YES"**
      - **TO ALL-CUSTOMERS-DONE-FOR-AGENT**
  - .END
    - GET NEXT AGENT
      - AT END MOVE "YES"
      - TO ALL-AGENTS-DONE

?1/ UNTIL ALL-AGENTS-DONE   = "YES"
?2/ UNTIL ALL-CUSTOMERS-DONE-FOR-AGENT = "YES"

Adding SALE is now almost mechanical. While we're at it, we will add the instructions to write the logical record and the end-of-file indication:

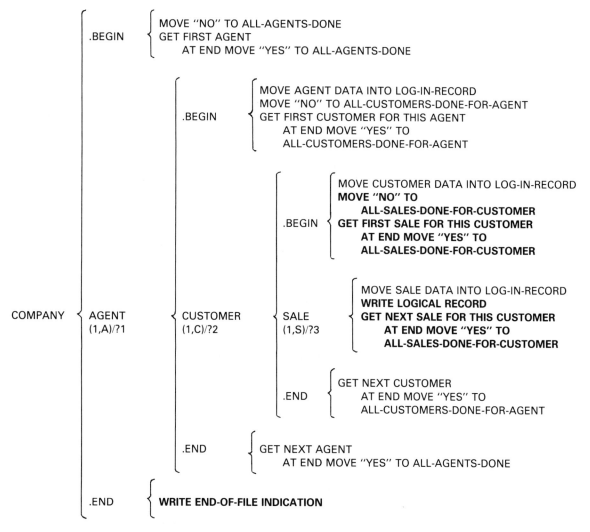

COMPANY
.BEGIN
MOVE "NO" TO ALL-AGENTS-DONE
GET FIRST AGENT
AT END MOVE "YES" TO ALL-AGENTS-DONE

AGENT (1,A)/?1
.BEGIN
MOVE AGENT DATA INTO LOG-IN-RECORD
MOVE "NO" TO ALL-CUSTOMERS-DONE-FOR-AGENT
GET FIRST CUSTOMER FOR THIS AGENT
AT END MOVE "YES" TO
ALL-CUSTOMERS-DONE-FOR-AGENT

CUSTOMER (1,C)/?2
.BEGIN
MOVE CUSTOMER DATA INTO LOG-IN-RECORD
MOVE "NO" TO
ALL-SALES-DONE-FOR-CUSTOMER
GET FIRST SALE FOR THIS CUSTOMER
AT END MOVE "YES" TO
ALL-SALES-DONE-FOR-CUSTOMER

SALE (1,S)/?3
MOVE SALE DATA INTO LOG-IN-RECORD
WRITE LOGICAL RECORD
GET NEXT SALE FOR THIS CUSTOMER
AT END MOVE "YES" TO
ALL-SALES-DONE-FOR-CUSTOMER

.END
GET NEXT CUSTOMER
AT END MOVE "YES" TO
ALL-CUSTOMERS-DONE-FOR-AGENT

.END
GET NEXT AGENT
AT END MOVE "YES" TO ALL-AGENTS-DONE

.END
WRITE END-OF-FILE INDICATION

?1/ UNTIL ALL-AGENTS-DONE   = "YES"
?2/ UNTIL ALL-CUSTOMERS-DONE-FOR-AGENT = "YES"
?3/ UNTIL ALL-SALES-DONE-FOR-CUSTOMER   = "YES"

To recap, we derived this structure from repeated application of the rule: read once to begin, and again when a record is consumed.

An inverted version of this data base routine is discussed in Sections 15.5 and 15.6.

If you are not studying inversion, please skip to Section 15.7

15.4 INVERTING THE OVERDETAILED DRIVER

If you want to create an input **sub**routine, here is how to restructure the solution of Section 15.1. The subroutine will be called by the main line LOM like this:

MAINLINE LOM: COMPANY
- CALL "PIM"
- DEPT (1,D) { PROJECT (1,P) { CALL "PIM" }

That is, after the first call it will be called once per PROJECT. Thus, we have to invert the input mapping structure with respect to PROJECT, not WORKER as we might have at first guessed.

That is, invert the input mapping with respect to the rightmost universal in the LOM. In the current example this gives:

PIM'
- COMPANY-BEGIN (0,1)/?X1
  - OPEN INPUT WORKER-FILE
  - MOVE "NO" TO EOF, L-EOF
  - READ WORKER-FILE
    - AT END MOVE "YES" TO EOF
- PROJECT (0,1)/?X2
  - DEPT-BEGIN (0,1)/?X3
    - MOVE IN-DEPT# TO CURR-DEPT#
    - MOVE IN-DEPT# INTO LOG-IN-RECORD
  - .BEGIN
    - **MOVE IN-PROJ-ID TO CURR-PROJ-ID**
    - **MOVE IN-PROJ-ID INTO LOG-IN-RECORD**
    - **SET PROJECT-COST TO 0**
  - WORKER (1,W)/?X4
    - **ADD WORKER-COST TO PROJECT-COST**
    - **READ WORKER-FILE**
      - **AT END MOVE "YES" TO EOF**
  - .END
    - **MOVE PROJECT-COST RECORD**
      - **INTO LOG-IN-PROJECT-COST**
    - ("write" logical record)
  - ⊕
- COMPANY-END (0,1)
  - CLOSE WORKER-FILE
  - MOVE "YES" TO END-LOGICAL-INPUT
  - ("write" end-of-file indication)

?X1/ ON 1
?X2/ IF PHYS-EOF = "NO"
?X3/ (ON 1) OR (IF IN-DEPT# > CURR-DEPT#)
?X4/ UNTIL (PHYS-EOF = "YES") OR (IN-DEPT# > CURR-DEPT#) OR (IN-PROJ-ID > CURR-PROJ-ID)

Notice that the superstructure is the regular inverted form from previous chapters. The only difference is the PROJECT-BEGIN/WORKER/PROJECT-END logic, which is emphasized in the diagram: it is needed to collect WORKER costs into a PROJECT cost. And it is carried over intact from the uninverted form, right down to the looping footnote ?X4 on the repetition of WORKER. (The other footnotes are copied from the model in Chapter 14.)

Translating this into COBOL should by now be a mechanical exercise, as long as you remember the assumed GOBACK at the end of the PIM.

Of course, we didn't need the PROJECT-COST field; we could have simply accumulated WORKER-COST into the LOG-IN-PROJECT-COST field being passed back to the main line. We introduced PROJECT-COST to emphasize that PROJECT-END is where the value gets "returned" to the main line.

15.5 DATA BASE: INVERTED MAPPING

Anyone committed to separating the input structure from the output production will want to invert the data base routine of Section 15.3. The general form will be familiar from our earlier work. It is:

```
                  COMPANY-BEGIN
                  (0,1)/?X1

                                                       AGENT-BEGIN
                                    CUSTOMER-BEGIN      (0,1)/?X3
                                    (0,1)/?X4
                                                       .PROCESSING

      PIM'        SALE              .PROCESSING
                  (0,1)/?X2
                                                       .PROCESSING

                                    CUSTOMER-END
                    ⊕               (0,1)/?X5          AGENT-END
                                                       (0,1)/?X6

                  COMPANY-END
                  (0,1)
```

The footnote analysis is the same as the one we went through for driver files in Chapter 14. The results are:

```
?X1/ ON 1
?X2/ IF ALL-AGENTS-DONE = "NO"
?X3/ (ON 1) OR (IF ALL-CUSTOMERS-DONE-FOR-AGENT = "YES")
?X4/ (ON 1) OR (IF ALL-SALES-DONE-FOR-CUSTOMER  = "YES")
?X5/ IF ALL-SALES-DONE-FOR-CUSTOMER  = "YES"
?X6/ IF ALL-CUSTOMERS-DONE-FOR-AGENT = "YES"
```

15.6 INVERSION: THE PROBLEM WITH ZERO

Notice that the inverted structures we have developed work properly only because all our repetitions have a minimum of 1 time. If there can be zero agents in the company, or zero customers to an agent, or zero sales to a customer, then the inverted routine fails. (There is no problem with the **un**inverted routine.)

Convincing yourself of this may take some doing. The basic point is that the inverted PIM is a straight sequential flow: there is no turning back. By the time we figure out there are no sales records for a customer, it's too late to go back and get the next customer. And even if you introduce a loop to churn through customers until you find one with sales, what if you get to end-of-agent before that happens? How can you go back to AGENT-BEGIN? Another loop?

You could get a solution going with a combination of loops and switches; but I have seen no systematic approach to the problem.

If coroutines are unavailable, there are at least three alternatives:

1. Run the input mapping as a separate stand-alone program that creates a temporary file to be read by the LOM.

2. Dispense with the PIM altogether and put all the data base input statements directly into the main line LOM. They go in the same places: if it's AGENT-BEGIN in the PIM, it's AGENT-BEGIN in the LOM. (This may require inserting the hidden hierarchies into the LOM.) As noted above, it's the inversion that causes the difficulty, not the basic structure of the logic.

3. Create the PIM subroutine by Jackson's **program** inversion (rather than by hierarchy inversion), as described in Chapter 21.

Recall the discussion of whether it's worthwhile having a separate input mapping in general (Section 13.4). The put-it-all-in-the-LOM school would cite the inversion difficulties we've just seen as support for their anti-input-mapping position (in situations where coroutines are unavailable).

15.7 SUMMARY

This chapter presents three situations with no driver file: overdetailed driver, splitting input records, and accessing a database. Each of them succumbs to the read-once-to-begin-and-again-when-consumed rule.

The splitting-input-records problem is the first one we've seen that has a structure clash between input and output. Thus, it *requires* an input mapping: there is no way to put the input logic drectly into the LOM.

The absence of a driver file doesn't affect inversion strategy. We still create the uninverted form first, then study it to work out the footnotes for the inverted version. (The data base problem with 0 repetitions is one case where no inversion is possible using these techniques.)

15.8 EXERCISES

1. In Chapter 7 we met the report shown here:

| "ACCOUNTS PAYABLE TOTAL IS" | AP-TOTAL |

Create an input mapping for this report, given a physical input file with this structure:

PIF: COMPANY { ACCOUNT PAYABLE (0,A) { . . AMOUNT-OUTSTANDING . . }

Do you need the END-LOGICAL-INPUT signal in this case?

2. In the data-base solution of Section 15.3, show that all three levels can share the same ALL-DONE switch.

3. If you have access to a data base management system, adapt the data base solution shown here to the syntax of your DBMS. Code and test a simple example.

4. Here is a problem where the physical input file has a structure clash (boundary clash) with the LOS. Suppose the project report from Chapters 5–7 has an input file in the right order, but the records on the input file are blocked in groups of 10, as in Section 15.2. Design the main line LOM and the input subroutine. (*Hint*: They should look a lot like the LOM from Chapter 7 and the input subroutine in Section 15.2, respectively.)

5. What is the basic problem in trying to invert a structure with a repetition that can occur 0 times? (*Hint*: Consider zero-to-*n* as an alternation between one-to-*n* and null. How do you invert an expression with an alternation?)

16

Select, Unstring, and Sort

This chapter deals with some common problems with physical input mappings: selecting from an input file, unstringing data, and reordering an input file.

16.1 SELECTION

We have already seen the basic idea behind selecting from an input file. That was in Chapter 14, when we saw that a sequential file (e.g., CITY) in the right order could be treated as a direct access file. Now we will look at the problem from a slightly different viewpoint.

The user wants a list of all male employees:

LOS: COMPANY { MALE-EMPLOYEE (0,M) { .NAME

Obviously, the logical input file has the same structure as the LOS. The physical input file, however, has both males and females on it:

PIF: COMPANY { EMPLOYEE (1,E) { MALE (0,1) { ⊕ FEMALE (0,1) {

To write a stand-alone input mapping for this file is trivial: just cycle through the file, writing males and not writing females. Section 16.5 shows how to invert it.

16.2 *STRING MANIPULATION*

String manipulation is an area where data structured design really shines. We will look at a very simple problem to illustrate the principle.

Suppose that DEPT-NAME on the input file can have some leading spaces. We have to get rid of them before passing the name along in the logical input record; we must also supply the length of the department name. To keep things simple, we will suppose that the name cannot have imbedded blanks. We can diagram IN-DEPT-NAME this way:

```
                          ┌  BLANK       {
                          │  (0,LB)
                          │
                          │
                          │  NAME        {  NONBLANK    {
IN-DEPT-NAME    {         │              {  (1,N)
                          │
                          │
                          │  BLANK       {
                          └  (0,TB)
```

We will assume that the name fields are 25 characters long. We physically declare IN-DEPT-NAME to consist of IN-CHAR repeated 25 times, and LOG-DEPT-NAME to consist of LOG-CHAR, also repeated 25 times. Then it is almost self-evident how we get the following logic:

```
                   ┌  .BEGIN          {  MOVE SPACES TO LOG-NAME
                   │                  {  MOVE 1 TO IN-SUB, LOG-SUB
                   │
                   │
                   │  SKIP-BLANK       {  ADD 1 TO IN-SUB
                   │  (0,LB)/?1
                   │
BUILD LOG-NAME  {  │
                   │
                   │                   ┌  MOVE IN-CHAR (IN-SUB)
                   │  MOVE-CHAR        {      TO LOG-CHAR (LOG-SUB)
                   │  (1,N)/?2         └  ADD 1 TO IN-SUB, LOG-SUB
                   │
                   │
                   └  .END             {  COMPUTE LOG-LENGTH = LOG-SUB - 1
```

?1/ UNTIL (IN-SUB > 25) OR (IN-CHAR (IN-SUB) > " ")
?2/ UNTIL (IN-SUB > 25) OR (IN-CHAR (IN-SUB) = " ")

16.3 *INCREDIBLY SLOW SORT*

We have mostly been creating input mappings in which there is no structure clash between physical input and LOS. We noted that a PIM is absolutely necessary when there *is* a structure clash. We dealt with one case of a boundary clash: things in the right order, but cut up differently. (See Chapter 15, Exercise 4.)

Now we turn to a second type of structure clash, also identified by Jackson: the **ordering clash**. For this we need new approaches.

A company wants a list of all its products in alphabetical order:

APPLE PEELER
BABY BOTTLE
BRICK
CARBON PAPER
DOORSTOP
.
.

So the main line logic is trivially:

MAINLINE LOM: COMPANY
- .BEGIN — GET PRODUCT
- PRODUCT (1,P) — PRINT NAME / GET PRODUCT

And the logical input file is:

LIF: COMPANY — PRODUCT (1,P) — .NAME

The product "file" is actually designed to be used as a table, just as we used departments in Section 14.3. It is in order by PRODUCT-NUMBER:

PIF: COMPANY — PRODUCT (1,P) — .NUMBER / .NAME

So we have an ordering clash: we need the products in name order, but they're given to us in number order.

We'll work this example from first principles; then we'll look at the general solutions to ordering clashes.

The framework of the PIM is obviously:

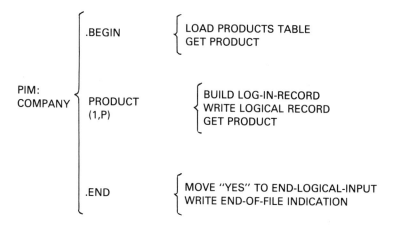

The nub is finding the next product to pass. We can look at the product file as:

The next product is the one whose name is the "minimum" (lowest in alphabetical order) of all unreturned products:

So we'll need some way to exclude products whose names have already been returned. The simplest is to replace a product's name with HIGH-VALUES. This has the additional advantage that we can then calculate the MIN over all products, already returned or not, and still get the right answer. The logic for calculating the MIN is then similar to the way we've calculated totals many times, but based here, of course, on the structure of the input file:

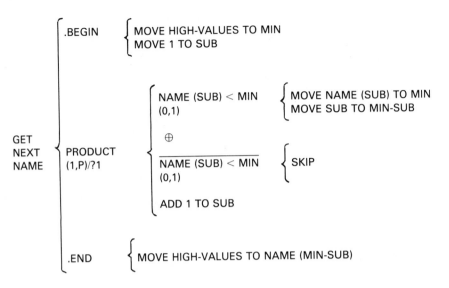

GET NEXT NAME
- .BEGIN
  - MOVE HIGH-VALUES TO MIN
  - MOVE 1 TO SUB
- PRODUCT (1,P)/?1
  - NAME (SUB) < MIN (0,1)
    - MOVE NAME (SUB) TO MIN
    - MOVE SUB TO MIN-SUB
  - ⊕
  - $\overline{\text{NAME (SUB)} < \text{MIN}}$ (0,1)
    - SKIP
  - ADD 1 TO SUB
- .END
  - MOVE HIGH-VALUES TO NAME (MIN-SUB)

?1/ UNTIL SUB > NUMBER-OF-ENTRIES

This is grotesquely inefficient and could easily be tuned. Instead of calculating the MIN over all the entries, for example, we could segregate the ones that have already been returned so they needn't be examined again. We might use a swapping arrangement. On the first call from the main line, swap the minimum element with the first one in the table:

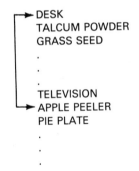

DESK
TALCUM POWDER
GRASS SEED
.
.
.
TELEVISION
APPLE PEELER
PIE PLATE
.
.
.

Then the search for the *n*th NAME could be confined to elements *n* through *P*.

The point of this exercise is to show that we already have enough tricks in our bag to resolve ordering clashes. But we don't want to reinvent the sort every time. From now on we will assume you have a utility subroutine that can sort a table in core, and another that can sort a file.

16.4 SORT VS. B.O.M.

We need a report of total sales, year to date, by country. The sample is:

```
┌─────────────────────────────────────────────────┐
│              YTD SALES BY COUNTRY               │
│                                                 │
│    COUNTRY CODE                        SALES    │
│                                                 │
│         01                            56,917    │
│         02                         1,365,312    │
│         03                           736,589    │
│          .                               .      │
│          .                               .      │
│          .                               .      │
│                                                 │
└─────────────────────────────────────────────────┘
```

So of course the logical input file is:

$$\text{LIF: COMPANY} \left\{ \begin{array}{l} \text{COUNTRY} \\ \text{(1,C)} \end{array} \right. \left\{ \begin{array}{l} \underline{.CODE} \\ .SALES \end{array} \right.$$

Unfortunately, the physical input file is:

$$\text{PIF: COMPANY} \left\{ \begin{array}{l} \text{INVOICE} \\ \text{(1,I)} \end{array} \right. \left\{ \begin{array}{l} \underline{.DATE} \\ .COUNTRY\text{-}CODE \\ .AMOUNT \end{array} \right.$$

That is, the invoices are sorted in date order.

There are two basic ways of resolving this. One is to first sort the input in COUNTRY-CODE order:

$$\text{SORTED PIF: COMPANY} \left\{ \begin{array}{l} \text{COUNTRY} \\ \text{(1,C)} \end{array} \right. \left\{ \begin{array}{l} \text{INVOICE} \\ \text{(1,IN)} \end{array} \right. \left\{ \begin{array}{l} \underline{.COUNTRY\text{-}CODE} \\ .AMOUNT \end{array} \right.$$

(where we no longer care about the date); and then create logic to summarize the invoices by country. This will be the same as the logic to summarize worker by project, as we worked out in Chapter 15.

The second possible approach is to use a matrix. (This is what Orr calls the B.O.M., or Big Ole Matrix, approach.) Define a table like this:

```
01  COUNTRY-SALES-TABLE.
    05  COUNTRY-SALES          PIC .....   OCCURS 200.
```

where we have assumed that 200 is the maximum value of COUNTRY-CODE. Then, instead of having to sort and summarize a potentially enormous file of invoices, we can get by with reading the file only once:

```
BUILD
TABLE:

COMPANY   ┌  .BEGIN   ┌ OPEN INPUT INVOICE-FILE
          │           │ MOVE "NO" TO PHYS-EOF
          │           │ READ INVOICE-FILE
          │           └     AT END MOVE "YES" TO PHYS-EOF
          │
          │  INVOICE  ┌ ADD INVOICE-AMOUNT TO
          │  (1,I)/?T1 │    COUNTRY-SALES (INVOICE-COUNTRY-CODE)
          │           │ READ INVOICE-FILE
          │           └     AT END MOVE "YES" TO PHYS-EOF
          │
          └  .END     ┤ CLOSE INVOICE-FILE
```

?T1/ UNTIL PHYS-EOF = "YES"

This will leave us with a table of sales in order by country. So the logic of the input mapping will be:

```
PIM
COMPANY   ┌  .BEGIN    ┌ BUILD TABLE (see above)
          │            └ MOVE 1 TO SUB
          │
          │  COUNTRY   ┌ MOVE COUNTRY-SALES (SUB)
          │  (1,C)/?1  │    INTO LOG-IN-RECORD
          │            │ WRITE LOGICAL RECORD
          │            └ ADD 1 TO SUB
          │
          └  .END      ┌ MOVE "YES" TO END-LOGICAL-INPUT
                       └ WRITE END-OF-FILE INDICATION
```

?1/UNTIL SUB < 200

This problem was kept simple in order to illustrate the difference between sort-and-summarize and big-ole-matrix as clearly as possible. It can easily be made more realistic. For instance, if the user wants the report to show COMPANY-NAME instead of COMPANY-CODE, it is only necessary to add a table lookup to COMPANY-PROC. And if some country codes are unassigned, then we will have a sequential search for the next assigned code instead of setting SUB = 1 or adding 1 to SUB.

If you are not studying inversion, please skip to Section 16.6.

16.5 *INVERTING THE SELECTION LOGIC*

What if we want to invert the selection routine of Section 16.1? We've said that we need to invert with respect to the rightmost universal in the LOM: in this case, MALE-EMPLOYEE. But how do you do that here?

We have to redraw the physical input file so it is in an invertible form. We can look at the file as consisting of some (possibly zero) male employees, interspersed with collections of female employees. By grouping any female employees with the immediately following males, we get this structure:

```
                         ┌ MALE-GROUP ┌ FEMALE-EE
                         │            │ (F1)
PIF: COMPANY ┤           │            │
                         │            └ MALE-EE
                         │
                         └ EOF-GROUP  ┌ FEMALE-EE
                                      │ (F2)
```

This is logically identical to the diagram in Section 16.1. But it's also essentially the same as our desired logical input file: a sequence of male records followed by an EOF marker. The only difference is that we have "groups" instead of records. So let's treat the groups the way we normally treat records. The result is:

```
              ┌ .BEGIN        ┌ GET GROUP
              │
              │ MALE-GROUP    ┌ BUILD LOG-IN-RECORD
PIM: COMPANY ┤  (1,M)        ┤ WRITE LOGICAL RECORD
              │               └ GET GROUP
              │
              └ .END          ┌ MOVE "YES" TO END-LOGICAL-INPUT
                              └ WRITE END-OF-FILE INDICATION
```

What will the GET GROUP look like? Well, the structure of a group is:

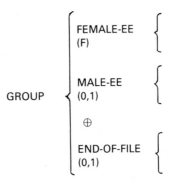

GROUP
- FEMALE-EE (F)
- MALE-EE (0,1)
- ⊕
- END-OF-FILE (0,1)

Some female employees (possibly zero) are followed by either a male employee or the end-of-file mark.

So applying the read-once-to-begin-again-when-consumed rule, we get:

GET GROUP
- FEMALE-EE (F)/?3
  - READ EE-FILE
    - AT END MOVE "YES" TO PHYS-EOF
- MALE-EE (0,1)/?4
  - MOVE IN-RECORD TO MALE-RECORD
  - READ EE-FILE
    - AT END MOVE "YES" TO PHYS-EOF

?3/ UNTIL (PHYS-EOF = "YES") OR (SEX = MALE)
?4/ IF PHYS-EOF = "NO"

where the end-of-file universal disappears because no processing is needed there.

Instead of GET GROUP, this structure can be called GET MALE or GET NEXT VALID-RECORD.   It provides a general model for selection problems.

For completeness, we observe that the inverted form will look like this after getting a little more physical, and changing the name of the above GET GROUP routine to GET MALE:

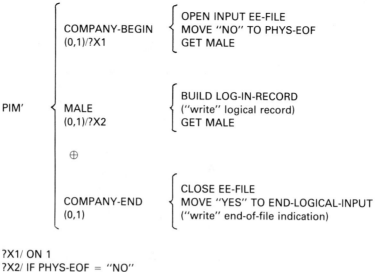

PIM'
- COMPANY-BEGIN (0,1)/?X1
  - OPEN INPUT EE-FILE
  - MOVE "NO" TO PHYS-EOF
  - GET MALE
- MALE (0,1)/?X2
  - BUILD LOG-IN-RECORD ("write" logical record)
  - GET MALE
- ⊕
- COMPANY-END (0,1)
  - CLOSE EE-FILE
  - MOVE "YES" TO END-LOGICAL-INPUT ("write" end-of-file indication)

?X1/ ON 1
?X2/ IF PHYS-EOF = "NO"

16.6 SUMMARY

This chapter dealt with three independent problems.

Selection. The nub of an inverted selection routine is the get-next-valid-record logic, which has this structure:

GET GROUP
- INVALID (I)/?3
  - READ INPUT
    - AT END MOVE "YES" TO PHYS-EOF
- VALID (0,1)/?4
  - MOVE IN-RECORD TO VALID-RECORD
  - READ EE-FILE
    - AT END MOVE "YES" TO PHYS-EOF

?3/ UNTIL (PHYS-EOF = "YES") OR (RECORD IS VALID)
?4/ IF PHYS-EOF = "NO"

String manipulation. String manipulation presents no new issues; it's a classic setting for data structured program design.

Ordering clash. When the PIF has an ordering clash with the LOS, there are two options:

- Sort: we developed a crude one based on a statement of the required output; or
- Big Ole Matrix: accumulate data in-core, in the format needed for output.

16.7 EXERCISES

1. Develop the inverted forms of the input mappings in sections 16.3 and 16.4.
2. Write a cross-reference utility for your favorite language. It should read a source program and produce a report showing, for each unique fieldname in the program, the number of every line where it is referenced. (This is the hardest, and most interesting, exercise in the book.)

FURTHER READING

For an introduction to sorting algorithms, see Chapter 2 of *Algorithms + Data Structures = Programs* by Wirth.

17

File Merge and Update

We have introduced most of our principles via reporting programs, but there is more to life than reports. In this chapter we derive logic to pass any number of transaction files against a master file, updating the master. We use the traditional Ken Orr and Associates setting for the problem.

Suppose we own three department stores. Each store supplies us with a daily tape of its transactions, sorted in customer number order. The transactions can add, change, or delete a customer.

We are to pass a day's transactions against the customer master file to produce a new master file. If a customer has transactions at more than one store, we want to process their store 1 transactions first, then store 2 transactions, then store 3.

17.1 STAND-ALONE MERGE PIM

As a first step we develop a physical input mapping to merge the transaction files. In this section we create the uninverted form; in the next we will invert it.

It's not clear how to base the process structure on three independent input files. So we take another tack and examine the logical input file we have to produce, in the hope that it will provide a superstructure for processing the input files.

For each customer on the LIF, all store 1 transactions come before all store 2 transactions, which in turn come before all store 3 transactions. So we have the following diagram:

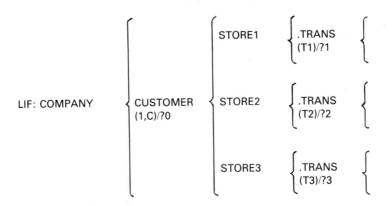

LIF: COMPANY {
 CUSTOMER (1,C)/?0 {
  STORE1 { .TRANS (T1)/?1 {
  STORE2 { .TRANS (T2)/?2 {
  STORE3 { .TRANS (T3)/?3 {

Suppose we try this as the basis for the PIM structure. Then how do we allocate the READs?

Any transactions from file 1 will be written to the LIF from the STORE1-TRANS bracket, so that is where they are consumed. Thus, by the read-once-to-begin-again-when-consumed rule, we need to read FILE1 once at COMPANY-BEGIN, and again in STORE1-TRANS.

And of course the situation for files 2 and 3 is similar. The resulting process is as follows:

PIM: COMPANY {

.BEGIN {
 OPEN INPUT FILE1, FILE2, FILE3
 MOVE "NO" TO 1-EOF, 2-EOF, 3-EOF
 READ FILE1, FILE2, FILE3

CUSTOMER (1,C)/?0 {

 STORE1 { TRANS (T1)/?1 {
  WRITE 1-TX TO LOG-IN-FILE
  READ FILE1

 STORE2 { .TRANS (T2)/?2 {
  WRITE 2-TX TO LOG-IN-FILE
  READ FILE2

 STORE3 { .TRANS (T3)/?3 {
  WRITE 3-TX TO LOG-IN-FILE
  READ FILE3

.END {
 CLOSE FILE1, FILE2, FILE3
 WRITE END-OF-FILE

That is, for each customer we first spin through any FILE1 records, then any FILE2 records, then any FILE3 records.

Now all we have to do is work out the footnotes. Roughly speaking, we want them to work like this:

```
?0/ UNTIL ALL CUSTOMERS PROCESSED
?1/ UNTIL FILE1 CUSTOMER# > CURRENT CUSTOMER#
?2/ UNTIL FILE2 CUSTOMER# > CURRENT CUSTOMER#
?3/ UNTIL FILE3 CUSTOMER# > CURRENT CUSTOMER#
```

We just have to make this rigorous.

Footnotes ?1 to ?3 refer to CURRENT CUSTOMER#. How will we determine the current customer? By examining the three input files to see which customer number is next in line for processing. We are tempted to write:

```
SET CURR-CUST# = MINIMUM (I1-CUST#, I2-CUST#, I3-CUST#)
```

where I1-CUST# is the next customer number on FILE1, I2-CUST# is next on FILE2, and so on.

That is, the lowest available customer number is the one we want. But end-of-file rears its ugly head: we don't want a file competing in the lowest number sweepstakes if it is out of records. Luckily, there's a simple way around the problem: the compound keys introduced in Chapter 9. Define keys as follows:

```
01  C-KEY.
    02  C-EOF           PIC XXX.
    02  C-CUST-NO       PIC ....

01  1-KEY.
    02  1-EOF           PIC XXX.
    02  1-CUST-NO       PIC ....
```

and so on. Naturally, this means we have to do our READs as follows, according to Chapter 9:

```
                    ┌  READ FILE1
                    │      AT END MOVE "YES" TO 1-EOF
                    │
*READ FILE1         ┤
                    │  1-EOF = "NO"    ┌ MOVE I1-CUST-NO TO 1-CUST-NO
                    │  (0,1)           ┤
                    └                  └
```

with the equivalent for files 2 and 3.

With this under control we can write:

```
SET C-KEY = MINIMUM (1-KEY, 2-KEY, 3-KEY)
```

and be confident that end-of-file will be handled properly. Because "YES" tests higher than "NO", any at-end file will be disqualified as long as some other file still has records; and when all the files are at-end, C-EOF will automatically be set to "YES".

We will set C-KEY according to the read-once-to-begin-again-when-consumed rule: once at COMPANY-BEGIN, again at CUSTOMER-END. Then it is easy to see how the above rough-cut footnotes translate into the following versions:

```
                  ⎧         ⎧ OPEN INPUT FILE1, FILE2, FILE3
                  ⎪ .BEGIN  ⎨ MOVE "NO" TO 1-EOF, 2-EOF, 3-EOF
                  ⎪         ⎪ READ FILE1*, FILE2*, FILE3*
                  ⎪         ⎩ SET C-KEY = MIN (1-KEY, 2-KEY, 3-KEY)
                  ⎪
                  ⎪                         ⎧          ⎧ MOVE 1-TX TO LOG-IN-RECORD
                  ⎪                  STORE1 ⎨ .TRANS   ⎨ WRITE LOGICAL RECORD
                  ⎪                         ⎩ (T1)/?1  ⎩ READ FILE1*
                  ⎪
                  ⎪                         ⎧          ⎧ MOVE 2-TX TO LOG-IN-RECORD
PIM:      ⎧ CUSTOMER ⎨           STORE2 ⎨ .TRANS   ⎨ WRITE LOGICAL RECORD
COMPANY   ⎨ (1,C)/?0               ⎩ (T2)/?2  ⎩ READ FILE2*
          ⎪
          ⎪                         ⎧          ⎧ MOVE 3-TX TO LOG-IN-RECORD
          ⎪                  STORE3 ⎨ .TRANS   ⎨ WRITE LOGICAL RECORD
          ⎪                         ⎩ (T3)/?3  ⎩ READ FILE3*
          ⎪
          ⎪                  .END   ⎰ SET C-KEY = MIN (1-KEY, 2-KEY, 3-KEY)
          ⎪
          ⎪         ⎧ CLOSE FILE1, FILE2, FILE3
          ⎩ .END    ⎨ WRITE END-OF-FILE INDICATION
```

?0/ UNTIL C-EOF = "YES"
?1/ UNTIL 1-KEY > C-KEY
?2/ UNTIL 2-KEY > C-KEY
?3/ UNTIL 3-KEY > C-KEY

For completeness we repeat the asterisked READ instructions:

```
                  ⎧ READ FILE1
                  ⎪     AT END MOVE "YES" TO 1-EOF
*READ FILE1       ⎨
                  ⎪ 1-EOF = "NO"   ⎰ MOVE I1-CUST-NO TO 1-CUST-NO
                  ⎩ (0,1)
```

with the equivalent for files 2 and 3.

Section 17.4 discusses inversion of this merge logic.

17.2 UPDATING A MASTER FILE

Recall that the whole point in working out the merge PIM was to pass the transactions against a master file. We now turn our attention to the updating problem; to keep things simple we will initially assume that there is only one transaction file.

We will pass a file of transactions against a **sequential** master file to produce a new, updated master. We will also produce a transaction log showing the outcome of each transaction. Here is a sample of the log:

```
                    TRANSACTION LOG

CUSTOMER#     TRANSACTION     RESULT

    386         ADD           ADD REJECTED--MASTER EXISTS
    427         ADD           ADD ACCEPTED
    427         CHANGE        CHANGE PROCESSED
    493         CHANGE        CHANGE REJECTED--NO MASTER
    546         DELETE        MASTER DELETED
    718         DELETE        CANNOT DELETE--NO MASTER
```

The other output is the new master file, which consists of customer records. We will derive the composite output structure by applying the LFUD technique we first met in Chapter 6: List atoms, give Frequency, do Universal analysis, draw Diagram. We begin LFUD by listing each output item and its frequency of appearance:

DATA ELEMENT	APPEARS
REPORT LABEL	1/COMPANY
CUSTOMER NUMBER	1/TRANSACTION
"ADD"	1/ADD
"CHANGE"	1/CHANGE
"DELETE"	1/DELETE
"ADD REJECTED . . . "	1/INVALID ADD
"ADD ACCEPTED"	1/VALID ADD
"CHANGE PROCESSED"	1/VALID CHANGE
"CHANGE REJECTED . . . "	1/INVALID CHANGE
"MASTER DELETED"	1/VALID DELETE
"CANNOT DELETE . . . "	1/INVALID DELETE
NEW MASTER	1/UNDELETED MASTER

Notice that the last item (NEW MASTER) is from the new master file; all the others are from the transaction log. The universal analysis is:

```
UNIVERSAL                OCCURS

COMPANY                  1
TRANSACTION              0,T/CUSTOMER

ADD                      0,1/TRANSACTION
CHANGE                   0,1/TRANSACTION
DELETE                   0,1/TRANSACTION

VALID ADD                0,1/ADD
INVALID ADD              0,1/ADD

VALID CHANGE             0,1/CHANGE
INVALID CHANGE           0,1/CHANGE

VALID DELETE             0,1/DELETE
INVALID DELETE           0,1/DELETE

UNDELETED CUSTOMER       0,1/CUSTOMER
```

A new entry appears in the universal analysis OCCURS column: CUS-TOMER. It obviously is related to COMPANY like this:

```
CUSTOMER                 1,C/COMPANY
```

Thus the LOM structure is:

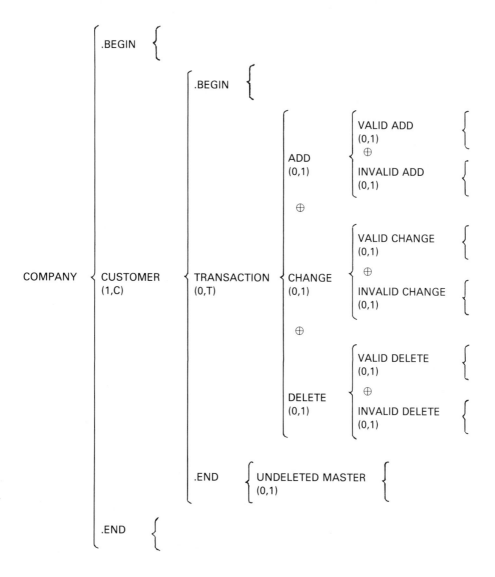

Filling in the details is just a matter of applying principles we have seen many times. The basic decision from which all else follows is to keep an up-to-date copy of the master for any customer we process. We start each customer by storing the old master (if there is one) in working storage. We keep that copy up to date with all transactions for this customer, and then write it if the last valid transaction wasn't a delete.

The result is shown in the following set of figures. Routines marked * are detailed later in the set:

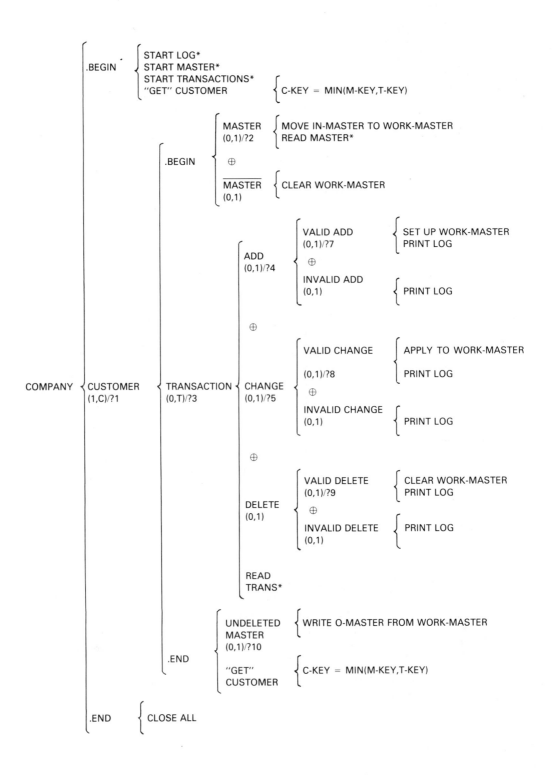

COMPANY ⟨ CUSTOMER (1,C)/?1

.BEGIN
- START LOG*
- START MASTER*
- START TRANSACTIONS*
- "GET" CUSTOMER { C-KEY = MIN(M-KEY,T-KEY)

.BEGIN
- MASTER (0,1)/?2 { MOVE IN-MASTER TO WORK-MASTER / READ MASTER*
- ⊕
- $\overline{\text{MASTER}}$ (0,1) { CLEAR WORK-MASTER

TRANSACTION (0,T)/?3

ADD (0,1)/?4
- VALID ADD (0,1)/?7 { SET UP WORK-MASTER / PRINT LOG
- ⊕
- INVALID ADD (0,1) { PRINT LOG

⊕

CHANGE (0,1)/?5
- VALID CHANGE (0,1)/?8 { APPLY TO WORK-MASTER / PRINT LOG
- ⊕
- INVALID CHANGE (0,1) { PRINT LOG

⊕

DELETE (0,1)
- VALID DELETE (0,1)/?9 { CLEAR WORK-MASTER / PRINT LOG
- ⊕
- INVALID DELETE (0,1) { PRINT LOG

READ TRANS*

.END
- UNDELETED MASTER (0,1)/?10 { WRITE O-MASTER FROM WORK-MASTER
- "GET" CUSTOMER { C-KEY = MIN(M-KEY,T-KEY)

.END { CLOSE ALL

*COMPANY-BEGIN {

    START LOG { OPEN OUTPUT LOGFILE
                     BUILD HEADING LINES

    START MASTER { OPEN INPUT MASTIN, OUTPUT MASTOUT
                       MOVE "NO" TO M-EOF
                       READ MASTER*

    START TRANSACTIONS { OPEN INPUT TRANS
                              MOVE "NO" TO T-EOF
                              READ TRANS*

    GET FIRST CUSTOMER { C-KEY = MIN (M-KEY, T-KEY)

}

*READ MASTER {

    READ MASTER
        AT END MOVE "YES" TO M-EOF

    M-EOF = "NO"
    (0,1) { MOVE IM-CUST# TO M-CUST#

}

*READ TRANS {

    READ TRANS
        AT END MOVE "YES" TO M-EOF

    T-EOF = "NO"
    (0,1) { MOVE IT-CUST# TO T-CUST#

}

Control Keys

```
01  M-KEY.
    02  M-EOF      PIC XXX.
    02  M-CUSTNO   PIC ...

01  T-KEY.
    02  T-EOF      PIC XXX.
    02  T-CUSTNO   PIC ...

01  C-KEY.
    02  C-EOF      PIC XXX.
    02  C-CUSTNO   PIC ...
```

Footnotes

```
?1/  UNTIL C-EOF = "YES"
?2/  IF M-KEY = C-KEY
?3/  UNTIL T-KEY > C-KEY

?4/  IF IT-TRANSCODE = "A"
?5/  IF IT-TRANSCODE = "C"
?6/  IF IT-TRANSCODE = "D"

?7/  IF WORK-MASTER = SPACES
?8/  IF WORK-MASTER > SPACES
?9/  IF WORK-MASTER > SPACES
?10/ IF WORK-MASTER > SPACES
```

17.3 *NOTES ON THE FILE UPDATE ALGORITHM*

This file update structure has been around for a long time. I first learned it from Ken Orr in 1978; I don't know how long he had been using it. Here are some of the other places it has appeared:

- Barry Dwyer published it in "One More Time: How to Update a Master File" in 1981.
- It was previously discovered by Dijkstra's colleague, W.H.J. Feijen; his solution appeared in Dijkstra's 1976 book, *A Discipline of Programming*.
- Art Huber of IBM Canada has given me a copy of a memo that flowcharts essentially this technique. The memo attributes it to someone named Grosch at the Esso Baton Rouge refinery. It seems to date from sometime in the sixties.

Historical interest aside, I had always been suspicious of the derivation given in the previous section. Listing all the run log messages and then using their frequencies of appearance to generate the program structure seemed contrived: it was as if someone had come up with the algorithm first and worked out a derivation to match it.

But I have had to recant. A student recently brought me quite a different problem, and it practically solved itself when we applied this technique of designing from the log.

But what if no log exists? Will it be impossible to design the process because there's no interesting data structure?

No, it won't be impossible. But we do have to add another technique to our kit. It is based on the idea that outputs require actions, and that these actions take place under certain conditions. These conditions generate brackets.

Suppose we have no transaction log. Then the only output is the customer record.

Now we ask ourselves: What are the actions that must be taken in order to get us to the point where we can decide if we have a customer to write? We list these actions, along with their frequencies; obviously, these frequencies will become universals.

Once again, we must first make the decision that we will keep a copy of the customer master up to date as each transaction comes through. Then the following table is fairly easy to create:

```
ACTION              FREQUENCY = CONDITION

set up master       1/old customer
erase master        1/DELETE on existing master
reject              1/ADD on existing master
                  + 1/CHANGE on nonexisting master
                  + 1/DELETE on nonexisting master
process add         1/ADD with no master
process change      1/CHANGE with master
process delete      1/DELETE with master
write master        1/undeleted master
```

We can then perform a universal analysis of these frequencies; it will end up looking essentially the same as the one we derived from the log.

This process of adding structure to accommodate processing required for the output is not new. In Chapter 12 we did essentially the same thing. As we worked the field TOTAL PAYABLE back to available input items, we created about a dozen extra brackets.

For more information on this approach, see the survey of Warnier in Chapters 18 and 19. It is a standard part of his approach to list processing actions required and to generate decision tables of the conditions under which they will take place. His decision tables are used in deriving his bracket structure.

As we mentioned earlier in the book, the naked data structures of the output and input will not always be enough to structure your program. When they aren't, you can often move farther along the road by starting from your required outputs and pushing each back to its appropriate inputs.

And occasionally, as in the file-matching example, you can make progress by looking at required inputs and asking what processing is required for each.

_____

If you are not studying inversion please skip to Section 17.5.

17.4 INVERTING THE MERGE

How can we invert the file merge of Section 17.1? We want to invert with respect to the rightmost universal in the LIF, which in this case is TRANSACTION. So the inverted PIM will have the following general form. Note in this diagram that *as above* refers to the version in Section 17.1.

?X1/ ON 1
?X2/ IF C-EOF - "NO"

But what will go in the body of the transaction bracket? The uninverted PIM shows that each transaction is either from STORE1 or from STORE2 or from STORE3. Thus we can write:

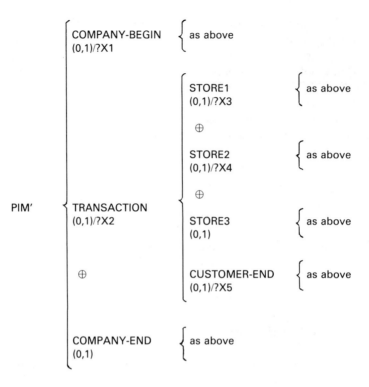

```
?X1/ ON 1
?X2/ IF C-EOF - "NO"
```

It remains only to work out the conditions ?X3 to ?X5. Looking at the uninverted conditions, it's clear that we will pick a transaction from FILE1 whenever it has the current key:

```
?X3/ IF 1-KEY = C-KEY
```

Similarly, we will pick from FILE2 if FILE1 isn't suitable and FILE2 is:

```
?X4/ IF (1-KEY > C-KEY) AND (2-KEY = C-KEY)
```

Finally, we will be at CUSTOMER-END if none of the files is suitable:

```
?X5/ IF (1-KEY > C-KEY) AND (2-KEY > C-KEY) AND (3-KEY > C-KEY)
```

Combining the above figures gives the complete solution in one diagram:

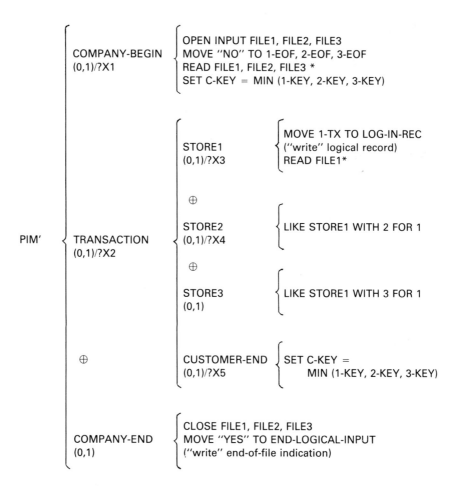

PIM' {
COMPANY-BEGIN
(0,1)/?X1
{
OPEN INPUT FILE1, FILE2, FILE3
MOVE "NO" TO 1-EOF, 2-EOF, 3-EOF
READ FILE1, FILE2, FILE3 *
SET C-KEY = MIN (1-KEY, 2-KEY, 3-KEY)
}

TRANSACTION
(0,1)/?X2
{
STORE1
(0,1)/?X3
{
MOVE 1-TX TO LOG-IN-REC
("write" logical record)
READ FILE1*
}

⊕

STORE2
(0,1)/?X4
{ LIKE STORE1 WITH 2 FOR 1 }

⊕

STORE3
(0,1)
{ LIKE STORE1 WITH 3 FOR 1 }
}

⊕

CUSTOMER-END
(0,1)/?X5
{
SET C-KEY =
MIN (1-KEY, 2-KEY, 3-KEY)
}

COMPANY-END
(0,1)
{
CLOSE FILE1, FILE2, FILE3
MOVE "YES" TO END-LOGICAL-INPUT
("write" end-of-file indication)
}
}

?X1/ ON 1
?X2/ IF C-EOF = "NO"
?X3/ IF 1-KEY = C-KEY
?X4/ IF (1-KEY > C-KEY) AND (2-KEY = C-KEY)
?X5/ IF (1-KEY > C-KEY) AND (2-KEY > C-KEY) AND (3-KEY > C-KEY) .

Here is the READ routine referred to in several places above:

*READ FILEn {
READ FILEn
AT END MOVE "YES" TO n-EOF

n-EOF = "NO"
(0,1)
{ MOVE In-CUST-NO TO n-CUST-NO }
}

17.5 SUMMARY

The main message of this chapter is in the merge algorithm of Section 17.1 and the master file update algorithm in Section 17.2.

Naturally, the update algorithm will use the merge routine to provide the next transaction if there is more than one transaction file.

17.6 EXERCISES

1. If your language lacks a MIN function, work out the code to calculate:

```
C-KEY = MIN (1-KEY, 2-KEY, ..., n-KEY)
```

with *n*-1 unnested IFs and *n* MOVES.

2. Find a way to eliminate Ċ-KEY from the inverted merge algorithm (Section 17.4) by expressing all footnotes in terms of the keys of the input files only. Which solution do you prefer? Why?

3. Code and test the update algorithm, using a physical input mapping for two transaction files.

4. Derive the process structure for an update to a *direct access* master file.

Part IV

Other Voices

Parts I through III explored the program design techniques of Ken Orr. Now we will look briefly at the work of other people in the field.

The bulk of this part is devoted to the other two major theoreticians of data structured program design: Jean-Dominique Warnier and Michael Jackson. We devote two chapters to each, outlining some of their ideas and contrasting them with Orr's.

The final chapter, "Goal Directed Programming," is not about data structured design at all. It is included because it relates closely to Orr's ideas on the primacy of output.

I haven't studied with any of the people whose ideas are presented in this Part, so what follows is strictly my interpretation of their writing. You should be sure to consult the original works for authoritative statements.

18

Warnier:
The Basics

Jean-Dominique Warnier was the first proponent of data structured program design. He has been publishing books in French since the 1960s, and they have been translated into Spanish, Japanese, English, Portuguese, Dutch, Italian, and Romanian.

His work was first translated into English in 1976, when *Logical Construction of Programs* (LCP) appeared. Since then there have been translations of *Program Modification* (1978), describing techniques of program maintenance; and *Logical Construction of Systems* (1981), discussing data base design.

In this chapter and the next we will survey some main ideas in LCP (Logical Construction of Programs), stressing the points where Warnier's ideas differ from Orr's. The discussion will not make you a master of Warnier's techniques; it is designed to ease your entry into LCP by relating its concepts to ones you're already familiar with.

18.1 WHAT'S DIFFERENT ABOUT WARNIER?

Warnier's work can present special problems to people familiar with Orr's ideas. Warnier diagrams look so much like Warnier/Orr diagrams that it's easy to mistakenly think you know what's going on.

Of course there are major similarities between the two schools. Both teach data structured program design (data structure $\longrightarrow$ process structure $\longrightarrow$ code); and Warnier/Orr diagrams are clearly an outgrowth of Warnier diagrams. But confusion often arises over the differences. Here are some of the main ones.

1. **Brackets:** Orr uses Warnier/Orr diagrams throughout the design process, carrying them almost to code. Warnier uses Warnier diagrams only for data structure and for the first cut at process structure; then he switches to other tools.

2. **Process Structure:** Orr tends to derive the main line process structure from the *output* data structure, relegating the input structure to the physical input mapping. Warnier derives the process structure from the *input* data structure, which in turn is diagrammed with one eye on the output.

3. **Optimization:** Orr leaves optimization of the process structure to individual intuition and experience. Warnier devotes a good deal of attention to reducing the number of operations required in the process structure.

4. **Structure Clashes:** Orr deals with structure clashes by hierarchy inversion. Warnier doesn't explicitly deal with structure clashes; he does introduce the concept of processing **phases** (use of counters and switches), which can be used to handle them.

5. **Code:** Orr gives explicit instructions on deriving COBOL code from the process structure. Warnier stays strictly away from code.

18.2 DATA STRUCTURE

With that background we can look at some details of Warnier's techniques. We will see how Warnier would deal with a problem we treated extensively in Parts II and III: the project report. Recall that the logical data layout was:

Warnier's goal, of course, is to derive the process structure. In his case the process structure is essentially a list of instructions held together by GO TOs. Here is how he gets it.

He starts, as we did, by diagramming the output. The Warnier diagram of the output would look like this, as far as I can tell (Warnier's books seem to have no examples of report headings or treatment of literals in general):

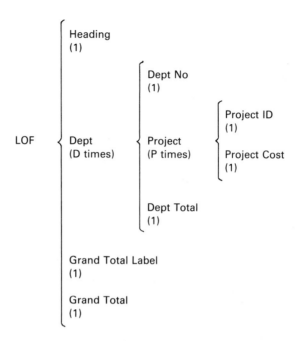

Note the slight notational differences: (D times) where we've written (**1**,D); (1) where we've written nothing.   We'll see later how Warnier expresses (**0**,D).

Note that the diagram is called LOF, for logical output file.   Equivalent terms in English translations of Warnier's books are "output" and "results."

So far so good: except for notational differences we have drawn the LOS that we saw in Chapter 5.   Now the differences begin: Warnier draws a diagram of the *input* file.   In Part III we worked through several possible input files.   Here we'll use the assumption from Section 15.1: a file containing one record for each worker on each project.

| LIF | Dept (D times) | Project (P times) | Worker (W times) | Dept No (1) Project ID (1) Worker Cost (1) |

Notice that Warnier frequently uses a broken-line bracket to show the decomposition of a universal (Worker) if all its elements are atoms.   LIF, of course, stands for logical input file.   Warnier's books often call this "Data" or "Input" or "Input Data" instead.   Note that Warnier's LIF is an entirely different thing from the LIF we described in Part III.

18.3 PROCESS STRUCTURE

Warnier now derives the process structure from the *input* data structure and gets:

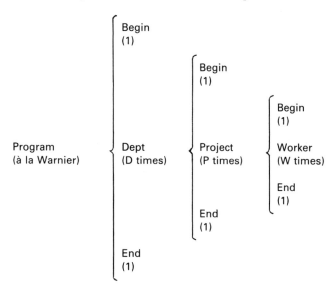

Note that this is fundamentally different from what we came up with in Chapter 7 (LOM) using Orr's techniques:

Warnier bases his process structure on the input, so he has a Worker level of structure that doesn't appear in Orr's LOM. Orr's LOM is completely independent of the input; Warnier's program structure *depends* on the input.

Because of this input derivation, Warnier inserts a validation step at this point: compare the process structure diagram with the output structure diagram

(LOF) to make sure you still have a place for everything. Essentially, this means that the input diagram must contain the output diagram as a subset.

Now Warnier pulls a switch: he abandons the bracket diagram and switches to a flowchart:

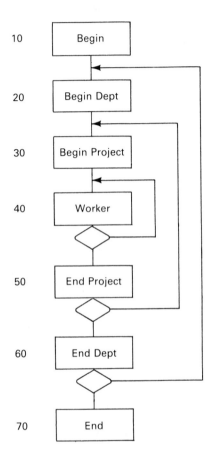

This flowchart is produced according to strict rules, including:

1. Each atom (undivided element) on the Warnier diagram becomes a process box: e.g., Begin, Begin Dept, Worker. Each box is called a **logical sequence**.
2. The boxes are numbered, usually by 10s.
3. The End box for each repetition is *immediately* followed by a decision diamond:

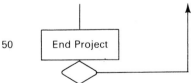

The decision diamond controls loop repetition. Recall that in a Warnier diagram the expression (*P* times) means **one**-to-*P* times; therefore, all Warnier's loops are bottom tested. If you could use a refresher on top-and bottom-tested loops, see Chapter 3 of this book.

18.4 OPERATIONS

We have converted Warnier's structure diagram to a flowchart. Now we must allocate operations to it. Recall how, with Orr's techniques in Chapter 7, we inserted the operations for:

- calculations
- output
- input

and in Chapter 9 we added instructions for:

- loop control.

Warnier does the same thing, though in slightly different order. He starts with inputs and uses the old rule about reading once to begin (box 10, Begin), and again when a record is consumed (box 40, Worker).

Sequence	Instruction
10	Read the first record of the file
40	Read another record of the file or the end-of-file record

Note that the program will not work if the input file is empty: the first read will return EOF and the rest of the logic will choke on it. More on this later. Also note that Warnier doesn't have to call a logical read routine: his process structure comes from the *input* structure, so he can do a physical read.

So much for input; now for loop control. Warnier divides this into "branch instructions" and "preparation of branch instructions." By branch he means a conditional branch:

```
IF (condition) THEN GO TO (target sequence)
```

The branches are the decision diamonds on the flowchart: in this case, the loop control tests. The branches on the project report problem are essentially the same as the loop control conditions we came up with in Chapter 9. Once again, using prefix in- (input) for the most recently read record, and curr- for the current value of any field, we have:

Sequence	Instruction	Next Seq
40	if in-project-key = curr-project-key	40
50	if in-dept-key = curr-dept-key	30
60	if not end-of-file	20

The first entry in this list means: at sequence (box) 40, insert the statement "If in-project-key = curr-project-key then go to sequence 40". The keys are similar to the concatenated keys we used in Chapter 9. Project-key, for example, is:

Dept No	Project ID	= Project-key

That is, each key contains any higher-level control codes. Warnier doesn't include an EOF switch in the key; instead, he moves HIGH-VALUES to the control fields at end of file.

The second half of loop control is "preparation of branch instructions"—that is, storing values for the branch conditions to test. Recall that in Chapter 9 we wrote:

DEPT.BEGIN { MOVE IN-DEPT-NO TO CURR-DEPT-NO

Similarly, here we need to write:

Sequence	Instruction
20	Move in-dept-no to curr-dept-no
30	Move in-project-id to curr-project-id

Warnier introduces two terms that will be important to us later:

- the **reference criterion** (e.g., curr-project-key) in Working-Storage; and
- the **identification criterion** (e.g., in-project-key) of the input record.

Each branch instruction compares a reference criterion to an identification criterion. Preparing branch instructions consists of making the reference criterion available if it's not automatically present. That's what we just did by moving the "in" values to the "curr" values.

Next come calculations, which are the same ones we derived in Chapter 7:

```
10    Clear grand-total
20    Clear dept-total
30    Clear project-cost
40    Add worker-cost to project-cost
50    Add project-cost to dept-total
60    Add dept-total to grand-total
```

Finally come the output instructions. Once again, these are the same as the ones we came up with previously:

```
10    Produce heading
20    Move dept-no to detail-dept-no
30    Move project-id to detail-project-id
50    Move project-cost to detail-project-cost
50    Output and clear detail line
60    Produce dept-total line
70    Produce grand-total line
```

We now have the complete collection of instructions for the program. Here they are again:

	Sequence		Instruction	Next Seq
INPUT	10		Read the first record of the file	
	40		Read another record of the file or the end-of-file record	
BRANCH	40		if in-project-key = curr-project-key	40
	50		if in-dept-key = curr-dept-key	30
	60		if not end-of-file	20
BRANCH PREP	20		Move in-dept-no to curr-dept-no	
	30		Move in-project-id to curr-project-id	
CALCULATION	10		Clear grand-total	
	20		Clear dept-total	
	30		Clear project-cost	
	40		Add worker-cost to project-cost	
	50		Add project-cost to dept-total	
	60		Add dept-total to grand-total	
OUTPUT	10		Produce heading	
	20		Move dept-no to detail-dept-no	
	30		Move project-id to detail-project-id	
	50		Move project-cost to detail-project-cost	
	50		Output and clear detail line	
	60		Produce dept-total line	
	70		Produce grand-total line	

Now we sort the above instructions to get the **detailed instruction list**, which Warnier sometimes calls Pi. Sort first on sequence number. Within a sequence the order is usually:

- preparation of branches
- preparation of calculations, and calculations
- preparation of outputs, and outputs
- inputs
- branches

Thus we have:

10	Clear grand-total	
10	Produce heading	
10	Read the first record of the file	
20	Move in-dept-no to curr-dept-no	
20	Clear dept-total	
20	Move dept-no to detail-dept-no	
30	Move in-project-id to curr-project-id	
30	Clear project-cost	
30	Move project-id to detail-project-id	
40	Add worker-cost to project-cost	
40	Read another record of the file or the end-of-file record	
40	if in-project-key = curr-project-key	40
50	Add project-cost to dept-total	
50	Move project-cost to detail-project-cost	
50	Output and clear detail line	
50	if in-dept-key = curr-dept-key	30
60	Add dept-total to grand-total	
60	Produce dept-total line	
60	if not end-of-file	20
70	Produce grand-total line	

Finally, there's another validation. Just as we earlier validated the program structure diagram by comparing it to the output, we must now do the same thing for the detailed instruction list. This second validation completes the development.

18.5 THE STORY SO FAR

Here is a summary of LCP steps we have covered so far:

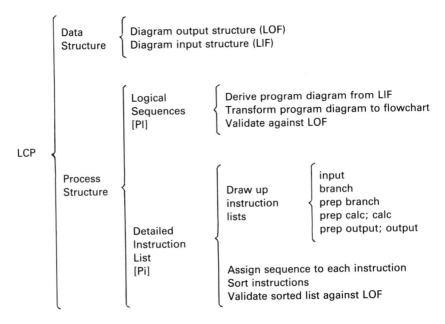

Note the main differences from Orr's approach.

1. Warnier bases process structure on *input* data structure. Orr uses output.
2. Warnier's detail process structure is a flowchart with conditional GO TOs. Orr's introduction of footnotes (?1/UNTIL EOF = "YES" and the like) lets him stick with Warnier/Orr diagrams.
3. Warnier stops when he gets to process structure. Orr goes on to give COBOL coding rules.

A couple of other differences are worth noting. I find Warnier's use of sequence numbers for the process structure less natural then Orr's use of names: "40" doesn't mean as much as "1/worker." On the other hand, Warnier's stress on the need to explicitly work out the branch (loop and selection) and preparation of branch instructions seems very useful.

18.6 ALTERNATIVES

We have seen how Warnier handles sequence and repetition. Now we turn to the third basic construct, called "alternative structure" in the English translation.

Warnier diagrams *output* alternatives just like Orr does. *Input* alternatives present a new wrinkle. Suppose some processing depends on whether or not the employee is male. Where Orr would draw:

$$\left\{ \begin{array}{l} . \\ \text{SEX} = \text{M} \quad \left\{ \; . . . \right. \\ (0,1) \\ . \end{array} \right.$$

Warnier normally writes:

$$\left\{ \begin{array}{l} . \\ . \\ \text{CODE [M, 0 or 1]} \\ . \end{array} \right.$$

When he needs to know whether the percent discount is > 0, he writes:

$$\left\{ \begin{array}{l} . \\ . \\ \text{DISCOUNT\% [>0, 0 or 1]} \\ . \end{array} \right.$$

On the other hand, LCP sometimes uses the same notation as Orr:

$$\left\{ \begin{array}{l} \text{OS} < \text{MIN} \\ \text{(0 or 1)} \\ \\ \oplus \\ \\ \text{OS} >= \text{MIN} \\ \text{(0 or 1)} \end{array} \right.$$

There seems to be no statement of when to use the square-bracket notation and when to use the Orr-like notation.

Finally, here is how Warnier diagrams an alternative in the *program* structure. For this input data:

$$\left\{ \begin{array}{l} . \\ . \\ \text{SEX [M, 0 or 1]} \\ . \end{array} \right.$$

he creates this program structure diagram:

$$\left\{ \begin{array}{l} . \\ . \\ \text{Begin} \\ \text{(1)} \\ \\ \text{M} \\ \text{(0 or 1)} \\ \\ \overline{\text{M}} \\ \text{(0 or 1)} \\ \\ \text{End} \\ \text{(1)} \\ . \\ . \end{array} \right.$$

There are two differences here from Orr's techniques:

1. Begin and End are introduced for alternation, just as they are for repetition. Begin will be where the actual making of the test for M or $\overline{\text{M}}$ takes place.
2. There is no exclusive or symbol ($\oplus$) between M and $\overline{\text{M}}$. The reason isn't stated in LCP.

This structure diagram yields the following flowchart:

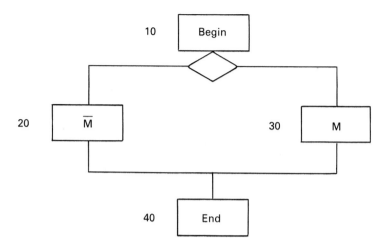

The following branch instructions are inserted in the detailed instruction list to handle the selection:

Sequence	Instruction	Next Seq
10	if sex = M	30
20		40

(Notice the unconditional branch in sequence 20.) Naturally, the detailed instruction list will also contain whatever processing logic is needed for M (20) and $\overline{\text{M}}$ (30).

Before leaving alternation we should tie up a loose end from the discussion of repetition. Recall that when Warnier writes:

Trans file { Transaction
               (T times)

he means that T is at least 1. In other words "(T times)" means the same as Orr's "(1,T)". But how does Warnier handle a repetition that may occur 0 times: Orr's "(0,T)"? He does it by combining repetition with alternation:

LIF { Trans file   { Transaction
        (0 or 1)   (T times)

That is, zero-to-T is just a one-to-T that may or may not occur. The resulting program structure is:

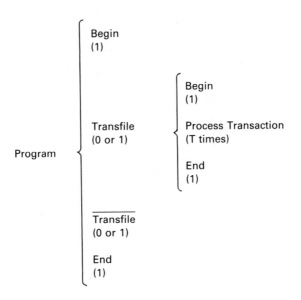

Program
{
  Begin
  (1)

  Transfile
  (0 or 1)
  {
    Begin
    (1)

    Process Transaction
    (T times)

    End
    (1)
  }

  T̅r̅a̅n̅s̅f̅i̅l̅e̅
  (0 or 1)

  End
  (1)
}

This gives the flowchart:

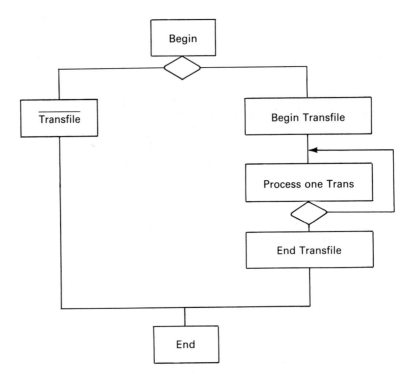

The repetition has been nested within the alternation.

18.7 "COMPLEX" STRUCTURES

So far we have dealt with simple breakdowns: each level of bracket has introduced one repetition:

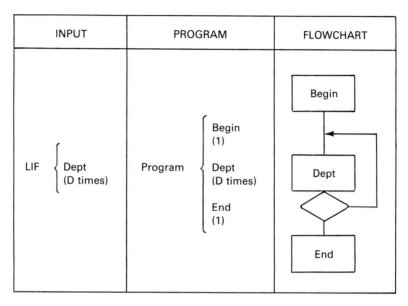

or one selection:

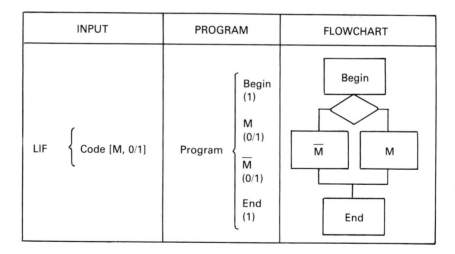

A "complex" structure, by contrast, is one where a bracket has two or more structures immediately to its right, be they repetitive or alternative or a mixture.

For example, suppose each customer of a bank has a customer record, followed by one or more account records, followed by an optional credit card record. Diagrammatically:

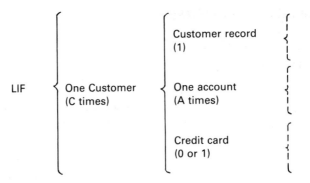

LIF { One Customer (C times) { Customer record (1) / One account (A times) / Credit card (0 or 1)

The only interesting thing about complex structures is that the "End" sequence for each substructure is merged with the "Begin" sequence of the next to form an "Intermediate" sequence:

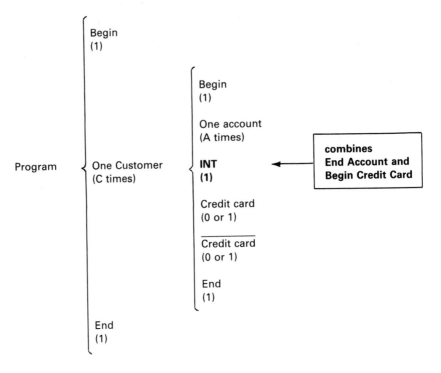

Program { Begin (1) / One Customer (C times) { Begin (1) / One account (A times) / INT (1) / Credit card (0 or 1) / Credit card (0 or 1) / End (1) / End (1)

combines
**End Account and
Begin Credit Card**

Notice that the customer record proper will be handled in the "Begin" sequence. The flowchart is:

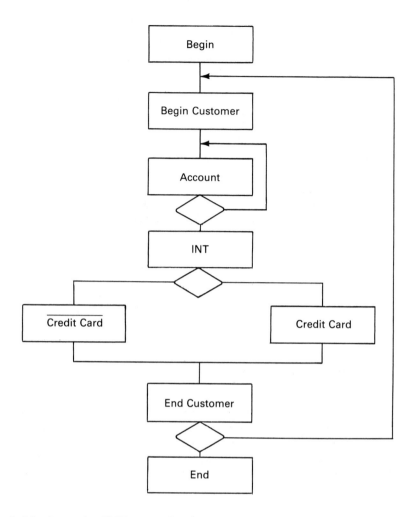

Aside from the INT, complex input structures present no novel features. Except this. Sometimes output actions depend on some *combination* of input conditions. Warnier refers to this phenomenon as "complex alternative input structure" and devotes about a hundred pages to it. We should at least start a new chapter.

18.8 SUMMARY

For a more detailed summary of Warnier's techniques, see the end of the next chapter, or the Appendix. The stages we have seen so far are:

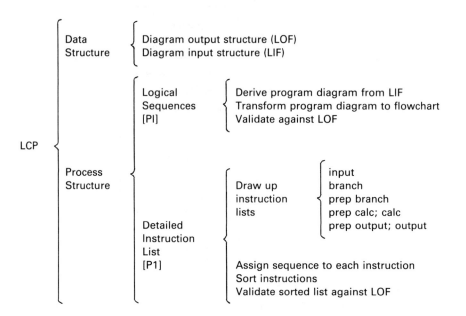

LCP
- Data Structure
  - Diagram output structure (LOF)
  - Diagram input structure (LIF)
- Process Structure
  - Logical Sequences [PI]
    - Derive program diagram from LIF
    - Transform program diagram to flowchart
    - Validate against LOF
  - Detailed Instruction List [P1]
    - Draw up instruction lists
      - input
      - branch
      - prep branch
      - prep calc; calc
      - prep output; output
    - Assign sequence to each instruction
    - Sort instructions
    - Validate sorted list against LOF

FURTHER READING

For a detailed exposition of the material we have been summarizing, see Warnier's *Logical Construction of Programs* if you can find a copy; it's out of print in English in North America.   It is currently being retranslated from the 1981 French edition.

If you can read French and can't wait for the new English version, see the French original, *Construction et transformation des programmes (L.C.P.)* (7th Ed.).

19

Warnier: Optimization and Phases

In the previous chapter we discussed Warnier's basic approach to data structured program design. We saw how he derives the program structure from the input data structure when the input is pure repetition, pure alternation, or a mixture of repetition and alternation.

In this chapter we will examine two more areas:

1. "Complex alternative input": What to do when the output actions depend on *combinations* of conditions.
2. "Processing phases": What to do when the output depends on things that don't appear directly in the input.

Again we can only touch the major ideas. The goal is not to completely cover Warnier's techniques; the goal is to provide a bridge from what you already know.

We start with complex alternative input.

19.1 COMPLEX ALTERNATIVE INPUT

We said that complex alternative input means that the output actions depend on *combinations* of input conditions. Warnier has two approaches to this. One is based on the conditions; the other on the actions.

To illustrate the difference, consider a company that wants to compute and print the percent discount of its customers. There are three different discount calculations; we will call them D1, D2, and D3:

```
D1  applies to big    nearby  customers
D2     "      " big    remote     "
D3     "      " small  nearby     "
```

There is no discount for small, remote customers.
Thus, the LOF is:

$$
\text{LOF} \left\{ \text{Customer} \atop \text{(C1 times)} \right. \left\{ {\text{Name} \atop (1)} \atop {\text{Discount [D1,D2,D3]} \atop (1)} \right.
$$

Warnier often writes actions [D1,D2,D3] in square brackets on his LOF diagrams. Warnier also diagrams the case in which no output is produced:

$$
\overline{\text{Output}} \left\{ \text{Customer} \atop \text{(C2 times)} \right.
$$

Note that C1 + C2 = total number of customers.

Now we'll derive the LIF. There are two codes on the input customer record: code B (with values 0 or 1) says whether the customer is big; code N (values 0 or 1) says whether it's nearby. Thus:

B (or B = 1) means the customer is big
$\overline{B}$ (or B = 0) means the customer is small

and similarly for N = nearby. Thus the logical input file is:

$$
\text{LIF} \left\{ \text{Customer} \atop \text{(C times)} \right. \left\{ {\text{Name}} \atop {\text{code [B, 0 or 1]} \atop {+ \atop \text{code [N, 0 or 1]}}} \right.
$$

The + sign between the B entry and the N entry means that they are *not* mutually exclusive: either or both can hold. This is what's meant by complex alternative input.

Let's look at the two possible approaches to programming that Warnier presents for this input, then see how he would decide between them. His first approach is based on input conditions. It has this program structure diagram:

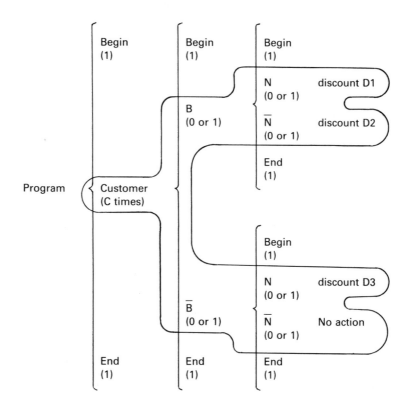

If you focus on the area that is marked above, ignoring all those Begins and Ends, you will recognize a plain old condition sandwich à la Orr (with the difference that Warnier doesn't insert curly brackets before the actions "discount D1" and the like).

Warnier calls this a tree structure—for reasons that will become apparent if you tilt your head to the right. It is essentially what in other contexts is called a "decision tree." It consists of nesting the conditions: within each value of B we test each value of N. (Note that Warnier forbids codes with more than two values; if he needs a multivalued code, he creates enough artifical two-value codes to cover all the values.)

This gives the following flowchart:

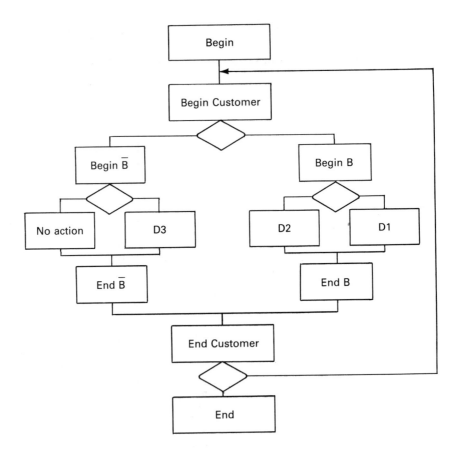

So that's one approach: the tree structure, based on input conditions.

Now here is the second possible approach; this one is based on the actions. The discount problem has three possible actions: D1, D2, and D3. Without even asking what conditions lead to these actions, we can diagram a structure with one alternative for each action:

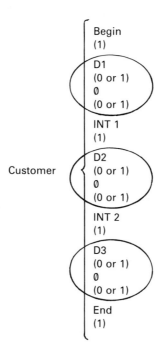

Customer

Begin
(1)

D1
(0 or 1)
∅
(0 or 1)

INT 1
(1)

D2
(0 or 1)
∅
(0 or 1)

INT 2
(1)

D3
(0 or 1)
∅
(0 or 1)

End
(1)

The circled pairs of entries in the diagram represent one alternative structure for each action. Warnier's program structures always show both branches of each alternative, even when one of them is empty (∅). In a structure of the sort we are now describing, the alternative to each action will always be empty. And of course the actions have INTermediate entries separating them, just as the complex repetitions and complex mixed entries did in the last chapter.

This is called a "complex alternative structure." To save space we'll call it CAPS (Complex Alternative Program Structure) from now on.

The flowchart from this CAPS is a straightforward sequence of alternatives. Notice that we have written the conditions (B.N = big nearby; B.$\overline{\text{N}}$ = big remote; $\overline{\text{B}}$.N = small nearby) on the branches for each action:

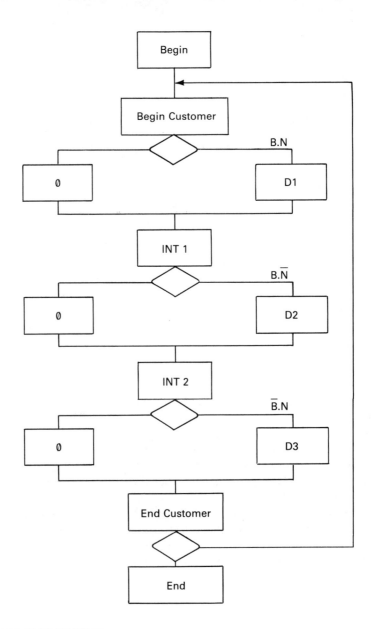

19.2 WHEN TO USE WHICH

We have seen Warnier's two ways of handling complex alternative input (i.e., actions that depend on combinations of conditions):

PROGRAM STRUCTURE	BASED ON	TECHNIQUE
Tree	Input conditions	Nest conditions
CAPS	Output actions	One alternative per action

How do you decide when to use which of them?

Orr normally opts for the tree structure, which will always work; there's never a *need* to use the CAPS. Warnier's introduction of CAPS is based largely on considerations of efficiency: how shall we minimize the number of operations the computer has to perform? His treatment is also interesting because it can also produce clearer diagrams.

Warnier uses logic tables to decide between tree and CAPS. (The English translation usually calls them truth tables, sometimes decision tables.) The table for our discount example is:

◄ conditions ►   ◄——————— actions ———————►

B N	D1	D2	D3	Print	$\overline{\text{Output}}$
0 0					X
0 1			X	X	
1 0		X		X	
1 1	X			X	

For example, the circled third row means: For big (B = 1) remote (N = 0) customers, compute discount D2 and then print. That is, the 0s and 1s give the combinations of conditions; the Xs show which actions to take for a given combination of conditions.

If you're familiar with decision tables, you may recognize this more readily if you interchange rows and columns:

B	0	0	1	1
N	0	1	0	1
D1				X
D2			X	
D3		X		
Print		X	X	X
$\overline{\text{Output}}$	X			

But we'll stick to Warnier's format, which we repeat for convenient reference:

B N	D1	D2	D3	Print	$\overline{\text{Output}}$
0 0					X
0 1			X	X	
1 0		X		X	
1 1	X			X	

And at last we come to the point of introducing these tables: Warnier's criterion for deciding between tree and CAPS depends on comparing columns in the table. To state his criterion, we must introduce a couple of terms.

Consider action columns L and Q in a hypothetical table:

L	Q
X	
X	
	X
	X
X	
	X
	X

We say L and Q are **disjoint**: no horizontal row has an X for both L and Q. That is, no input can result in both action L and action Q taking place.

Here is a different setup:

S	U
X	X
X	
X	X

We say that U is **included** in S: in any row where action U has an X, action S also has one.

We can use these terms to give Warnier's rule for deciding between tree structure and CAPS. Compare each pair of columns in the logic table:

IF . . .	THEN USE . . .
there are <u>only</u> disjoints and inclusions	tree
there are <u>no</u> disjoints, <u>no</u> inclusions	CAPS
otherwise (some disjoint-or-included, some not)	combination

So to return to our discount calculation:

B N	D1	D2	D3	PRINT	$\overline{\text{Output}}$
0 0					X
0 1			X	X	
1 0		X		X	
1 1	X			X	

There are 10 **pairs** of action columns to check: D1-D2, D1-D3, D1-Print, D1-Output, D2-D3, D2-Print, etc. You can verify that there are seven disjoints and three inclusions. Thus this table fits the criteria for a **tree** structure: it only has disjoints and inclusions.

But consider this table:

A B C	W	X	Y	Z
0 0 0	X		X	
0 0 1	X			
0 1 0	X	X	X	X
0 1 1	X	X		X
1 0 0			X	X
1 0 1				X
1 1 0		X	X	
1 1 1		X		

Once again, the checking takes a little time: there are six pairs of action columns to examine. But you can easily satisfy yourself that there are no disjoints and no inclusions. So this table will be implemented by a CAPS; that is, the program structure is a series of four alternatives, one for each of the actions (W, X, Y, Z).

Finally, consider:

E G	P	Q	R	S
0 0	X			X
0 1	X	X		
1 0				X
1 1			X	

P-Q is an inclusion; P-R is disjoint; Q-R is disjoint. So far so good: all are disjoints or inclusions, and we are heading for a tree structure. But S breaks the pattern: P-S is neither disjoint nor inclusive.

So the tree structure for actions P, Q, and R will presumably be followed by a simple alternative for S. (What is the condition on this alternative; i.e., under what condition is action S carried out?)

19.3 BUILDING TREES AND LINKING TABLES

We have spent several pages outlining Warnier's criterion for deciding between tree and CAPS approaches, but have only given the lay of the land. LCP contains the details.

Warnier devotes considerable attention to the techniques for building a tree once you've decided you need one; the goal is minimizing machine usage by making the condition tests in the right order. He uses Boolean algebra, and what are variously called Karnaugh maps or Veitch diagrams, to simplify the logical conditions for each action. Here again, a detailed treatment is well beyond the scope of this book; LCP discusses the matter thoroughly.

Warnier also discusses the situation in which combined conditions on one bracket of a Warnier diagram are bound up with combined conditions on the bracket to the left. The solution, chain-linked truth tables, has a chapter to itself in Warnier's book.

One thing about this attention to conditions and actions is worth noting here. Warnier bases program structure on input data structure. But he first looks carefully at all the actions needed to produce the outputs; that's how he determines which input conditions must be distinguished. In other words, the input data structure can be drawn only when you know the actions needed to produce the output; so Warnier is not as remote from Orr's output orientation as may at first appear.

19.4 THE PROCESSING PHASES:
SWITCHES, COUNTERS, CALCULATIONS

This completes our discussion of Warnier's optimization and simplification techniques. We now move on to the second question this chapter promised to answer: what do you do when the actions depend on information that isn't directly available on the input file(s)?

Warnier derives program structure from the input data structure. But sometimes the control information required just doesn't appear in the input data, at least not in ready-to-use form. Then it's necessary to use switches or counters or calculations to derive the control information from the input data. "Processing phases" is Warnier's name for such work. The concept of phases is particularly interesting to us because it provides Warnier's approach when faced with a structure clash.

In Chapter 18 we introduced Warnier's distinction between **reference** and **identification** criteria. Any conditional branch instruction (controlling a loop or a selection) compares an identification criterion associated with the input data to a reference criterion stored in core.

For example, in producing the project report the DEPT loop control instruction was:

```
SEQUENCE                INSTRUCTION                      NEXT SEQ

   50          If In-Dept-Key = Curr-Dept-Key               30
                           :              :
                           :              :
           identification....:            :.....reference
                criterion                      criterion
                 (input)                        (stored)
```

Similarly, in the selection sample we introduced the conditional branch:

```
   10                 If Code = M                           30
                           :    :
                           :    :
           identification.....:  :.....reference
                criterion           criterion
                 (input)             (fixed)
```

We said that if the reference criterion isn't fixed, it is necessary to create it. That is what preparation of branch instructions consisted of: setting up reference criteria. For example, in the project report we wrote:

```
   20         Move In-Dept-Num to Curr-Dept-Num
```

So we're used to establishing reference criteria. But what about identification criteria? For example, what if we need to:

- set a switch, or
- increment a counter, or
- calculate a value

and then compare the switch/counter/value with some reference criterion?

Whenever a branch instruction depends on such a switch/counter/value, Warnier says there is a change in processing phase. You handle a phase change in two steps:

1. The action to create the identification criterion is designed into the program just like any other action; and
2. The identification criterion then becomes input to a new phase of the program, which is designed according to all the rules we have discussed so far in these two chapters.

Here are some lightweight examples to show what this means.

Phase Change: Calculation. Suppose each customer has one or more loan records. We want a report listing the customers whose total loans exceed $10,000. Obviously, the structure of phase 1 will be:

$$
\text{Program}
\left\{
\begin{array}{l}
\text{Begin} \\
\text{(1)} \\[1em]
\text{Customer} \\
\text{(C times)} \\[1em]
\text{End} \\
\text{(1)}
\end{array}
\right.
\left\{
\begin{array}{l}
\text{Begin} \\
\text{(1)} \\[1em]
\text{Loan} \\
\text{(L times)} \\[1em]
\text{End} \\
\text{(1)}
\end{array}
\right.
$$

We will need to create an identification criterion called TOTAL-LOANS. It will be the job of phase 1 to create it by initializing it to zero in Begin Customer, and adding LOAN-AMOUNT to it in Loan.

In phase 2 we will either list the customer or not, depending on whether or not TOTAL-LOANS exceeds $10,000. The input to phase 2 is:

$$
\begin{array}{l}
\text{UNIVERSAL:} \\
\text{1 CUSTOMER}
\end{array}
\left\{
\begin{array}{l}
\text{TOTAL-LOANS} > 10{,}000 \\
\text{(0 or 1)}
\end{array}
\right.
$$

So the phase 2 subprogram is:

$$
\text{process one customer}
\left\{
\begin{array}{l}
\text{Begin} \\
\text{(1)} \\[1em]
\text{List customer} \\
\text{(0,1)} \\[1em]
0 \\
\text{(0,1)} \\[1em]
\text{End} \\
\text{(1)}
\end{array}
\right.
$$

This is merged into the phase 1 program, presumably at End Customer.

This is a very simple example; it can easily become more complicated. For example, we might want to send a dunning letter to nearby (code N) customers whose loans exceeded \$10,000; terminate remote customers whose loans exceeded \$10,000; and send a statement of account to remote customers whose loans are \$10,000 or less. Then the input to phase two will be the complex alternative:

$$\text{Phase 2} \begin{cases} \text{UNIVERSAL:} \\ \text{1 CUSTOMER} \end{cases} \begin{cases} \text{CODE [N, 0 or 1]} \\ \\ + \\ \\ \text{TOTAL-LOANS} > 10{,}000 \\ \text{(0 or 1)} \end{cases}$$

Then we will be into truth tables, tree structures, and the like. As we said, the structure of phase 2 is derived from its input according to all the principles we have discussed in these two chapters.

Phase Change: Counting. (The one-page rule revisited.) Recall the one-page rule. For chapter after chapter we maintained the fiction that all our reports are one page long—that is, that the physical output structure is the same as the logical one. Eventually (Chapters 10 and 11) we saw how inversion could handle page breaks by resolving the structure clash between the concurrent logical and physical structures of the report file.

Warnier doesn't discuss concurrency, structure clashes, or inversion. Instead he says that if we want a page skip after 54 lines, then to-skip-or-not-to-skip is a characteristic of a line. But you can't tell from looking at a line that it is the 54th: it carries no "skip code" on it. Thus, the test for page skip must involve a change of phase: we must create an identification criterion that can be tested.

We do this by introducing LINE-COUNTER. The input to phase 2 is then:

$$\text{Phase 2} \begin{cases} \text{UNIVERSAL:} \\ \text{1 LINE} \end{cases} \begin{cases} \text{LINE-COUNTER} > 54 \\ \text{(0 or 1)} \end{cases}$$

So the phase 2 subprogram is:

$$\text{Process One Line} \begin{cases} \text{Begin} \\ \text{(1)} \\ \\ \text{Change Page} \\ \text{(0 or 1)} \\ \\ \emptyset \\ \text{(0 or 1)} \\ \\ \text{End} \\ \text{(1)} \end{cases}$$

It is, of course, the job of phase 1 to initialize LINE-COUNTER, and phase 1 could even increment it. But it's hard to see how any logic except Change Page could be responsible for **re**initializing LINE-COUNTER on the second and subsequent pages.

Phase Change: Switch Setting. We are writing a validation program for a transaction file. All errors on each transaction are to be reported. If a transaction has no errors, it is to be written to a Validated Transaction file for later processing.

There is no identification criterion on the input transaction record that will let us determine immediately if it is valid. Only by making each error-check in turn will we find out.

We introduce a switch (VALID-TRANSACTION), which we set to "YES" at the beginning of each new transaction, and change its value to "NO" any time we find an error. This switch then becomes an identification criterion that can be tested at the end of error checking to determine if the transaction should be written.

If you would like to pursue the matter further, you might have a look at Jackson's ideas on backtracking (Chapter 21) and consider how they apply in such a situation.

This completes our survey of processing phases. To put it in a nutshell: any time an identification criterion is not present in the input data, we must derive it and then test it in a new phase.

19.5 PROGRAM MODIFICATION

Warnier is one of the few people to have seriously addressed program modification: the revision of a program to satisfy new requests from the program's end users. Space won't permit a detailed treatment of his techniques.

But if you use the diagram in the chapter summary (Section 19.6) as your guide and work through it, making any revisions dictated by the user's new requirement, you will be essentially doing what he says. For more details see his book *Program Modification*: you now have enough background to follow the techniques and terminology.

One passage from *Program Modification* bears retelling. He reports a survey of several dozen DP shops in government, retailing, banking, manufacturing, and service bureaus. Each shop reported how many test runs it took, on the average, to get a program working. The results, covering several thousand programs, were as follows:

- shops using trial-and-error design methods averaged 20–30 test runs per program
- shops using more or less Warnier's principles, without the validation steps, averaged 4–10 test runs per program
- shops where programmers have thorough experience in LCP and perform thorough validations average fewer than 2 test runs per program

19.6 SUMMARY

One major theme of this chapter was what to do when one or more actions depend on a *combination* of input conditions. After drawing up a logic table relating the conditions and actions, proceed as follows:

IF THE COLUMNS TAKEN PAIRWISE HAVE . . .	USE	BASED ON
only disjoints and inclusions	tree	input conditions (nested)
no disjoints, no inclusions	CAPS	output actions (one alternative per action)
some disjoint-or-included, some not	mix	

The other main thread dealt with conditions whose reference field (identification criterion) doesn't exist on the input record. This field will be a switch, counter, or computed item. The instructions to compute it become part of the regular structure. The processing *based* on its value becomes a new "phase."

To put the last few sections in place, the following figure shows LCP in a nutshell. The material from this chapter is highlighted.

LCP
- DATA STRUCTURE
  - OUTPUT
    - diagram LOF
  - INPUT
    - diagram LIF
  - $\overline{\text{OUTPUT}}$
    - diagram absence of results
  - **PHASES**
    - for each identification criterion **not** on LIF
      - diagram phase input note actions needed to produce id criterion
  - **TABLES**
    - if action(s) depend on combination of conditions (i.e., + sign appears)
      - draw truth/ decision tables
- PROCESS STRUCTURE
  - LOGICAL SEQUENCES
    - DRAW PROGRAM STRUCTURE
      - diagram left to right: use LIF, **phase diagrams, and tables. (Tables control choice of caps vs. tree vs. mixed structure.)**
    - CREATE FLOWCHART
      - derive flowchart from program structure diagram
      - number the sequences (boxes)
    - VALIDATE FLOWCHART
      - validate flowchart by LOF, output, and phase diagrams
  - DETAILED INSTRUCTION LIST
    - DRAW UP INSTRUCTION LIST
      - input
      - branch
      - prep branch
      - prep calc and calc
      - prep output and output
      - subroutine calls
    - ALLOCATE INSTRUCTIONS
      - assign logical sequence number to each instruction
      - sort instructions
      - validate sorted list against LOF, output, and phase diagrams

FURTHER READING

For more details on the material in this chapter, see Part II of Warnier's *Logical Construction of Programs*.

20

Jackson:
The Basics

The third major theoretician of data structured program design is Michael Jackson. His ideas, as set out in his *Principles of Program Design* (1975), have been especially influential in the United Kingdom and northern Europe. He recently set out his thoughts on all phases of system creation in *System Development* (1983); we won't consider that work here.

In this chapter we will introduce Jackson's notation and basic techniques; in the following one we will explore the areas where he differs most sharply from Warnier and Orr.

As was the case with Warnier, we have space only to touch the highlights. Once again, the objective is to ease your entry into further study by building a bridge from what you already know.

20.1 JACKSON STEP 1: DIAGRAM DATA STRUCTURE

Jackson, like Warnier and Orr, begins by diagramming the data structure. But he uses boxes, not brackets. Here, for each of the three basic structures, are the Warnier/Orr diagram (on the left) and the Jackson diagram (on the right).

Sequence: A consists of B, followed by C, followed by D:

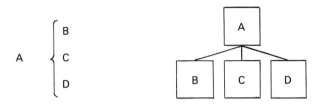

Alternation (Selection): E consists of G or H, but not both:

The little circle in the upper right-hand corner of the G and H boxes means that E is a selection between G and H.

Repetition (Iteration): J consists of zero or more repetitions of K:

The asterisk in the K box means that J is an iteration (repetition) of zero or more Ks. Note that we said *zero* or more. Just as Warnier insists all repetitions occur one or more times, Jackson maintains the correct lower limit is zero.

Warnier had to find a way of dealing with zero or more: he says it's a one-or-more that may not exist. And similarly, Jackson sometimes needs a way for one-or-more. He diagrams it as:

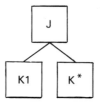

where K1 is the first K.

That's how Jackson draws data structures. We can now look at how he uses the diagrams to develop programs. We will explore Jackson's methods using a version of—you guessed it—the project report. The logical data layout is:

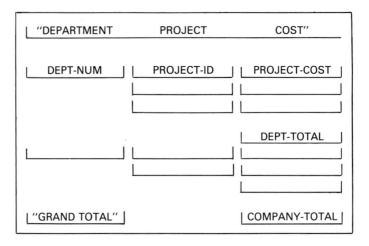

For reference, Orr's diagram of this output—his LOS—is as follows:

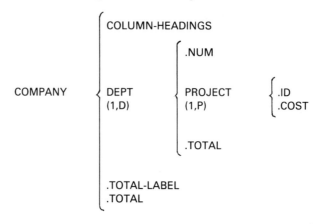

You might expect Jackson's diagram of the same output to be a simple translation of Orr's LOS into the box format. But it's not quite that simple. Jackson forbids "mixed constructs"; that is, each level of the diagram must be exactly *one* of sequence or selection or iteration. So, for example, you couldn't write:

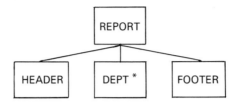

This combines sequence (header, then departments, then footer) with iteration (the * indicates DEPT is repeated).

The ban on mixed constructs means that a Jackson diagram normally has one or two more levels than the Warnier/Orr diagram of the same problem. And that's the case here. The Jackson diagram would be something like this, with RREPORT BODY and RDEPT BODY introduced to avoid mixed constructs:

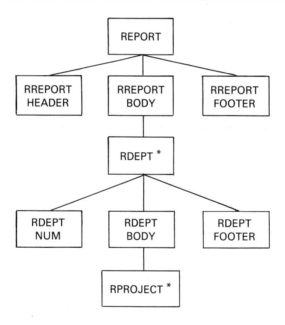

This diagram ignores page breaks. We will meet program inversion, Jackson's technique for handling structure clashes, in the next chapter.

A couple of minor points:

- The Jackson and Orr diagrams aren't exactly equivalent because of the zero-or-more vs. one-or-more question, but it turns out not to make much difference here.
- Orr's diagram shows individual data elements, while Jackson's stops basically at the print-line level. We've been forced to create a box for RDEPT NUM,

since it occurs only once per department. Jackson might prefer to call this something like RDEPT HEADER.

Jackson's next step is to diagram the input data. Let's stick with the same input file we assumed when we discussed Warnier: the file with WORKER records. The Warnier/Orr diagram is:

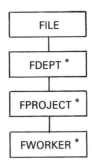

COMPANY { DEPT (1,D) { PROJECT (1,P) { WORKER (1,W) { DEPT-NUM PROJ-ID .NAME .COST

Jackson would diagram this as:

```
        ┌──────────┐
        │   FILE   │
        └────┬─────┘
        ┌────┴─────┐
        │ FDEPT *  │
        └────┬─────┘
        ┌────┴──────┐
        │ FPROJECT *│
        └────┬──────┘
        ┌────┴──────┐
        │ FWORKER * │
        └───────────┘
```

This completes the diagramming of the input and output files.

20.2 JACKSON STEP 2: PROGRAM STRUCTURE

Having diagrammed the data structures, Jackson's next step is to attempt to merge them into a program structure. He does this by looking for **correspondences** between the input and output. Like this:

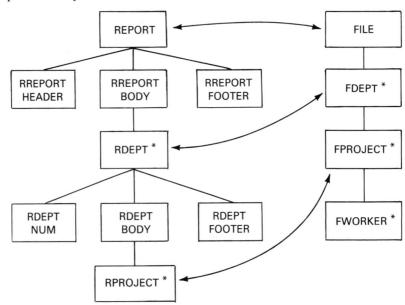

Here everything works: FILE corresponds to REPORT. FDEPT corresponds to RDEPT: there is the same number of FDEPTs as of RDEPTs, and they correspond pairwise. (Unlike Warnier's and Orr's diagrams, Jackson's don't identify the number of occurrences—(0,D) or whatever. You just have to remember whether things occur the same number of times.) Similarly, FPROJECT corresponds to RPROJECT: within an FDEPT/RDEPT pair, there is the same number of FPROJECTs and RPROJECTs and they correspond pairwise.

To put it another way: there is no structure clash here. So we get the program structure by combining the two diagrams—that is, by merging them:

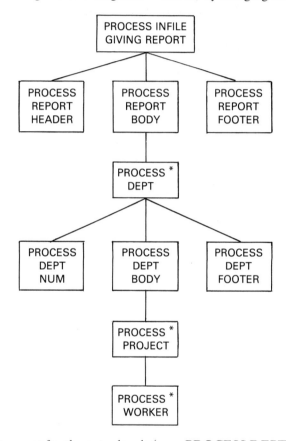

Notice that except for the extra levels (e.g., PROCESS DEPT BODY) caused by shunning mixed constructs, this is rather like what Warnier would come up with—see Section 18.3.

So some of Jackson's differences from Warnier are more apparent than real. Jackson *combines* data structures to get the program structure. Warnier uses the input structure only; but since he then validates it against the output, it often looks a lot like Jackson's combination.

And notice that Orr is different from both of them: he derives the main line structure exclusively from the output; the input structure is buried in the logical read routine. His solution to this problem, therefore, has no WORKER level.

20.3 JACKSON STEP 3: LIST AND ALLOCATE OPERATIONS

We have derived Jackson's program structure diagram; now we have to put some flesh on the bones. At this point Warnier surprised us by switching to flowcharts. Jackson also pulls a switch (though not to flowcharts), but he postpones it a bit.

First he allocates **operations** to the program structure diagram. He has you list all the operations you can think of. He gives no methodical procedure for telling when you've finished, since he finds that none is necessary in practice.

We might as well use the list we came up with for Warnier, with a few additions to be explained in a minute. We follow Jackson's conventions and write A: = B for MOVE B TO A.

```
 1. READ INFILE
 2. OPEN INFILE
 3. CLOSE INFILE
 4. OPEN PFILE
 5. CLOSE PFILE
 6. GRAND-TOTAL       := 0
 7. DEPT-TOTAL        := 0
 8. PROJ-COST         := 0
 9. PROJ-COST         := PROJ-COST     + WORKER-COST
10. DEPT-TOTAL        := DEPT-TOTAL    + PROJ-COST
11. GRAND-TOTAL       := GRAND-TOTAL   + DEPT-TOTAL
12. MOVE DEPT-NUM       INTO DETAIL-LINE
13. MOVE PROJECT-ID     INTO DETAIL-LINE
14. MOVE PROJECT-COST   INTO DETAIL-LINE
15. PRINT AND CLEAR DETAIL-LINE
16. BUILD AND PRINT DEPT-FOOTER-LINE
17. BUILD AND PRINT REPORT-FOOTER-LINE
18. CURR-DEPT-NUM     := IN-DEPT-NUM
19. CURR-PROJECT-ID   := IN-PROJECT-ID
20. STOP
21. PRINT REPORT HEADER
```

Note that Jackson often uses compound keys (NDEPTKEY, CWORKKEY, etc.) of the sort we discussed in Chapter 9. For example:

But in the interest of simplicity, we have not used compound keys here.

Note also that Jackson's list of operations depends on the language the program will be written in: if that language needs OPEN and CLOSE as COBOL does, then they must be included in the list. By contrast, Warnier leaves language-dependent instructions to be added at coding time. And Orr adds them to the augmented process structure, leaving them out of the basic structure.

For each instruction you now ask yourself: this must be executed once per what? This tells you where to write the instruction's number on the program structure diagram. The instruction numbers are written in boxes added to the program structure diagram for this purpose:

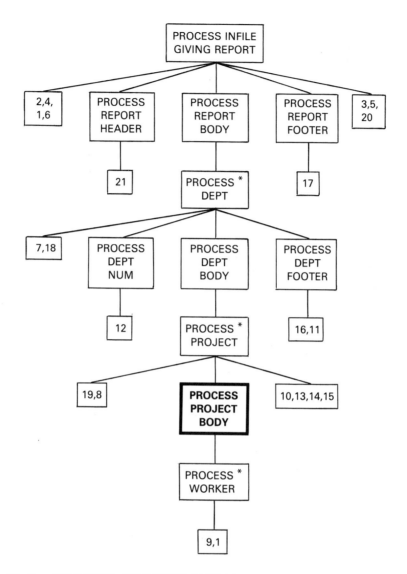

Notice PROCESS PROJECT BODY, which appears above PROCESS WORKER. This avoids the mixed constructs that would occur if the boxed instructions (19, 8, 10, 13, 14, 17) were **sequenced** with the **repetition** of WORKER.

20.4 JACKSON STEP 4: SCHEMATIC LOGIC

There's still something missing: the selection and looping conditions. Orr handles them by footnotes on Warnier/Orr diagrams; Warnier calls them "branch instructions" and shows them on his flowchart. Jackson handles them by introducing "schematic logic," a sort of pseudocode. The syntax of schematic logic is as follows. Keywords are underlined; **do** indicates a component not broken down further on this diagram.

Sequence:

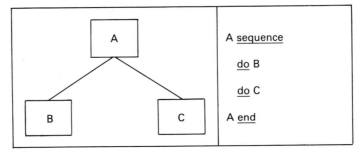

Alternation (Selection):

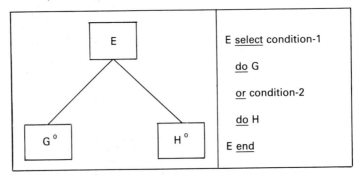

Repetition (Iteration):

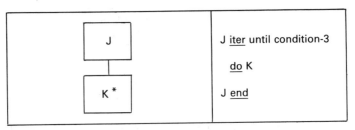

We use these rules to derive the report program's schematic logic from the program structure diagram of a couple of pages back. The result is approximately like this:

```
PROCINFILE seq
    open INFILE; open PFILE; GRAND-TOTAL:=0; read INFILE;
    PREPHDR seq
        print report header;
    PREPHDR end
    PREPBODY iter until EOF="YES"
        PDEPT seq
            CURR-DEPT-NUM := IN-DEPT-NUM;
            DEPT-TOTAL    := 0;
            PDEPTNUM seq
                move DEPT-NUM into DETAIL-LINE;
            PDEPTNUM end
            PDEPTBODY iter until EOF="YES" or CURR-DEPT-NUM not= IN-DEPT-NUM
                PPROJECT seq
                    CURR-PROJECT-ID := IN-PROJECT-ID;
                    PROJECT-COST    := 0;
                    PPROJECTBODY iter until EOF="YES"
                                         or CURR-DEPT-NUM    not= IN-DEPT-NUM
                                         or CURR-PROJECT-ID not= IN-PROJECT-ID
                        PWORKER seq
                            PROJECT-COST := PROJECT-COST + WORKER-COST;
                            read INFILE;
                        PWORKER end
                    PPROJECTBODY end
                    move PROJECT-ID   into DETAIL-LINE;
                    move PROJECT-COST into DETAIL-LINE;
                    print and clear DETAIL-LINE;
                    DEPT-TOTAL := DEPT-TOTAL + PROJECT-COST;
                PPROJECT end
            PDEPTBODY end
            PDEPTFTR seq
                build and print DEPT-FOOTER-LINE;
                GRAND-TOTAL := GRAND-TOTAL + DEPT-TOTAL;
            PDEPTFTR end
        PDEPT end
    PREPBODY end
    PREPFTR seq
        build and print REPORT-FOOTER-LINE;
    PREPFTR end
    close INFILE; close PFILE; stop;
PROCINFILE end
```

This is basically a form of pseudocode; it leaves us at the same stage as a Warnier/Orr diagram with footnotes.

20.5 JACKSON STEP 5: CODE

Now we must turn the schematic logic into code. Jackson offers two ways of doing this. The first is the same one we've been using throughout the book: each box becomes a paragraph, iterations are controlled by PERFORM. . .UNTIL, and so on. There's no need to discuss this further.

The second coding technique is totally different. It is designed to completely eliminate PERFORMs, for reasons we'll discuss later; the only control structure used is GO TO. Jackson calls this "nest-free" or "PERFORM-free" procedure code.

Once again, here are the three basic constructs. For each we show the schematic logic we've already discussed; beside it is the PERFORM-free logic outline, showing the names of the COBOL paragraphs, and any needed GO TOs.

Sequence:

A <u>sequence</u>	ASEQ.
	B--.
<u>do</u> B	. . . .
	BEND.
	C--.
<u>do</u> C	. . . .
	CEND.
A <u>end</u>	AEND.

Notice the hyphens in B-- and C--. They mean the complete names depend on which constructs are involved. For example, if B is itself a sequence of other processes, its lead paragraph will be named BSEQ rather than B. If C is an iteration, its lead paragraph will be CITER. And so on.

Alternation:

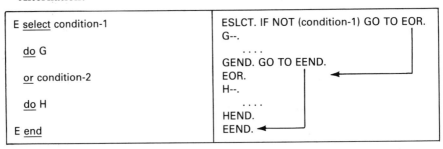

E <u>select</u> condition-1	ESLCT. IF NOT (condition-1) GO TO EOR.
	G--.
<u>do</u> G	. . . .
	GEND. GO TO EEND.
<u>or</u> condition-2	EOR.
	H--.
<u>do</u> H	. . . .
	HEND.
E <u>end</u>	EEND.

Repetition:

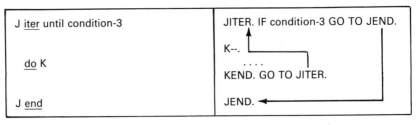

J <u>iter</u> until condition-3	JITER. IF condition-3 GO TO JEND.
	K--.
<u>do</u> K	. . . .
	KEND. GO TO JITER.
J <u>end</u>	JEND.

So the nest-free logic for the project report would be something like this:

```
PPROC-INFILE-SEQ.
    MOVE "NO" TO EOF.
    OPEN INPUT PROJECT-FILE.
    OPEN OUTPUT PRINT-FILE.
    MOVE ZERO TO GRAND-TOTAL.
    READ PROJECT-FILE AT END MOVE "YES" TO EOF.
PREP-HDR-SEQ.
    WRITE PRINT-LINE FROM REP-HDR-LINE
        AFTER ADVANCING TO-TOP-OF-PAGE.
PREP-HDR-END.
PREP-BODY-ITER.
    IF EOF = "YES" GO TO PREP-BODY-END.
PDEPT-SEQ.
    MOVE IN-DEPT-NUM      TO CURR-DEPT-NUM.
    MOVE ZERO             TO DEPT-TOTAL.
PDEPT-NUM-SEQ.
    MOVE CURR-DEPT-NUM TO DE-DEPT-NUM.
PDEPT-NUM-END.
PDEPT-BODY-ITER.
    IF EOF = "YES"
    OR CURR-DEPT-NUM NOT = IN-DEPT-NUM
        GO TO PDEPT-BODY-END.
PPROJECT-SEQ.
    MOVE IN-PROJECT-ID    TO CURR-PROJECT-ID.
    MOVE ZERO             TO PROJECT-COST.
PPROJECT-BODY-ITER.
    IF EOF = "YES"
    OR CURR-DEPT-NUM    NOT = IN-DEPT-NUM
    OR CURR-PROJECT-ID  NOT = IN-PROJECT-ID
        GO TO PPROJECT-BODY-END.
PWORKER-SEQ.
    ADD IN-WORKER-COST TO PROJECT-COST.
    READ PROJECT-FILE AT END MOVE "YES" TO EOF.
PWORKER-END.  GO TO PPROJECT-BODY-ITER.
PPROJECT-BODY-END.
    MOVE CURR-PROJECT-ID  TO DE-PROJECT-ID.
    MOVE PROJECT-COST     TO DE-PROJECT-COST.
    WRITE PRINT-LINE FROM DETAIL-LINE AFTER ADVANCING 1.
    MOVE SPACES TO DETAIL-LINE.
    ADD PROJECT-COST TO DEPT-TOTAL.
PPROJECT-END.     GO TO PDEPT-BODY-ITER.
PDEPT-BODY-END.
PDEPT-FTR-SEQ.
    MOVE DEPT-TOTAL TO DF-DEPT-TOTAL.
    WRITE PRINT-LINE FROM DEPT-FTR-LINE AFTER ADVANCING 1.
    ADD DEPT-TOTAL TO GRAND-TOTAL.
PDEPT-FTR-END.
PDEPT-END.        GO TO PREP-BODY-ITER.
PREP-BODY-END.
PREP-FTR-SEQ.
    MOVE GRAND-TOTAL TO RF-GRAND-TOTAL.
    WRITE PRINT-LINE FROM REP-FTR-LINE.
PREP-FTR-END.
    CLOSE PROJECT-FILE.
    CLOSE PRINT-FILE.
    STOP RUN.
PPROC-INFILE-END.
```

It might be made easier to read by judicious indentation.

Once again we find a striking similarity between the apparently remote techniques of Jackson and Warnier. Jackson's nest-free coding is essentially identical to Warnier's sorted instruction list: both use the GO TO as the only control structure. The difference is that Jackson uses paragraph names instead of numbers, and has a few more of them because his ban on mixed constructs introduces some extra levels.

20.6 *SOME THOUGHTS ON TOOLS*

There is no doubt that Jackson's boxes are more pictorial than brackets. Nevertheless, I think the brackets are preferable for a couple of reasons.

First, brackets are useful all the way from data structure through process structure to code structure. With boxes we must eventually switch to schematic logic because there isn't room to write details in the boxes.

But the second reason seems to me to be more important. It has to do with the nature of hierarchies. There are at least two kinds of hierarchy in the world: we can call them **chain-of-command** and **subset** hierarchies. A chain-of-command hierarchy consists of independent units, all but one of which are subordinate to others. For example:

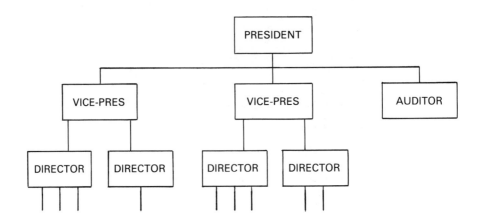

and so on. Each unit *commands* those below it on the chart. The president has his or her own existence, distinct from the vice presidents, and would still exist even if they didn't.

A subset hierarchy, on the other hand, consists of successively narrower groupings. Consider, for example, this catalog of an animal fancier's menagerie:

PETS	DOGS	HUNTERS	Rex, Rover
		LAP DOGS	ChiChi
		MONGRELS	Ruff
	CATS	SIAMESE	Rafael
		OTHER	Simon, Midnight, Tom

This collection of pets *consists of* dogs and cats; it has no existence apart from them. That's what distinguishes a subset hierarchy from chain of command.

Those, then, are the two types of hierarchies. How should they be diagrammed?

The organization-chart diagram we drew for our executives is the standard way of representing chain-of-command hierarchies. It is often used in programming. Consider this program structure diagram, for example:

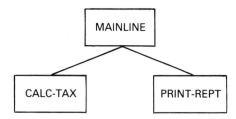

The standard meaning of this diagram is: MAINLINE is a piece of logic to accomplish some function. It contains perhaps dozens or hundreds of lines of code. It invokes two lower-level functions to carry out its task: CALC-TAX and PRINT-REPT. Most people find this interpretation quite natural; in fact we used it several times earlier in the book without explanation.

But this is not what the diagram means in Jackson's method. In his notation it means that MAINLINE **consists** of CALC-TAX and PRINT-REPT. Take them away and there's nothing left.

In other words, it seems to me that Jackson's diagrams risk confusion by making a subset hierarchy look like a chain of command.

The chance of confusion seems especially great for data structures. Here is a common sort of data-base diagram. It represents a department record to which some project records are attached:

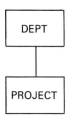

That is, for each department we have a DEPT record and perhaps some PROJECT records. But the Jackson interpretation of this diagram would be that DEPT *consists of* a PROJECT record; there is no separate department record.

I think things are clearer all around if we reserve the box diagrams for chain-of-command hierarchies; that's their established meaning. For representing a subset hierarchy, Warnier/Orr diagrams seem the clear choice:

```
                              ⎧         ⎧ HUNTERS   ⎧ Rex
                              ⎪         ⎪           ⎩ Rover
                              ⎪         ⎪
                   ⎧   DOGS   ⎨   LAP DOGS { ChiChi
                   ⎪          ⎪
                   ⎪          ⎩   MONGRELS { Ruff
            PETS   ⎨
                   ⎪          ⎧   SIAMESE  { Rafael
                   ⎪          ⎪
                   ⎩   CATS   ⎨                      ⎧ Simon
                              ⎩   OTHER    ⎨ Midnight
                                                     ⎩ Tom
```

Strictly speaking, entries at the same level in the above diagram (e.g., DOGS and CATS) should be separated by a plus sign + to show that order is not material here. But the plus sign is often omitted.

20.7 SUMMARY

Here is a brief summary of Jackson's techniques as we have seen them so far:

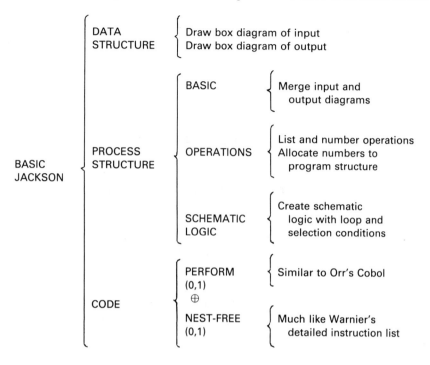

FURTHER READING

For details of the material sketched in this chapter, see Chapters 1 to 3 of *Principles of Program Design* by Jackson. You may also want to look at Chapters 4 and 5, which we won't be treating.

For a tutorial on Jackson's ideas on both program design and system design, see Cameron's book, *JSP & JSD: The Jackson Approach to Software Development.*

21

Jackson: Backtracking and Inversion

In the previous chapter we introduced Jackson's basic methods by applying them to a simple problem. Now we will look at two of Jackson's more advanced techniques: backtracking and program inversion. These techniques attack many of the same problems as Warnier's processing phases, described in Chapter 19.

Recall Warnier's processing phases. If you need an identification criterion that's not on the input, then you must develop it, be it switch or counter or calculated field. You use the switch/counter/calculation as input to a new processing phase.

Jackson's approach is to analyze *why* you need a field that is not on the input. He offers two reasons:

1. The need to make assumptions on insufficient evidence: he deals with this by "backtracking."
2. Structure clashes: he deals with these by "program inversion." (This is quite different from hierarchy inversion, which we discussed in Parts II and III.)

We turn first to backtracking.

21.1 BASIC BACKTRACKING

Suppose your grocery store begins to stock kiwi fruit. You've never seen it before, but you're the adventurous type. If it tastes good, you want to buy it and eat it; otherwise you want to leave it alone. Diagrammatically:

258

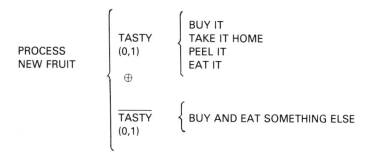

But how can you tell if it's tasty? Since a large man in a store uniform is standing nearby, nibbling is out of the question. Only one course is open: assume it tastes good. Buy it, take it home, peel it, and take a bite. In other words, do much of the processing that's appropriate to a tasty fruit. Only after that first bite will you know if kiwi fruit really is tasty.

If it is, you'll finish eating it. If you don't like it, however, you will naturally quit eating it—that is, stop the "tasty" processing. You will admit your assumption was wrong, and will go to not-tasty processing, which tells you to buy and eat something else.

This is the basic model behind Jackson's **backtracking**. If it's impossible to tell from the input which branch of a selection is correct, you **posit** (assume) that one of them is and begin the processing of that branch. Any time you discover evidence that contradicts the assumption, you **quit** processing that branch, **admit** the other one is correct, and go there to continue processing. We introduce the posit/quit/admit into our diagram the following way:

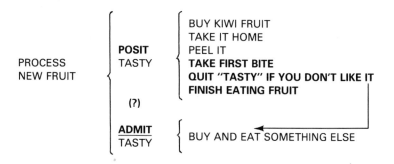

The symbol (?) is one I just made up to separate posit from admit on Warnier/Orr diagrams. For this is a new breed of diagram: the admit part gets done only if control transfers there from inside posit.

In fact the above logic may not be enough. If you don't like kiwi fruit, you will reach "admit not tasty" with an unpleasant substance in your mouth: this is the unavoidable *side effect* of the "posit tasty" processing. We must further refine (if that's the word) the solution:

```
                                    ┌ BUY KIWI FRUIT
                                    │ TAKE IT HOME
                        POSIT       │ PEEL IT
                        TASTY       { TAKE FIRST BITE
                                    │ QUIT "TASTY" IF YOU DON'T LIKE IT
                                    └ FINISH EATING FRUIT
PROCESS        {        (?)
NEW FRUIT
                        ADMIT       { EJECT FIRST BITE INTO SUITABLE RECEPTACLE
                        TASTY       { BUY AND EAT SOMETHING ELSE
```

We have now seen the basic principles of Jackson's backtracking. Here's an outline of the three phases or stages. (Note that Jackson's three phases of backtracking have nothing to do with Warnier's processing phases.)

```
                        SELECT      ┌ WRITE THE CHOICE AS AN ORDINARY
                                    │   TWO-PRONGED SELECTION WITH ⊕
                                    │
                                    └ FILL IN ACTIONS APPROPRIATE TO EACH PRONG

                                    ┌ CHANGE ⊕ to (?)
                                    │
                                    │ CHANGE FIRST ALTERNATIVE TO "POSIT"
                                    │
BACKTRACKING { POSIT/               { CHANGE SECOND ALTERNATIVE TO "ADMIT"
               ADMIT/               │
               QUIT                 │ INSERT A "QUIT" STATEMENT ANYWHERE
                                    │   THE "POSIT" COULD BE PROVED WRONG
                                    │   (THE KIWI FRUIT ONLY NEEDED ONE
                                    └   QUIT, BUT ANY NUMBER IS POSSIBLE)

               HANDLE
               SIDE                 { MORE ON THIS LATER
               EFFECTS
```

We'll now explore the technique in more detail.

21.2 IMPLEMENTING BACKTRACKING

This three-phase approach provides a useful avenue of attack for certain types of problems. But how shall we program the result?

One way is to use Jackson's PERFORM-free coding; then each quit is implemented as a GO TO to the admit logic. You will find the details in Jackson's book.

But suppose you're committed to PERFORMs. Then what will you do? How do you handle posit, admit, and (especially) quit?

Here is one approach. Jackson interprets quit as branching to the **start of admit**. If we regard it as branching to the **end of posit** instead, we have something more general on our hands. In fact, it is equivalent to the EXIT or BREAK statement.

EXIT or BREAK is often suggested as an addition to the big three structures of sequence, selection, and repetition. It provides a clean way to leave a routine (i.e., to leave a bracket):

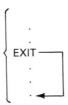

Suppose we have an EXIT or BREAK statement; then we can turn our diagram into something programmable by using a switch:

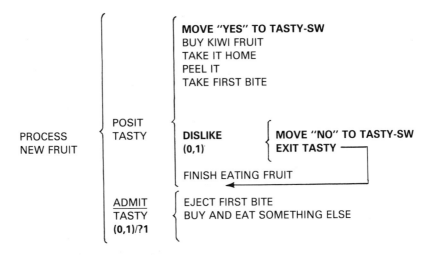

?1/ IF TASTY-SW = "NO"

The symbol (?) has disappeared: this is now a perfectly ordinary Warnier/Orr diagram where the posit always happens and the admit sometimes does. The line from EXIT to the end of posit is for pedagogical purposes; it's not part of the diagram, though I suppose it wouldn't hurt to include it.

The revised diagram can be coded in COBOL with PERFORMs, using the basic rules from Chapter 4. The EXIT is coded as GO TO the end of the POSIT-TASTY routine. Yes, the dreaded GO TO—but used here to express a useful, well controlled construct. The compiler always implements selection and repetition with GO TOs in the generated machine code; we are just playing compiler because of an unfortunate deficiency in the language.

Here is what the routine would look like in a COBOL that contained kiwi fruit extensions but still lacked an EXIT or BREAK statement:

```
NEW-FRUIT.
    PERFORM POSIT-TASTY THRU EXIT-POSIT-TASTY.
    IF TASTY-SW = "NO"
        PERFORM ADMIT-NOT-TASTY.
    GOBACK.

POSIT-TASTY.
    MOVE "YES" TO TASTY-SW.
    BUY NEW FRUIT.
    TAKE IT HOME.
    PEEL IT.
    TAKE FIRST BITE.
    IF DISLIKE
        MOVE "NO" TO TASTY-SW
        GO TO EXIT-POSIT-TASTY.
    FINISH EATING FRUIT.
EXIT-POSIT-TASTY.

ADMIT-NOT-TASTY.
    EJECT FIRST BITE.
    BUY AND EAT SOMETHING ELSE.
```

Jackson opposes this way of doing things: he prefers that you use PERFORM-free COBOL so the quit can go directly to the admit part. He thinks the switch TASTY-SW just obscures things.

You may be wondering what all the fuss is about. Why not put the ADMIT processing right after the DISLIKE test:

```
IF DISLIKE
    EJECT FIRST BITE
    BUY AND EAT SOMETHING ELSE
OTHERWISE
    FINISH EATING FRUIT.
```

In this case that would work fine, but this example has been kept simple. See Jackson's book for examples of backtracking with multiple quits (for example, the daisy-chain problem), where such simple tests don't make much sense.

21.3 ANOTHER BACKTRACKING EXAMPLE

Here is a more conventional data processing example of backtracking. Suppose the transaction file for a program consists of one card per transaction, sorted on customer number, with a card at the end of each customer group giving the total number of transactions for that customer:

$$
\text{COMPANY} \left\{ \text{CUSTOMER} \left\{ \begin{array}{l} \text{TRANS} \\ (1,T) \\ \\ \text{TOTCARD} \end{array} \right. \right.
$$

(1,C)

If the count shown on a customer's TOTCARD is accurate, all transactions for that customer (but not the total card) are written to a validated transaction file; if the count is wrong, all transactions for the customer (along with the total card) are written to an error file. Thus we need to distinguish good customer groups from bad, and the structure is:

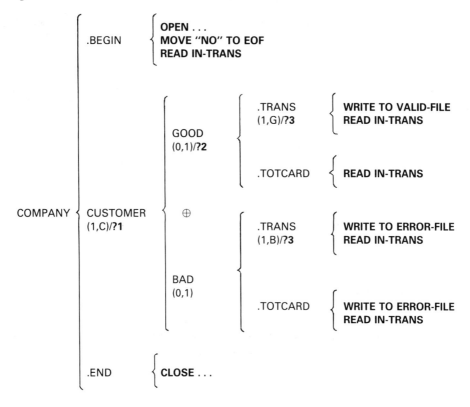

We can quickly go through Phase 1: insert the actions into the above selection diagram. The result is:

?1/ **UNTIL EOF = "YES"**
?2/ **. . .**
?3/ **UNTIL CARDTYPE = TOTAL**

There is no way to write footnote ?2 based on the input. We will need to make an assumption and be prepared to backtrack on it.

Now we can move to phase 2—switching to posit/quit/admit. In this case it's very simple to insert the quit:

```
                  ┌ .BEGIN    ┌ OPEN ...
                  │           │ MOVE "NO" TO EOF
                  │           └ READ IN-TRANS
                  │
                  │                                ┌ .BEGIN      { SET CALC-COUNT = 0
                  │                                │
                  │                    ┌ POSIT     │                          ┌ ADD 1 TO CALC-COUNT
                  │                    │  GOOD     │ .TRANS                   │ WRITE TO VALID-FILE
                  │                    │           │ (1,G)/?3                 └ READ IN-TRANS
                  │                    │           │
COMPANY ┤ CUSTOMER ┤ (?)              │            │                          ┌ QUIT GOOD IF CALC-COUNT
         │ (1,C)/?1  │                 │           │ .TOTCARD                 │   NOT = IN-COUNT
                  │                    │           │                          └ READ IN-TRANS
                  │                    │
                  │                    │           ┌ .TRANS                   ┌ WRITE TO ERROR-FILE
                  │                    │  ADMIT     │ (1,B)/?3                 └ READ IN-TRANS
                  │                    │  BAD       │
                  │                    │            │ .TOTCARD                 ┌ WRITE TO ERROR-FILE
                  │                                 │                          └ READ IN-TRANS
                  │
                  └ .END      { CLOSE ...
```

?1/ UNTIL EOF = "YES"
?3/ UNTIL CARDTYPE = TOTAL

Now for phase 3 of the backtracking: handling side effects. The big problem is the WRITE TO VALID-FILE in POSIT GOOD: by the time we get to ADMIT BAD, the transactions will already have been read and written. How can we unread and unwrite them?

Jackson devotes considerable attention to side effects, specifically to intolerable ones like having inedible food in your mouth or bad batches on the VALID-FILE.

He offers two basic approaches. Here is what they would mean in our example:

1. **Do and undo.** Acquire or create a write routine that, besides the usual OPEN, WRITE, and CLOSE operations, has two more: NOTE and RESTORE. NOTE will "remember" the current status of the file; RESTORE will restore the status as of the last NOTE.

   Then just NOTE the statuses of the INFILE and VALID-FILE at the start of POSIT GOOD, and RESTORE them to that state at the start of ADMIT BAD.

2. **Pretend.** Make the following changes in POSIT GOOD:

   - at the beginning of POSIT GOOD: OPEN SCRATCHFILE
   - change WRITE TO VALID-FILE to say WRITE TO SCRATCHFILE
   - at the end of POSIT GOOD, copy SCRATCHFILE to VALID-FILE and then close SCRATCHFILE
   - at the beginning of ADMIT BAD: copy SCRATCHFILE to ERROR-FILE and close SCRATCHFILE

   That is, just pretend to write to TRANSFILE as you process each card; really write to TRANSFILE after you have survived the quit.

The distinction may strike you as artificial; after all, an I/O routine that lets you "restore" TRANSFILE to what it was 20 records ago must have just pretended to print the lines in the first place. It must really have held them in core, or on a temporary file.

But there is an important difference between the two approaches. Once the sophisticated I/O routine is implemented, you can use it in any problem where it helps, whereas pretending is a technique you must reimplement every time it is used.

We have done all our exposition of backtracking using Warnier/Orr diagrams. (Note that we have redrawn the diagram at each phase of this problem for pedagogical purposes; in real life you would normally progress through all three phases on the same copy of the diagram, just adding a few lines at each stage.) But of course Jackson doesn't use Warnier/Orr diagrams.

We should show a solution using Jackson's tools. The schematic logic for phase 3 with "do and undo" would be something like this:

```
PFILE seq
    open IN-TRANS, VALID-FILE, ERROR-FILE; read IN-TRANS;
    PFILEBODY iter until EOF="YES"
        PCUST posit GOOD
            note IN-TRANS, VALID-FILE;
            CALC-COUNT := 0
            PGOODTXGRP iter until TOT-CARD-READ
                PGOODTX seq
                    CALC-COUNT := CALC-COUNT + 1;
                    write to VALID-FILE;
                    read IN-TRANS;
                PGOODTX end
            PGOODTXGRP end
            PGOODTOTCD seq
        PCUST    quit if CALC-COUNT not= IN-COUNT
                read IN-TRANS;
            PGOODTOTCD end
        PCUST admit BAD
            restore IN-TRANS, VALID-FILE;
            PBADTXGRP iter until TOT-CARD-READ
                PBADTX seq
                    write to ERROR-FILE;
                    read IN-TRANS;
                PBADTX end
            PBADTXGRP end
            PBADTOTCD seq
                write to ERROR-FILE;
                read IN-TRANS;
            PBADTOTCD end
        PCUST end
    PFILEBODY end
    close IN-TRANS, VALID-FILE, ERROR-FILE; stop
PFILE end
```

Backtracking seems to be a very useful tool. It brings together in a methodical way many techniques (switches, counters, saving-and-restoring, temporary files) that are often worked out only by trial and error.

21.4 BACKGROUND TO PROGRAM INVERSION

We turn now to Jackson's second major technique: program inversion. This is quite different from the hierarchy inversion we discussed in Parts II and III; we'll see the difference shortly.

Recall that in Chapter 13 we created a physical input mapping for the Employee Loan List. We wanted to create these coroutines:

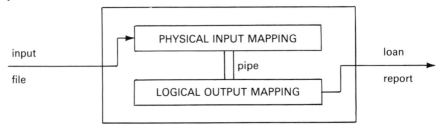

We easily worked out a data structured input mapping that could run as a coroutine. It looked like this:

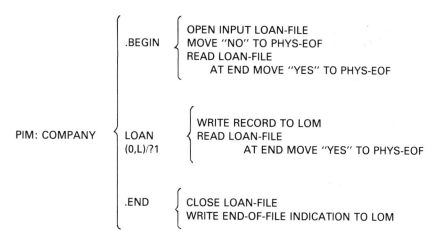

PIM: COMPANY
- .BEGIN
  - OPEN INPUT LOAN-FILE
  - MOVE "NO" TO PHYS-EOF
  - READ LOAN-FILE
    - AT END MOVE "YES" TO PHYS-EOF
- LOAN (0,L)/?1
  - WRITE RECORD TO LOM
  - READ LOAN-FILE
    - AT END MOVE "YES" TO PHYS-EOF
- .END
  - CLOSE LOAN-FILE
  - WRITE END-OF-FILE INDICATION TO LOM

?1/ UNTIL PHYS-EOF = "YES"

But unfortunately COBOL for most systems doesn't support such coroutines; we are forced into the subroutine mold:

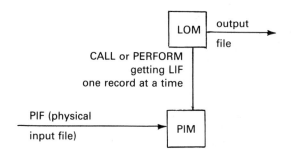

To make this work we **restructured** the PIM. We inverted the hierarchy of the file that the PIM had to produce. The result was this basic structure for the subroutine:

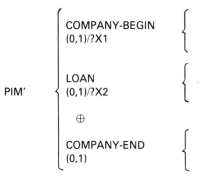

PIM'
- COMPANY-BEGIN (0,1)/?X1
- LOAN (0,1)/?X2
- ⊕
- COMPANY-END (0,1)

?X1/ IF FIRST TIME THROUGH
?X2/ IF NOT AT END OF PHYSICAL INPUT

This restructuring formed the basis of all our input subroutines in Part III.

21.5 PROGRAM INVERSION: PROGRAMMING WITH BOOKMARKS

Jackson's approach is different. He offers a way to make the PIM run as a subroutine *without restructuring it.*

Basically the idea is this. Write the PIM as if it were a stand-alone program or genuine coroutine. Then, whenever the PIM wants to "write" a record to the LOM, it just has to move the record into its linkage section and GOBACK. Like so:

```
PROCEDURE DIVISION USING END-LOGICAL-INPUT
                         LOG-IN-RECORD.
COMPANY.
      PERFORM COMPANY-BEGIN.
      PERFORM LOAN UNTIL PHYS-EOF = "YES".
      PERFORM COMPANY-END.
      GOBACK.

COMPANY-BEGIN.
      OPEN INPUT LOAN-FILE.
      MOVE "NO" TO PHYS-EOF.
      READ LOAN-FILE
        AT END MOVE "YES" TO PHYS-EOF.

LOAN.
      MOVE IN-EE-NAME     TO LOG-IN-EE-NAME.
      MOVE IN-LOAN-AMOUNT TO LOG-IN-LOAN-AMOUNT.
      GOBACK.
      READ LOAN-FILE
        AT END MOVE "YES" TO PHYS-EOF.

COMPANY-END.
      CLOSE LOAN-FILE.
      MOVE "YES" TO END-LOGICAL-INPUT.
```

But of course we have a problem: How will processing ever continue past the GOBACK? How will we read the next record? What will happen the next time the LOM is called?

Jackson's solution is to have the PIM *remember* where it is when it does a GOBACK. Then the next time it's called, it can pick up exactly where it left off, just as if nothing had happened.

To accomplish this he creates a field that acts as a sort of bookmark in the PIM; in fact, we will call the field BOOKMARK. (Jackson calls it QS, or the state variable, or the text pointer.)

The result is something like this:

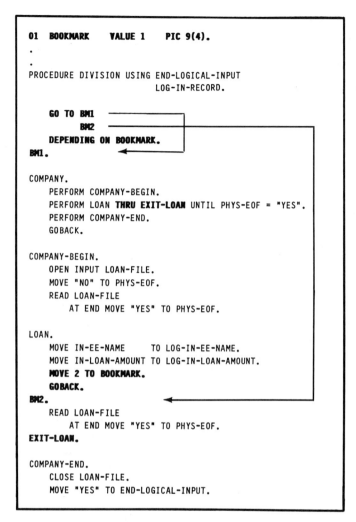

```
01  BOOKMARK    VALUE 1    PIC 9(4).
    .
    .
PROCEDURE DIVISION USING END-LOGICAL-INPUT
                        LOG-IN-RECORD.

    GO TO BM1
          BM2
    DEPENDING ON BOOKMARK.
BM1.

COMPANY.
    PERFORM COMPANY-BEGIN.
    PERFORM LOAN THRU EXIT-LOAN UNTIL PHYS-EOF = "YES".
    PERFORM COMPANY-END.
    GOBACK.

COMPANY-BEGIN.
    OPEN INPUT LOAN-FILE.
    MOVE "NO" TO PHYS-EOF.
    READ LOAN-FILE
        AT END MOVE "YES" TO PHYS-EOF.

LOAN.
    MOVE IN-EE-NAME      TO LOG-IN-EE-NAME.
    MOVE IN-LOAN-AMOUNT TO LOG-IN-LOAN-AMOUNT.
    MOVE 2 TO BOOKMARK.
    GOBACK.
BM2.
    READ LOAN-FILE
        AT END MOVE "YES" TO PHYS-EOF.
EXIT-LOAN.

COMPANY-END.
    CLOSE LOAN-FILE.
    MOVE "YES" TO END-LOGICAL-INPUT.
```

If your COBOL is rusty, it may help to know that:

$$\text{GO TO A1, A2, } \ldots \text{, An DEPENDING ON X}$$

means:

$$\text{IF X = 1 GO TO A1}$$
$$\text{ELSE IF X = 2 GO TO A2}$$
$$. \qquad .$$
$$. \qquad .$$
$$\text{ELSE IF X = n GO TO An.}$$

It works like this:

- Immediately before doing a "write" GOBACK, the subroutine points BOOK-MARK to just after the GOBACK. (Of course there can be any number of these "write" GOBACKs, though our example only had one.)
- When control returns to the module, the GO TO DEPENDING ON branches directly to the paragraph after the GOBACK and execution continues as if nothing had happened.

Thus, no restructuring is necessary for the PIM (or any other coroutine implemented as a subroutine). The process structure based on its original data structure works fine.

21.6 NOTES ON BOOKMARKS

Program inversion—programming with bookmarks—raises a number of issues. Here are some.

1. Never trust a PERFORM? The bookmarked code we developed above has its risks. It doesn't say anywhere in the COBOL language specification that PERFORM chains are to be maintained when a called module issues a GOBACK.

So a compiler writer is free to blow PERFORM pointers to smithereens on GOBACK. Then our clever logic to get back into the middle of the PERFORMed LOAN routine on re-entry will go for naught. The program will probably die when we get to EXIT-LOAN.

So what can you do?

One possibility is: relax. If your compiler currently maintains a module's PERFORM chains from one call to the next, you can go ahead and use bookmarks. If the compiler ever changes the rules, you can just merge the PIM and the LOM into a single compiled program, perhaps by making the PIM a section in the LOM. After a small change to replace the GOBACK by a PERFORM exit, your program will work again.

If this doesn't appeal to you, you may be interested to hear that it doesn't appeal to Jackson either. That is the main reason he devised the PERFORM-free (nest-free) COBOL we discussed in the previous chapter. If you don't have any PERFORMs, the compiler obviously can't destroy your PERFORM chains when you GOBACK.

(Incidentally, you don't have to abandon PERFORMs altogether. You're welcome to put calculations and edits and the like into PERFORMed routines, because control never returns to the caller during one of these routines.)

Before deciding to use the PERFORM-free code, take a careful look at the sample in the previous chapter to be sure you can live with it.

2. Initializing BOOKMARK. We initialized BOOKMARK with a VALUE clause. This causes the usual result of not being able to restart the routine during the same run. If this is a problem, you will have to rely on the LOM main line to either (1) call a separate entry point to kick things off, or (2) hold BOOKMARK in its working storage.

3. GO TO considered harmful? Some people may object to program inversion on the grounds that it uses a GO TO. I'm as wary of GO TOs as the next person, but this one doesn't disturb me. It is well defined and controlled; it's just doing the job that would be done in the machine code (with a GO TO) if the compiler and operating system were sophisticated enough to support coroutines directly.

Nevertheless, it is irresponsible to use this technique without management approval in programs to be maintained by other people; it takes getting used to, to say the least.

4. It's not as easy as it looks. We picked a straightforward example. If you do much playing with inversion, you will soon discover that there are headaches. If you are inverting a program and converting its input or output to CALLs or GOBACKs, what do you do with the OPEN and CLOSE statements? Sometimes you can just delete them, but sometimes that gets you into trouble. Jackson's book has an extensive discussion.

5. Only in a clash. It has only been implicit so far, and we should make it explicit: neither Warnier nor Jackson would write a separate input mapping in this case, where the input has the same structure as the output.

6. READ and WRITE. We have been using the PIM as an example; thus, the GOBACKs have simulated WRITEs. There is no difference in principle if you want to make the LOM a subroutine and the PIM the main line. Then the GO-BACKs in the inverted LOM will be simulating READs instead.

21.7 INTERLEAVING CLASHES

So far we have been dealing with what Jackson refers to as "boundary clashes": all data is there, in the right order, but the boundaries of pages (for example) don't correspond to the boundaries of departments.

We saw a second type of structure clash in Part III: an ordering clash. The input and output files were in different orders. Resolving the clash required either (1) a sort or (2) a Big Ole Matrix to let us get the file into core columnwise, then use it rowwise.

There is a third and final type of structure clash identified by Jackson: the interleaving clash. The typical example is provided by a company that rents rowboats. Every time a boat is rented, a "borrow" transaction is input to the system; when it is returned, a "return" transaction is input. Both transactions specify the boat number.

If there is only one boat, the stream of transactions for the day will have the structure:

DAY { SESSION (1,S) { BORROW {

RETURN {

But suppose the company prospers and buys more boats. Then the file will have interleaved files for all boats. Using the concurrency symbol + that we introduced in Chapter 10, we can draw:

```
        ┌                    ┌                    ┌ BORROW  {
        │                    │ SESSION   ┌
        │ BOAT 1   ┌         │ (1,S1)    └ RETURN  {
        │
        │          +
        │                    ┌                    ┌ BORROW  {
        │ BOAT 2             │ SESSION   ┌
DAY    ┤          ┤          │ (1,S2)    └ RETURN  {
        │          +
        │          .
        │          .
        │          +
        │                    ┌                    ┌ BORROW  {
        │ BOAT n             │ SESSION   ┌
        │                    │ (1,Sn)    ┤
        └                    └                    └ RETURN  {
```

This can be abbreviated to:

```
         ┌            ┌                  ┌ BORROW  {
         │ + BOAT     │ SESSION   ┌
DAY     ┤  (n)       ┤ (1,Sn)    ┤
         │            │                  └ RETURN  {
         └            └
```

Here we have used the convention introduced in Chapter 12: putting an operator (in this case +) before a repeated item has the effect of inserting the operator between all pairs of the repeated set.

In fact if we don't care about boats, just about sessions, we could look at this as:

```
         ┌               ┌ BORROW  {
         │ + SESSION     │
DAY     ┤  (1,S)        ┤
         │               │
         └               └ RETURN  {
```

The operator of the boat rental company wants a report of how many BOAT-HOURS of rentals there were today. Recalling that putting an operator in a box makes it arithmetic, we can write:

That is, take the sum over all sessions of the difference between RETURN-TIME and BORROW-TIME. One way to do this calculation is to ignore all the issues raised by concurrent sessions and write:

```
                        ┌ TOTAL-RETURN   ┌ [+] RETURN-TIME
                        │                │     (1,SN)
                        │                └
            BOAT-HOURS {  [−]
                        │
                        │ TOTAL-BORROW   ┌ [+] BORROW-TIME
                        └                └     (1,SN)
```

That is, add up all the return times, and subtract the total of the finish times.

Jackson opposes this approach. He argues that you may have answered the user's question today, but tomorrow he will be back with: What is the median length of a session? The length of the longest session? And so on. If your system is designed as shown above, you will have to throw it out and start again in order to answer the new questions.

True. Mind you, in this simple example the program diagrammed above can be implemented in what—an hour? If the user never comes back with more questions, you've saved him a lot of money. If he does come back, you've only lost an hour, and you've given him his first results much earlier than he otherwise would have gotten them.

Nevertheless, when the problem gets complicated enough to warrant a nontrivial solution, Jackson provides an interesting one that uses inversion. In outline his approach is as follows.

Since all those boat structures are in the file concurrently, he creates concurrent BOAT routines. And since all the boat structures are the same, he reduces all these BOAT routines to one. This single routine keeps a separate copy of its working storage in core or on disk for each boat and reloads it when a record for that boat needs processing. This copy is called the "state vector." Essentially, it is a direct access master record.

21.8 OTHER JACKSONISMS

There is more to Jackson than we have described here, and there is, of course, not room here for a full treatment. But it is worth making space for his rules of optimization. They should be engraved on the heart of every programmer:

1. Don't do it.
2. (For experts only) Don't do it yet.

That is, make the program right before you make it fast. Even when the program is right, don't optimize unless you have proof that the program spends a significant amount of time in the logic in question. Optimization costs money to implement, and it results in harder-to-understand code. There has to be a clear and sizeable benefit to offset these disadvantages.

21.9 SUMMARY

Backtracking is a technique to use when you can't tell from the input which of two alternatives holds. It is a formalized guessing game that looks like this:

BACKTRACKING

- SELECT
  - WRITE THE CHOICE AS AN ORDINARY TWO-PRONGED SELECTION WITH $\oplus$
  - FILL IN ACTIONS APPROPRIATE TO EACH PRONG
- POSIT/ADMIT/QUIT
  - CHANGE $\oplus$ TO (?)
  - CHANGE FIRST ALTERNATIVE TO "POSIT"
  - CHANGE SECOND ALTERNATIVE TO "ADMIT"
  - INSERT A "QUIT" STATEMENT ANYWHERE THE "POSIT" COULD BE PROVED WRONG
- HANDLE SIDE EFFECTS
  - DO AND UNDO (0,1)
    - SAVE STATUS AT BEGINNING OF POSIT
    - RESTORE IN ADMIT
  - $\oplus$
  - PRETEND (0,1)
    - USE SCRATCH FILES AND VARIABLES IN POSIT
    - TRANSFER TO REAL FILES AND VARIABLES AT END OF POSIT

Program inversion is programming with a bookmark. To make a coroutine into a subroutine you keep its structure intact, using GOBACK to handle I/O to the calling module:

- just before GOBACK, BOOKMARK is set to point at the next line;
- at module re-entry, GO TO DEPENDING ON branches to where execution left off.

Optimization:

1. Don't do it.
2. Don't do it yet.

Finally, here is an outline of some of the differences (other than boxes vs. brackets) between Jackson and Orr.

1. Jackson assumes you know which input to use; Orr uses the output to figure out which input is needed.
2. Jackson sticks to one structure per file; Orr often considers the same file to have different structures (e.g., logical and physical) concurrently.
3. Orr gives a procedure for deriving an exhaustive list of required instructions.
4. Jackson gives techniques (lookahead and backtracking) for dealing with "recognition difficulties."
5. Jackson resolves structure clashes by program inversion; Orr uses hierarchy inversion.

FURTHER READING

For more details on these and other subjects, see Chapters 6 to 10 of Jackson's *Principles of Program Design*.

22

Goal Directed Programming

Data structured program design is very useful, but it's not a panacea. There are problems where the input and output data structures just aren't very interesting: they aren't elaborate enough to provide the entire solution. A designer needs other tools. We saw an example in Chapter 17 when we considered how to derive the update routine in the absence of a transaction log.

When data structure doesn't solve your problem, there are lots of other approaches available. This isn't a book on every known approach to program design, so we won't attempt to cover them. Nevertheless, I can't resist offering a glimpse at goal directed programming, because it relates so closely to Orr's ideas on the primacy of output.

This chapter will develop the ideas informally, with virtually no reference to symbolic logic. The objective is to familiarize you with some basic concepts so you can see the big picture as you proceed with further reading.

22.1 BASIC CONCEPTS

Goal directed programming consists of

1. Describing how things should be after your program executes, and then
2. Working backward from this statement of the goal to create the program.

You can see that goal directed programming is closely related to Orr's output oriented approach; you could describe Orr's LOS as a statement of the goal.

We will re-examine one of our examples to introduce the new terminology, then see how goal directed programming can generalize the techniques we have been looking at.

Recall the Employee Loan program first described in Chapter 4. We wanted to produce a report describing all L employee loans outstanding. We can introduce a **goal** assertion into a bare bones process diagram:

LOAN PRINT PROGRAM

{**all L loans have been printed properly**}

We use braces to surround such **assertions**. An assertion is not an executable statement; it's more like a comment.

If our program satisfies this goal condition, it will be a success. We don't have much to start with; the **precondition** is that nothing has been done:

{**no loans have been printed properly**}

LOAN PRINT PROGRAM

{all L loans have been printed properly}

Suppose we know that we have to write a loop. We introduce the concept of **loop invariant:** an assertion that is true whenever the loop exit condition is tested. Looking at the goal and precondition, it is easy to derive the invariant for this loop:

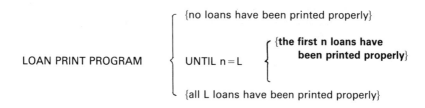

We have written the loop exit condition (UNTIL $n = L$) into the diagram rather than as a footnote, but the important thing here is the invariant itself. We say that whenever control reaches the top of the loop, the assertion will be true. The first time it will be true for $n = 0$; the second time for $n = 1$; and so on.

Filling in the body of the loop would be a straightforward exercise; we won't pursue it. The reason for going through this is to introduce the goal directed strategy for developing a loop. Briefly, it is this:

STRATEGY FOR
DEVELOPING
A LOOP

- WRITE THE GOAL ASSERTION G
- WRITE THE PRECONDITION P
- FROM G (AND MAYBE P) DEVELOP A LOOP INVARIANT I AND AN EXIT CONDITION X
- WRITE INITIALIZING LOGIC TO ESTABLISH I GIVEN P
- WRITE THE BODY OF THE LOOP TO MAINTAIN I AND PROGRESS TOWARD X

The first two points—write the goal and precondition—apply to all goal directed programming, not just to loops.

In looking at the loan report, we got only the most general idea how this strategy works. Here is a more detailed example. It is adapted from David Gries' book, *The Science of Programming*.

22.2 A DETAILED EXAMPLE OF GOAL DIRECTED PROGRAMMING

Suppose we are given a number N, which is greater than zero. We want to approximate its positive square root. That is, we want to find x, where x is the largest integer not exceeding $\sqrt{N}$.

$$0 =< x \quad \text{and} \quad x =< \sqrt{N} \quad \text{and} \quad \sqrt{N} < x+1$$

Our system, unfortunately, offers no square root function.

Step 1: State G and P. As with the loans program, we start by writing a goal assertion that must be satisfied when execution finishes. In fact we just wrote such an assertion. But we'd prefer one that didn't mention square root explicitly, since our system can't handle square root. So we square the last two expressions in the above figure and get:

$$0 \leq x \quad \text{and} \quad x \leq \sqrt{N} \quad \text{and} \quad \sqrt{N} < x+1$$

We now write the goal and preconditions into a Warnier/Orr diagram:

APPROXIMATE
THE SQUARE
ROOT OF N

$\{N>0\}$

?

$\{0 \leq x \ \text{and} \ x^2 \leq N \ \text{and} \ N < (x+1)^2\}$

Step 2: Pick I and X. Suppose we decide to try a loop. What should be its exit condition? One of the standard approaches of goal directed programming is to split up the goal condition: use part of it as an exit condition, the rest as the invariant. Using the last part for the exit condition gives:

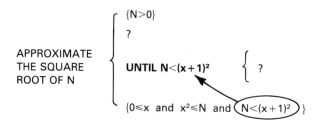

APPROXIMATE
THE SQUARE
ROOT OF N

$\{N>0\}$

?

UNTIL $N<(x+1)^2$?

$\{0 \leq x$ and $x^2 \leq N$ and $N<(x+1)^2\}$

For convenience we have again written the exit condition right into the diagram, rather than making it a footnote.

Now what? You can see that if we set things up so $(0 \leq x$ and $x^2 \leq N)$ is an invariant of the loop, we're finished. For when the loop terminates, we will have achieved our goal:

$$0 =< x$$ (because this is invariant)

and

$$x^2 \leq N$$ (because this is invariant)

and

$$N<(x+1)^2$$ (because this is the loop's exit condition)

We can represent the loop invariant diagrammatically as follows:

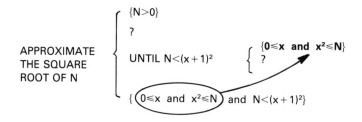

APPROXIMATE
THE SQUARE
ROOT OF N

$\{N>0\}$

?

UNTIL $N<(x+1)^2$ $\{0 \leq x$ and $x^2 \leq N\}$
?

$\{0 \leq x$ and $x^2 \leq N$ and $N<(x+1)^2\}$

This means that $(0 \leq x$ and $x^2 \leq N)$ holds whenever the exit condition is tested.

Step 3: Insert Instructions. So how can we hold $(0 \leq x$ and $x^2 \leq N)$ invariant? It's easy to see that we can start by setting x equal to zero: obviously $0 \leq 0$ and $0^2 \leq N$. Thus we have:

APPROXIMATE
THE SQUARE
ROOT OF N

$\{N>0\}$

SET $x=0$

UNTIL $N<(x+1)^2$ $\{0 \leq x$ and $x^2 \leq N\}$
?

$\{0 \leq x$ and $x^2 \leq N$ and $N<(x+1)^2\}$

So our only question is: What will we put in the body of the loop? We obviously can't leave it empty: the loop will go on forever. Suppose we try the simplest method of increasing x, which is to add 1 to it. Then we have:

APPROXIMATE
THE SQUARE
ROOT OF N

$\{N>0\}$

SET $x=0$

UNTIL $N<(x+1)^2$

$\{0\leq x$ and $x^2\leq N\}$

ADD 1 TO x

$\{0\leq x$ and $x^2\leq N$ and $N<(x+1)^2\}$

Obviously $(x+1)^2$ will eventually exceed N if you ADD 1 TO x often enough; so the loop will indeed terminate.

Step 4: Prove Invariance. We're into the home stretch. All that's left is to show that the invariant really is invariant: that it holds whenever the exit condition is tested.

Let B represent the value of x at the beginning of some cycle through the loop body. If $N<(B+1)^2$, the exit condition will be satisfied and will throw us out of the loop. So if we stay in the loop, $N<(B+1)^2$ must be false; in other words:

$(B+1)^2\leq N$

must be true.

During this cycle we add 1 to x. So the value of x at the beginning of the *next* cycle is $x=(B+1)$; and since we just saw that $(B+1)^2\leq N$, we have:

$x^2=(B+1)^2\leq N$

Which is what we had to prove: given $x^2\leq N$ at the beginning of one cycle, it will be true at the beginning of the next.

* * * * *

This has been a lengthy process; let's summarize it. We wanted to write a loop that would result in:

$0\leq x$ and $x^2\leq N$ and $N<(x+1)^2$

We used the last condition—$N<(x+1)^2$—as the loop exit condition and then arranged to hold the first two $0\leq x$ and $x^2\leq N$) invariant. Thus we knew that on exiting from the loop, both conditions will hold and we will have our result; we just had to show that we will in fact exit. We did that by observing that if we add 1 to x often enough, eventually we'll have $N<(x+1)^2$.

Along the way we became further acquainted with the very useful concept of loop invariant. A loop invariant is an assertion that is true whenever the exit condition of the loop is tested. The invariant is a powerful tool in dealing with loops.

The key is selecting the invariant. In the square root problem we did it by **splitting up** the result condition R. The loan print program in Section 22.1 shows a second strategy: **replacing a constant by a variable**. The result assertion is, "All L loans have been properly printed." We replaced the constant L by the variable n to get the invariant: "The first n loans have been properly printed."

And still other approaches can work depending on the problem. Gries' book tells you more.

This has been the critical material on goal directed programming. We now get into some other aspects of it that, while interesting, are less central to informal use of the techniques.

22.3 GUARDS AND DEMONS

Here is another example of goal-directed programming, also borrowed from Gries. Given X and Y, we have to find z such that z is the maximum of X and Y:

    z = MAX (X,Y)

We first restate the goal condition, since our language doesn't have a *MAX* function. We can restate it as shown here:

FIND MAX
$$
\begin{cases}
\{T\} \\
\\
\{(z=X \mid z=Y) \ \& \ (z \geqslant X) \ \& \ (z \geqslant Y)\}
\end{cases}
$$

We have used the symbol | for OR and the symbol & for AND. So the goal assertion says that:

z equals either X or Y,
and z is at least as big as both X and Y.

A little thought will show that this is what "$z = MAX(X,Y)$" means.

Incidentally, note the precondition $\{T\}$, which stands for True. Precondition T means the program must work whenever *anything* is true—i.e., no matter what the beginning state is. If T seems a bit abstract, you might replace it by, say, $1 = 1$. This means the program must work whenever $1 = 1$—i.e., anytime.

The assertion is now in a form we can work with. Examining the result, we see $z = X$ in it. This suggests MOVE X TO z as part of the program:

FIND MAX
$$
\begin{cases}
\{T\} \\
\\
\textbf{MOVE X TO z} \\
\\
\{(z=X \mid z=Y) \ \& \ (z \geqslant X) \ \& \ (z \geqslant Y)\}
\end{cases}
$$

But this yields the result only under certain conditions. What conditions? Well, since it sets $z = X$, it will obviously satisfy $(z - X|z = Y)$, as well as $z \geq X$.

But the third component of the result, $z \geq Y$, will hold only if $X \geq Y$. Thus we need:

```
                        ┌ {T}
                        │
          FIND MAX     ┤  IF X≥Y    { MOVE X TO z
                        │
                        └ {(z = X | z = Y) & (z≥X) & (z≥Y)}
```

And by an exactly symmetrical argument, we get:

```
                        ┌ {T}
                        │
                        │  IF X≥Y    { MOVE X TO z
                        │
          FIND MAX     ┤
                        │  IF Y≥X    { MOVE Y TO z
                        │
                        └ {(z = X | z = Y) & (z≥X) & (z≥Y)}
```

We're finished. Our two conditions cover every possible case, and each yields the desired result when it holds.

But this isn't right. Our solution shows $Y > X$ being tested *after* $X > Y$; but since our development was symmetrical, it is wrong to put either test before the other. We'd like to show the tests in parallel. Adapting from Dijkstra, we use the following notation to indicate that the tests are **parallel**:

```
                        ┌ {T}
                        │
                        │            ┌ X≥Y    { MOVE X TO z
                        │            │
          FIND MAX     ┤   IF       ┤  []
                        │            │
                        │            └ Y≥X    { MOVE Y TO z
                        │
                        └ {(z = X | z = Y) & (z≥X) & (z≥Y)}
```

Neat. But there's still a problem. What if $X = Y$: which path should be taken? The answer is: *We don't care*. Our derivation proved that either choice yields the desired result when it holds, so there's no reason to prefer either. We will leave it to the whim of the computer, fully expecting it to pick different paths on different occasions, even with the same data. If more than one condition holds, the computer will flip a coin or be instructed by a demon it employs for that purpose.

This is an example of what Dijkstra calls **guarded commands**. The guards are $(X \geq Y)$ and $(Y \geq X)$: they guard their respective brackets.

Here is a formal statement of what the guarded IF statement looks like and means. C stands for condition, A for action:

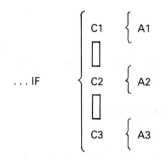

```
          ┌      C1  { A1
          │
          │      []
... IF   {       C2  { A2
          │
          │      []
          └      C3  { A3
```

This means:

IF ...	THEN ...
more than one Ci holds	randomly select one that holds and execute its Ai
exactly one Ci holds	execute its Ai
no Ci holds	execute no Ai

You may wonder why we move the IF off to the left by itself in the guarded IF command. We do it to distinguish this command from a similar concept for loops:

```
               ┌      C1  { A1
               │
               │      []
...DO         {       C2  { A2
  (0,n)        │
               │      []
               └      C3  { A3
```

This says: **On each cycle through the loop,** try to find a condition ($C1$, $C2$, $C3$) that applies:

IF ...	THEN ...
more than one Ci holds	randomly select one that holds and execute its Ai, then recycle
exactly one Ci holds	execute its Ai, then recycle
no Ci holds	exit from the loop

This can be handy for developing loops from the goal; space won't permit an example. Notice that the C_i's are conditions to *stay in* the loop, not exit conditions. Thus, you will have to negate portions of the result assertion to get them.

22.4 WEAKEST PRECONDITIONS

We have achieved satisfactory results, but they took a bit of arm waving. In order to make development beginning with the goal condition simpler and more reliable, Dijkstra developed the concept of **weakest preconditions**.

Suppose we want to write a program that will result in x being greater than 10. Then the goal is, of course:

$$\text{SET x} \left\{ {}_{\{x>10\}} \right.$$

Now let's consider a candidate program to accomplish the goal. We'll look at:

$$\text{SET x} \left\{ \begin{array}{l} \textbf{ADD 1 to x} \\ {}_{\{x>10\}} \end{array} \right.$$

Under what preconditions will this do the job? Obviously it will give the required result if and only if $(x>9)$ beforehand. We say that $(x>9)$ is the **weakest precondition** of $(x>10)$ for the code ADD 1 TO x. We can write:

$(x>9) = wp(\text{"ADD 1 to x"}, x>10)$

What do we mean by weakest? We mean the most general condition, the one that takes in as many situations as possible.

Suppose, for example, we happen to know that $x=37$ is true when this routine starts. Clearly the program will work in this case, since $37>9$. That is, $(x=37)$ is a precondition, but it's much narrower than $(x>9)$. Formally we can write:

$(x=37) \Rightarrow wp(\text{"ADD 1 to x"}, x>10)$

We can think of $\Rightarrow$ as meaning "satisfies."

What's all this in aid of? Well, suppose you write a series of statements S to achieve goal G. Then S will do the job for you if and only if:

$wp(S,G)$

holds before S is executed; that's what "wp" means.

Now suppose you carefully describe the situation you have to start from: let P be your actual precondition. Then obviously statements S will accomplish the goal G, provided:

$P \Rightarrow wp(S,G)$

Thus, if we had some way to work out $wp(S,G)$ for given S and G, we could tell whether or not S will work just by comparing $wp(S,G)$ with P. We could, in fact, *prove* that S will work.

Dijkstra provides a way of formally working out $wp(S,G)$. His rules let you mechanically derive the weakest precondition for given statements of any given goal or postcondition. For a detailed account see Gries' book, Chapters 7 to 12. (There are also half a dozen mentions of wp in Chapters 14 to 20.)

To prioritize: it seems to me that the critical concepts in this chapter are assertions and loop invariants. By all means learn guarded commands and weakest preconditions, but even without them, assertions and invariants can be useful in programming.

The idea of assertions was reportedly first introduced by Robert Floyd in 1967. He was also the first to develop loop invariants, which were carried further and made a basis for axiomatizing programs by Hoare in 1969. At this time the idea was mainly to discover a way of proving a given program correct.

But retrofitting proofs to programs was a painful and frustrating task. Far better was to develop the proof and the program hand in hand. From there it was but a small step to the idea that the developing proof could guide the development of the program; Dijkstra's introduction of guarded commands and weakest preconditions provided the needed tools.

Crudely speaking, you use the goal to develop invariants, guarded commands, and simple statements as required; then confirm that you have covered all cases by testing whether $P \Rightarrow wp(S,G)$.

22.5 SUMMARY

This chapter provided a very informal introduction to some of the tools of goal directed programming. The key step in this approach is, of course, formulating your goal: the assertion about the situation you want to exist when your program completes.

We saw examples of the use of the goal statement to derive loop invariants, loop exit conditions, selection conditions, and processing. A loop invariant is an assertion that always holds when the exit condition is tested.

Two of the more advanced features of goal directed programming are guarded commands (from which a demon takes his pick if more than one holds) and weakest preconditions (which provide a mechanical way of telling if given code will achieve a given goal for a given precondition).

FURTHER READING

For the next level of detail on this material, see *The Science of Programming* by Gries. On a first reading you may want to read Chapters 1 and 2, skim Chapters 3 to 12, and focus on Chapters 13 to 20. Note that the terms and symbols differ from those we have used. The precondition is normally called Q; the invariant is

P; the goal (result) is R; and the exit condition (negated) is called the guard and is represented by B (for Boolean).

With Gries under your belt, you will be in a position to tackle Dijkstra's *A Discipline of Programming*.

Berry discusses informal but thorough use of the concepts in this chapter in "Program Proofs Produced Practically."

A skeptical view on the usefulness of formal program proofs appears in "Social Processes and Proofs of Theorems and Programs" by DeMillo, Lipton, and Perlis.

Epilogue: What Next?

There is a large, growing body of work requiring programs; this will obviously increase the demand for programmers. But paradoxically it will ultimately limit the need. As the demand for systems grows, so will the market for products to automate system development: skeleton programs, higher-level languages, program generators, and the like.

Automation will change the nature of a programmer's work. Programmers who master a few techniques, then bank on meeting unending variants of the same old problems, will be the auto workers of the future. Knowledge of underlying principles was always desirable; with increasing automation such knowledge will be a basic survival strategy.

Which principles to master? Naturally, I recommend you start with a solid grounding in data structured design. But it would be a shame to stop there. It will become increasingly important for programmers to have more than one string to their bow.

Open-mindedness is no more prevalent in programming than anywhere else. We all tend to latch on to the techniques we met first or know best and shun "competing" methods. It's too bad. Programming is difficult, and we need all the help we can get.

This book takes some steps in the direction of cross fertilization by relating Orr's ideas to other areas of data structured design and to goal directed programming. But there's a lot more out there: data abstraction, information hiding, object-oriented programing, transform-centered design, SAPTAD, stepwise refinement . . . a programmer who masters them will become far more useful.

So what should you do? To start, consider the following.

1. **Try the techniques** of program design described in this book, and in Warnier's and Jackson's books. Decide from your own experience what their strengths and weaknesses are. Modify and adapt them.
2. **Get help.** Find someone who can show you broader horizons; find a colleague with whom you can compare notes, swap experiences, and argue. Get training.
3. **Expand your knowledge.** Study the work of Constantine, Wirth, Hoare, Parnas, Dijkstra. . . . Relate it to what you already know. Try the techniques; devise ways of bridging your methods and theirs.

The most useful programmers are the ones who understand principles and can bring fresh approaches to problems. Membership in this group requires practice and exploration. Luckily, the practicing and exploring are fun.

Appendix

Comparison of Orr, Warnier, Jackson

The table on the following pages summarizes the main steps in the methods of Orr, Warnier, and Jackson.

Data Structure

Fill in Output Definition Form
- **Data elements**
- **Appears 1/What**

Do universal analysis on appears column to get the logical output structure (LOS)

Orr

DATA ELEMENT	APPEARS	DETAILS
REPORT-TITLE	1/COMPANY(B)	
COLUMN-HEADINGS	1/COMPANY(B)	
DEPT-NUM	1/DEPT(B)	
PROJECT-ID	1/PROJECT	
PROJECT-COST	1/PROJECT	
DEPT-TOTAL	1/DEPT(E)	
COMPANY-TOTAL-LABEL	1/COMPANY(E)	
COMPANY-TOTAL	1/COMPANY(E)	

```
                                              REPORT-TITLE
                                              COLUMN-HEADINGS
                                                              .NUM
                            DEPT          PROJECT     .ID
              COMPANY       (1,D)         (1,P)       .COST
                                              .TOTAL

                            .TOTAL-LABEL
                            .TOTAL
```

Warnier

Define output

```
          Heading
          (1)
                       Dept No
                       (1)
                                    Project ID
          Dept         Project      (1)
LOF       (D times)    (P times)    Project Cost
                                    (1)
                       Dept Total
                       (1)
          Grand Total Label
          (1)
          Grand Total
          (1)
```

Define input

```
                                               Dept No
                                               (1)
          Dept        Project     Worker       Project ID
LIF       (D times)   (P times)   (W times)    (1)
                                               Worker Cost
                                               (1)
```

Jackson

Diagram output

```
                    REPORT
          ┌───────────┼───────────┐
      RREPORT     RREPORT      RREPORT
      HEADER       BODY        FOOTER
                    │
                 RDEPT *
          ┌─────────┼─────────┐
       RDEPT      RDEPT      RDEPT
        NUM        BODY      FOOTER
                    │
                RPROJECT *
```

Diagram input

```
      FILE
       │
     FDEPT *
       │
    FPROJECT *
       │
    FWORKER *
```

If missing identification criterion: new phase

If action depends on two conditions: table

PHASE 2 { UNIVERSAL: { TOTAL-LOANS > 10,000
         1 CUSTOMER   (0 or 1)

B N	D1	D2	D3	Print	$\overline{\text{Output}}$
0 0					X
0 1			X	X	
1 0		X		X	
1 1	X			X	

Process Structure

Orr

Finish worksheet
- Element types
- Calculations

DATA ELEMENT	APPEARS	†	DETAILS
REPORT-TITLE	1/COMPANY	L	"PROJECT STATUS REPORT"
COLUMN-HEADINGS	1/COMPANY	L	"DEPARTMENT PROJECT..."
DEPT-NUM	1/DEPT	*	
PROJECT-ID	1/PROJECT	*	
PROJECT-COST	1/PROJECT	*	
DEPT-TOTAL	1/DEPT	C	1.SET DEPT-TOTAL TO 0 2.ADD PROJECT-COST TO DEPT-TOTAL
COMPANY-TOTAL-LABEL	1/COMPANY	L	"GRAND TOTAL"
COMPANY-TOTAL	1/COMPANY	C	1.SET COMPANY-TOTAL TO 0 2.ADD DEPT-TOTAL TO COMPANY-TOTAL

Logical output mapping (LOM) = logical output structure (LOS) plus Calculations, Output, and Input

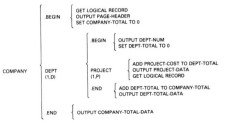

```
                  .BEGIN  { GET LOGICAL RECORD
                          { OUTPUT PAGE-HEADER
                          { SET COMPANY-TOTAL TO 0

                                  .BEGIN  { OUTPUT DEPT-NUM
                                          { SET DEPT-TOTAL TO 0

                                              { ADD PROJECT-COST TO DEPT-TOTAL
COMPANY  DEPT    PROJECT     { OUTPUT PROJECT-DATA
         (1,D)   (1,P)       { GET LOGICAL RECORD

                  .END    { ADD DEPT-TOTAL TO COMPANY-TOTAL
                          { OUTPUT DEPT-TOTAL-DATA

                  .END    { OUTPUT COMPANY-TOTAL-DATA
```

Warnier

Program structure: combine input, phase

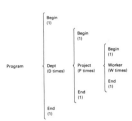

Turn into flowchart and validate

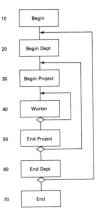

10	Begin
20	Begin Dept
30	Begin Project
40	Worker
50	End Project
60	End Dept
70	End

Jackson

Merge ⇒ Program structure (if clash: 2 programs)

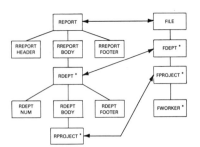

List operations

1. READ INFILE
2. OPEN INFILE
3. CLOSE INFILE
4. OPEN PFILE
5. CLOSE PFILE
6. GRAND-TOTAL   := 0
7. DEPT-TOTAL   := 0
8. PROJ-COST   := 0
9. PROJ-COST   := PROJ-COST + WORKER-COST
10. DEPT-TOTAL   := DEPT-TOTAL + PROJ-COST
11. GRAND-TOTAL   := GRAND-TOTAL + DEPT-TOTAL
12. MOVE DEPT-NUM   INTO DETAIL-LINE
13. MOVE PROJECT-ID   INTO DETAIL-LINE
14. MOVE PROJECT-COST INTO DETAIL-LINE
15. PRINT AND CLEAR DETAIL-LINE
16. BUILD AND PRINT DEPT-FOOTER-LINE
17. BUILD AND PRINT REPORT-FOOTER-LINE
18. CURR-DEPT-NUM   := IN-DEPT-NUM
19. CURR-PROJECT-ID   := IN-PROJECT-ID
20. STOP
21. PRINT REPORT HEADER

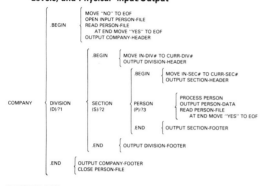

Augmented LOM = LOM plus Footnotes, Detail Levels, and Physical Input/Output

```
                    ┌ MOVE "NO" TO EOF
                    │ OPEN INPUT PERSON-FILE
         .BEGIN     │ READ PERSON-FILE
                    │   AT END MOVE "YES" TO EOF
                    └ OUTPUT COMPANY-HEADER

                                      ┌ MOVE IN-DIV# TO CURR-DIV#
                            .BEGIN    └ OUTPUT DIVISION-HEADER

                                              ┌ MOVE IN-SEC# TO CURR-SEC#
                                    .BEGIN    └ OUTPUT SECTION-HEADER

                                                      ┌ PROCESS PERSON
                                                      │ OUTPUT PERSON-DATA
                                           PERSON     │ READ PERSON-FILE
COMPANY   DIVISION     SECTION          (P)/?3        └   AT END MOVE "YES" TO EOF
          (D)/?1       (S)/?2
                                    .END      ┤ OUTPUT SECTION-FOOTER

                            .END      ┤ OUTPUT DIVISION-FOOTER

         .END     ┌ OUTPUT COMPANY-FOOTER
                  └ CLOSE PERSON-FILE
```

?1/ UNTIL EOF = "YES"
?2/ UNTIL (EOF = "YES") OR (IN-DIV# > CURR-DIV#)
?3/ UNTIL (EOF = "YES") OR (IN-DIV# > CURR-DIV#) OR (IN-SEC# > CURR-SEC#)

Use previous techniques plus hierarchy inversion if required to produce physical input mapping (PIM) and physical output mapping

```
                                        ┌ OPEN INPUT LOAN-FILE
                    COMPANY-BEGIN        │ MOVE "NO" TO PHYS-EOF
                    (0,1)/?X1            │ READ LOAN-FILE
                                         └   AT END MOVE "YES" TO PHYS-EOF

                                         ┌ BUILD LOG-IN-RECORD
PIM'                LOAN                  │ ("write" record to LPS)
                    (0,1)/?X2            │ READ LOAN-FILE
                                         └   AT END MOVE "YES" TO PHYS-EOF

                          ⊕

                    COMPANY-END          ┌ CLOSE LOAN-FILE
                    (0,1)                │ MOVE "YES" TO END-LOGICAL-INPUT
                                         └ ("write" end-of-file indication to LOM)

                    GOBACK
```

?X1/ on 1
?X2/ IF PHYS-EOF = "NO"

List instructions and allocate to flowchart

	Sequence	Instruction	Next Seq
INPUT	10	Read the first record of the file	
	40	Read another record of the file or the end-of-file record	
BRANCH	40	if in-project-key = curr-project-key	40
	50	if in-dept-key = curr-dept-key	30
	60	if not end-of-file	20
BRANCH PREP	20	Move in-dept-no to curr-dept-no	
	30	Move in-project-id to curr-project-id	
CALCULATION	10	Clear grand-total	
	20	Clear dept-total	
	30	Clear project-cost	
	40	Add worker-cost to project-cost	
	50	Add project-cost to dept-total	
	60	Add dept-total to grand-total	
OUTPUT	10	Produce heading	
	20	Move dept-no to detail-dept-no	
	30	Move project-id to detail-project-id	
	50	Move project-cost to detail-project-cost	
	50	Output and clear detail line	
	60	Produce dept-total line	
	70	Produce grand-total line	

Sort instructions and verify against output

10	Read the first record of the file	
10	Clear grand-total	
10	Produce heading	
20	Move in-dept-no to curr-dept-no	
20	Clear dept-total	
20	Move dept-no to detail-dept-no	
30	Move in-project-id to curr-project-id	
30	Move project-id to detail-project-id	
30	Clear project-cost	
40	Add worker-cost to project-cost	
40	Read another record of the file or the end-of-file record	
40	if in-project-key = curr-project-key	40
50	Add project-cost to dept-total	
50	Move project-cost to detail-project-cost	
50	Output and clear detail line	
50	if in-dept-key = curr-dept-key	30
60	Produce dept-total line	
60	Add dept-total to grand-total	
60	if not end-of-file	20
70	Produce grand-total line	

Write schematic logic with conditions (if trouble: look ahead or backtrack)

```
PROCINFILE seq
    open INFILE; open PFILE; GRAND-TOTAL: = 0; read INFILE;
    PREPHDR seq
        print report header;
    PREPHDR end
    PREPBODY iter until EOF = "YES"
        PDEPT seq
            CURR-DEPT-NUM := IN-DEPT-NUM;
            DEPT-TOTAL    := 0;
            PDEPTNUM seq
                move DEPT-NUM into DETAIL-LINE;
            PDEPTNUM end
            PDEPTBODY iter until EOF = "YES"
                         or CURR-DEPT-NUM not = IN-DEPT-NUM
                PPROJECT seq
                    .
                    .
                    .
                PPROJECT end
            PDEPTBODY end
            PDEPTFTR seq
                build and print DEPT-FOOTER-LINE;
                GRAND-TOTAL := GRAND-TOTAL + DEPT-TOTAL;
            PDEPTFTR end
        PDEPT end
    PREPBODY end
    PREPFTR seq
        build and print REPORT-FOOTER-LINE;
    PREPFTR end
    close INFILE; close PFILE; stop;
PROCINFILE end
```

If clash between input and output: invert program (with bookmark)

```
01  BOOKMARK    VALUE 1    PIC 9(4).

PROCEDURE DIVISION USING END-LOGICAL-INPUT
                         LOG-IN-RECORD.

    GO TO BM1
          BM2
    DEPENDING ON BOOKMARK.
BM1.

COMPANY.
    PERFORM COMPANY-BEGIN.
    PERFORM LOAN THRU EXIT-LOAN UNTIL PHYS-EOF = "YES".
    PERFORM COMPANY-END.
    GOBACK.

COMPANY-BEGIN.
    OPEN INPUT LOAN-FILE.
    MOVE "NO" TO PHYS-EOF.
    READ LOAN-FILE
        AT END MOVE "YES" TO PHYS-EOF.

LOAN.
    MOVE IN-EE-NAME       TO LOG-IN-EE-NAME.
    MOVE IN-LOAN-AMOUNT TO LOG-IN-LOAN-AMOUNT.
    MOVE 2 TO BOOKMARK.
    GOBACK.
BM2.
    READ LOAN-FILE
        AT END MOVE "YES" TO PHYS-EOF.
EXIT-LOAN.

COMPANY-END.
    CLOSE LOAN-FILE.
    MOVE "YES" TO END-LOGICAL-INPUT.
```

Appendix

Code

Apply 5 rules to get COBOL code

Orr

```
COMPANY.
    PERFORM COMPANY-BEGIN.
    PERFORM LOAN
        UNTIL EOF = "YES".
    PERFORM COMPANY-END.
    STOP RUN.

COMPANY-BEGIN.
    DISPLAY "LIST OF EMPLOYEE LOANS".
    OPEN INPUT LOAN-FILE.
    MOVE "NO" TO EOF.
    READ LOAN-FILE
        AT END MOVE "YES" TO EOF.

LOAN.
    MOVE LOAN-AMOUNT TO EDITED-AMOUNT.
    DISPLAY EE-NAME, EDITED-AMOUNT.
    READ LOAN-FILE
        AT END MOVE "YES" TO EOF.

COMPANY-END.
    DISPLAY "   END OF LOAN LIST".
    CLOSE LOAN-FILE.
```

Warnier

Code: either Orr-like or nest-free

Jackson

```
PPROC-INFILE-SEQ.
    MOVE "NO" TO EOF.
    OPEN INPUT PROJECT-FILE.
    OPEN OUTPUT PRINT-FILE.
    MOVE ZERO TO GRAND-TOTAL.
    READ PROJECT-FILE AT END MOVE "YES" TO EOF.
PREP-HDR-SEQ.
    WRITE PRINT-LINE FROM REP-HDR-LINE
        AFTER ADVANCING TO-TOP-OF-PAGE.
PREP-HDR-END.
PREP-BODY-ITER.
    IF EOF = "YES" GO TO PREP-BODY-END.
PDEPT-SEQ.
    MOVE IN-DEPT-NUM      TO CURR-DEPT-NUM.
    MOVE ZERO            TO DEPT-TOTAL.
PDEPT-NUM-SEQ.
    MOVE CURR-DEPT-NUM TO DE-DEPT-NUM.
PDEPT-NUM-END.
PDEPT-BODY-ITER.
    IF EOF = "YES"
    OR CURR-DEPT-NUM NOT = IN-DEPT-NUM
        GO TO PDEPT-BODY-END.
PPROJECT-SEQ.
    MOVE IN-PROJECT-ID     TO CURR-PROJECT-ID.
    MOVE ZERO             TO PROJECT-COST.

        .

PPROC-INFILE-END.
```

Bibliography

Berry, D. "Program proofs produced practically." *Proceedings, 6th annual DSSD User's Conference*. Topeka, KS: Ken Orr and Associates, 1981.

Bohm, C., and Jacopini, G. "Flow diagrams, Turing machines, and languages with only two formation rules." *Communications of the ACM*, May 1966, **9**:5, pp. 366–371.

Cameron, J. R. *JSP & JSD: The Jackson approach to software development*. Silver Spring, MD: IEEE Computer Society Press, 1983.

DeMarco, T. *Structured analysis and system specification*. New York: Yourdon, 1978.

DeMillo, R. A., Lipton, R. J., and Perlis, A. J. "Social processes and proofs of theorems and programs." *Communications of the ACM*, May 1979, **22**:5, pp. 271–230.

Dijkstra, E. W. *Discipline of programming*. Englewood Cliffs, NJ: Prentice-Hall, 1976.

Dwyer, B. "One more time: How to update a master file." *Communications of the ACM*, January 1981, **24**:1, pp. 3–8.

Gane, C., and Sarson, T. *Structured systems analysis: Tools and techniques*. New York: Improved Systems Technologies, 1977.

Gries, D. *The science of programming*. New York: Springer-Verlag, 1982.

Higgins, D. *Designing structured programs*. Englewood Cliffs, NJ: Prentice-Hall, 1983.

Hoare, C. A. R. "Communicating sequential processes," *Communications of the A.C.M.*, August 1978, **21**:8, pp. 666–677.

Jackson, M. *Principles of program design*. New York: Academic Press, 1975.

_____. *System development*. Englewood Cliffs, NJ: Prentice-Hall, 1983.

Knuth, D. E. *The art of computer programming*, Vol. 1: *Fundamental algorithms*. 2d ed. Reading, MA: Addison-Wesley, 1973.

Orr, K. T. *Structured requirements definition*. Topeka, KS: Ken Orr and Associates, 1981.

_____. *Structured systems development*. New York: Yourdon, 1977.

Parnas, D. L. "On the criteria to be used in decomposing systems into modules." *Communications of the A.C.M.*, December 1972, **5**:2, pp. 1053–58.

WARNIER, J.-D. *Logical construction of programs*. Boston: Martinus Nijhoff, 1975.

_____. *Logical construction of systems*. New York: Van Nostrand Reinhold, 1981.

_____. *Program modification*. Boston: Martinus Nijhoff, 1978.

Warnier's books in the original French include:

_____. *Construction et transformation des programmes (L.C.P.)*. (7th Edition). Paris: Les Editions d'Organisation, 1983.

_____. *Guide des utilisateurs du systeme informatique*. Paris: Les Editions d'Organisation, 1979.

_____. *Pratique de l'organization des donnees d'un systeme*. Paris: Les Editions d'Organisation, 1974.

_____. *La transformation des programmes*. Paris: Les Editions d'Organisation, 1975.

_____. *Les procedures de traitement et leurs donnees*. Paris: Les Editions d'Organisation, 1979.

_____. *Pratique de la construction d'un ensemble de donnees*. Paris: Les Editions d'Organisation, 1976.

Wirth, N. *Algorithms + data structures = programs*. Englewood Cliffs, NJ: Prentice-Hall, 1976.

YATES, J., and THOMAS, R. *User guide to the UNIX system*. Berkeley, CA: Osborne-McGraw, 1982.

YOURDON, E.N., and CONSTANTINE, L. *Structured design*. New York: Yourdon, 1978.

Index

P

Packaging, 82
Page breaks, 42
Paragraph, 25
Parallel tests, 282
Parnas, David, 83
Pascal, 34, 77
Payroll system problem, 105
PERFORM, 25, 30, 270
PERFORM-free coding, 252, 260, 270
PERFORM UNTIL, 25, 30
Perlis, A. J., 286
Phases, Jackson, 260
Physical:
    data structure, 98
    input file, 152
    input mapping, 136
    output mapping, 98, 101
    output structure, 42, 93
    print routine, 101
Pi, 215
PIF, 152
PIM, 136, 138, 163, 266
Pipe, 98, 138
    vanishing, 102
PL/1, 77
Place for everything, 49
Plus sign, 94, 226, 256
POM, 98–99
Posit, 259
Precondition, 277
    weakest, 284
Preparing branch instructions, 213
Prime symbol, 145, 163
PRINT A LINE subroutine, 116
Problem:
    accounting report, 51, 69
    accounts payable, 68
    city report, 149
    DEPT table, 152
    expense report, 53, 71, 155, 158–59
    kiwi fruit, 258
    loan list, 30, 140, 266
    payroll system, 105
    project list, 158

    project report, 39, 47, 60, 84, 169
    public school, 93
    rowboat, 271
    Shakespeare, 19
Process structure, 16, 211
Processing phases, 234
Program, 81
    inversion, 266
    modification, 238
    structure, 246
Programming, goal directed, 276
Project:
    list problem, 158
    report problem, 39, 47, 60, 84, 169
Proof of correctness, 285
Public school problem, 93

Q

Quit, 259

R

READ INTO, 87
Read-once-to-begin-again-when-
    consumed rule, 34, 64, 68, 92, 194
Record, logical, 63
Redundant occurrence, 66
Reference criterion, 214, 235
Repetition, 7, 13, 20, 25
Replacing a constant by a variable, 281
Report, sample, 39, 40
REPORT-BEGIN-SW, 118
Required elements, 65, 67, 158
Requirements definition, user, 38
Rightmost universal, 178, 189
Rowboat problem, 271
Run-unit, 81

S

Sample, 39–40
Sarson, Trish, 133
Sections, 77, 80
Segmentation, 81